Acknowledgments

Michiel Schriever
Art Direction

Luke Pauw
Sr. Graphic Designer

Elise O'Keefe
Copy Editor

Alan Harris
Technical Editor

Peter Verboom
Video Producer

Lenni Rodrigues & Linda Sellheim
Project Leads

Lenni Rodrigues
Program Development Manager

Richard Lane
Senior Manager, Customer Learning

Paul Mailhot
Sr. Director, Autodesk Learning

Special thanks go out to:

Laura Lewin, Kathryn Spencer, Rebecca Pease, Carmela Bourassa, Tonya Holder, Mary Ruijs, Amer Yassine, Marc Dahan, Sebastien Primeau, Steven Schain, Luc St-Onge, Paul Verrall, Sarah Blay, Roberto Ziche.

Cover Image
Roadside Romeo is a production of Yash Raj Films

Primary Author

Marc-André Guindon | NeoReel

Marc-André Guindon is the founder of NeoReel Inc. (www.NeoReel.com), a Montreal-based production facility. He is an Autodesk® Maya® Master and an advanced user of Autodesk® MotionBuilder® software. Marc-André and NeoReel have partnered with Autodesk Inc. on several projects, including the *Learning Maya* series from version 6.0 to present.

www.NeoReel.com

Marc-André has established complex pipelines and developed numerous plug-ins and tools, such as Animation Layers for Maya and Visual MEL Studio, for a variety of projects in the film, television and game industries. His latest film projects include pre-visualization on *G-Force* (Walt Disney Productions), *The Day the Earth Stood Still* (20th Century Fox), *Journey 3D* (Walden Media), among others. He also served in the game industry to integrate motion capture for *Prey* (2K Games) for the Xbox 360™, *Arena Football*™ (EA Sports) and the *Outlaw Sports Game Series* (2K Games).

Marc-André continues to seek challenges for himself, NeoReel, and his talented crew.

Table of Contents

Project 03

Project 04

Introduction

Autodesk® Maya® software is a character animation and visual effects system designed for professional artists. Built on a procedural architecture called the Dependency Graph, Maya software offers incredible power and flexibility for generating digital images of animated characters and scenes.

This tutorial book gives you hands-on experience with Maya software as you complete a series of project-based lessons. In the projects found in this book, you will model, animate, texture map, add visual effects, and render.

How to use this book

How you use *Learning Autodesk Maya 2010 | Foundation* will depend on your experience with computer graphics and 3D animation. This book moves at a fast pace and is designed to help you develop your 3D skills. If this is your first experience with 3D software, it is suggested that you read through each lesson and watch the accompanying demo files on DVD, which may help clarify the steps for you before you begin to work through the tutorial projects. If you are already familiar with Maya software or another 3D package, you might choose to look through the book's index to focus on those areas you would like to improve.

Updates to this book

In an effort to ensure your continued success with the lessons in this book, please visit our Web site for the latest updates available: *www.autodesk.com/learningtools-updates*.

Windows and Macintosh

This book is written to cover Windows and Macintosh platforms. Graphics and text have been modified where applicable. You may notice that your screen varies slightly from the illustrations, depending on the platform you are using.

Things to watch for

Window focus may differ. For example, if you are on Windows, you have to click on the panel with your middle mouse button to make it active.

To select multiple attributes in Windows, use the **Ctrl** key. On Macintosh, use the **Command** key. To modify pivot position in Windows, use the **Insert** key. On Macintosh, use the **Home** key.

Autodesk packaging

This book can be used with either **Autodesk® Maya® Complete 2010**, **Autodesk® Maya® Unlimited 2010,** or the corresponding version of **Autodesk® Maya® Personal Learning Edition**, as the lessons included here focus on functionality shared among all three software packages.

As a bonus feature, this hands-on book will also introduce you to compositing in Autodesk® Toxik™.

Learning Autodesk Maya DVD-ROM

The *Learning Autodesk Maya 2010* DVD-ROM contains several resources to accelerate your learning experience including:

- Learning Maya support files

- Instructor-led videos to guide you through the projects in the book

- A link to a trial version of Autodesk Toxik software

- Autodesk Maya reference guides

Installing support files

Before beginning the lessons in this book, you will need to install the lesson support files. Copy the project directories found in the *support_files* folder on the DVD disc to the *Maya\projects* directory on your computer. Launch Maya software and set the project by going to **File** → **Project** → **Set...** and selecting the appropriate project.

Windows: *C:\Documents and Settings\username\My Documents\maya\projects*

Macintosh: *Macintosh HD:Users:username:Documents:maya:projects*

Introduction
Understanding Maya

To understand Autodesk® Maya® software, it helps to understand how it works at a conceptual level. This introduction is designed to give you the story about Maya software. In other words, the focus of this introduction will be on how different Maya concepts are woven together to create an integrated workspace.

While this book teaches you how to model, animate, and render, these concepts are taught with a particular focus on how the underlying architecture in Maya software supports the creation of animated sequences.

You will soon learn that Maya architecture can be explained by a single line—nodes with attributes that are connected. As you work through the book, the meaning of this statement will become clearer and you will learn to appreciate how the Maya interface lets you focus on the act of creation, while giving you access to the power inherent in the underlying architecture.

The user interface (UI)

The Maya user interface (UI) includes a number of tools, editors, and controls. You can access these using the main menus or special context-sensitive marking menus. You can also use shelves to store important icons or hotkeys to speed up workflow. Maya software is designed to let you configure the UI as you see fit.

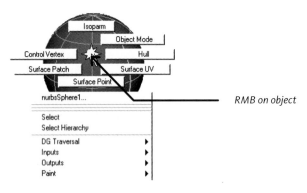

RMB on object

Marking menu

To work with objects, you can enter values using coordinate entry or you can use more interactive 3D manipulators. Manipulator handles let you edit your objects with a simple click+drag.

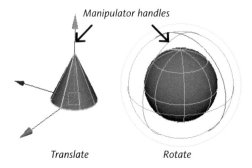

Manipulator handles

Translate   *Rotate*

Maya manipulators

The Maya UI supports multiple levels of undo and redo and includes a drag-and-drop paradigm for accessing many parts of the workspace.

Working in 3D

In Maya software, you will build and animate objects in three dimensions. These dimensions are defined by the cardinal axes that are labeled as X, Y, and Z. These represent the length (X), height (Y), and depth (Z) of your scene. These axes are represented by colors—red for X, green for Y, and blue for Z.

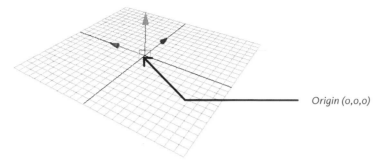

Origin (0,0,0)

The cardinal axes

The Maya default has the Y-axis pointing up (also referred to as Y-up).

As you position, scale, and rotate your objects, these three axes will serve as your main points of reference. The center of this coordinate system is called the origin and has a value of 0, 0, 0.

UV coordinate space

As you build surfaces in Maya software, they are created with their own coordinate space that is defined by U in one direction and V in another. You can use these coordinates when you are working with curve-on-surface objects or when you are positioning textures on a surface.

One corner of the surface acts as the origin of the system and all coordinates lie directly on the surface.

You can make surfaces live in order to work directly in the UV coordinate space. You will also encounter U and V attributes when you place textures onto surfaces.

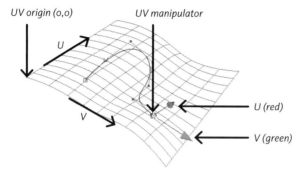

UV coordinates on a live surface

Views

In Maya software, you visualize your scenes using view panels that let you see into the 3D world.

Perspective views let you see your scene as if you were looking at it with your own eyes or through the lens of a camera.

Orthographic views are parallel to the scene and offer a more objective view. They focus on two axes at a time and are referred to as the top, side, and front views.

In many cases, you will require several views to help you define the proper location of your objects. An object's position that looks good in the top view may not make sense in a side view. Maya software lets you view multiple views at one time to help coordinate what you see.

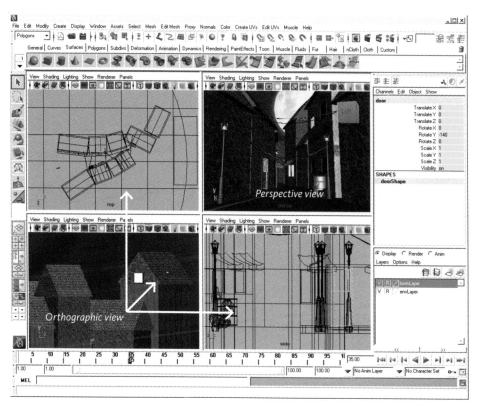

Orthographic and Perspective views

Cameras

To achieve a particular view, you look through a digital camera. An Orthographic camera defines the view using a parallel plane and a direction, while a Perspective camera uses an eye point, a look at point, and a focal length.

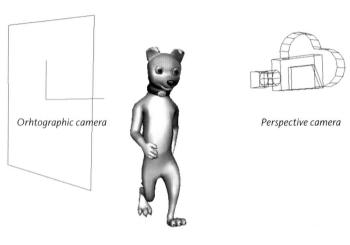

Orhtographic camera   Perspective camera

Orthographic and Perspective cameras

Image planes

When you work with cameras, it is possible to attach special backdrop objects called image planes to the camera. An image plane can be placed onto the camera so that as the camera moves, the plane stays aligned.

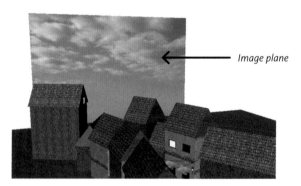

Image plane attached to a camera

The image plane has several attributes that allow you to track and scale the image. These attributes can be animated to give the appearance that the plane is moving.

Image plane seen looking through the camera

The Dependency Graph

The Maya system architecture uses a procedural paradigm that lets you integrate traditional keyframe animation, inverse kinematics, dynamics, and scripting into a node-based architecture that is called the dependency graph. As mentioned on the first page of this introduction, the dependency graph could be described as nodes with attributes that are connected. This node-based architecture gives Maya software its flexible procedural qualities.

Below is a diagram showing a primitive sphere's dependency graph. A procedural input node defines the shape of the sphere by connecting attributes on each node.

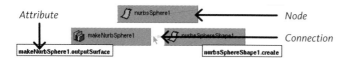

The dependency graph

Tip: *When multiple attributes are connected between two nodes, the connection is drawn with a thicker line. Hover your mouse cursor over the connection to see its content.*

Nodes

Every element, whether it is a curve, surface, deformer, light, texture, expression, modeling operation, or animation curve, is described by either a single node or a series of connected nodes.

A node is a generic object type. Different nodes are designed with specific attributes so that the node can accomplish a specific task. Nodes define all object types including geometry, shading, and lighting.

Shown below are three typical node types as they appear on a primitive sphere:

Transform nodes contain positioning information for your objects. When you move, rotate, or scale, this is the node you are affecting.

Shape nodes contain all the component information that represents the actual look of the sphere.

Input nodes represent options that drive the creation of your sphere's shape, such as radius or endsweep.

The Maya UI presents these nodes to you in many ways. Below is an image of the Channel Box where you can edit and animate node attributes.

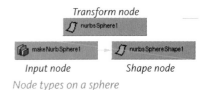

Transform node

Input node   *Shape node*

Node types on a sphere

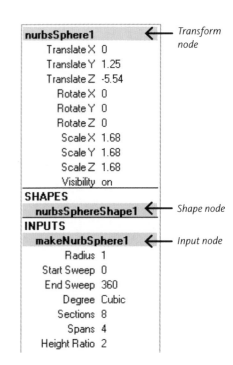

Channel Box

Attributes

Each node is defined by a series of attributes that relate to what the node is designed to accomplish. In the case of a transform node, Translate X is an attribute. In the case of a shader node, Color Red is an attribute. It is possible for you to assign values to the attributes. You can work with attributes in a number of UI windows, including the Attribute Editor, the Channel Box, and the Spread Sheet Editor.

Attribute Editor

One important feature is that you can animate virtually every attribute on any node. This helps give Maya software its animation power. You should note that attributes are also referred to as channels.

Connections

Nodes do not exist in isolation. A finished animation results when you begin making connections between attributes on different nodes. These connections are also known as dependencies. In modeling, these connections are sometimes referred to as construction history.

Most of these connections are created automatically by the Maya UI as a result of using commands or tools. If you desire, you can also build and edit these connections explicitly using the Connection Editor, by entering MEL (Maya Embedded Language) commands, or by writing MEL-based expressions.

Pivots

Transform nodes are all built with a special component known as the pivot point. Just like your arm pivots around your elbow, the pivot helps you rotate a transform node. By changing the location of the pivot point, you get different results.

Pivots are basically the stationary point from which you rotate or scale objects. When animating, you sometimes need to build hierarchies where one transform node rotates the object and a second transform node scales. Each node can have its own pivot location to help you get the effect you want.

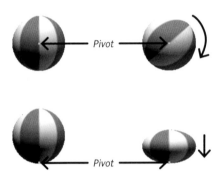

Rotation and scaling pivots

Hierarchies

When you are building scenes, you have learned that you can build dependency connections to link node attributes. When working with transform nodes or joint nodes, you can also build hierarchies, which create a different kind of relationship between your objects.

In a hierarchy, one transform node is parented to another. When Maya software works with these nodes, it looks first at the top node, or root node, then down the hierarchy. Therefore, motion from the upper nodes is transferred down into the lower nodes. In the diagram below, if the group1 node is rotated, then the two lower nodes will rotate with it. If the nurbsCone node is rotated, the upper nodes are not affected.

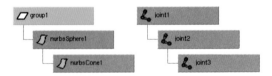

Object and joint hierarchy nodes

Joint hierarchies are used when you are building characters. When you create joints, the joint pivots act as limb joints while bones are drawn between them to help visualize the joint chain. By default, these hierarchies work just like object hierarchies. Rotating one node rotates all of the lower nodes at the same time.

You will learn more about joint hierarchies later in this introduction (see "Skeletons and Joints"), where you will also learn how inverse kinematics can reverse the flow of the hierarchy.

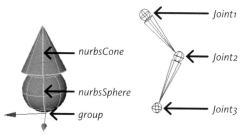

Object and joint hierarchies

MEL and Python scripting

MEL stands for Maya Embedded Language. In Maya software, every time you use a tool or open a window, you are using MEL. MEL can be used to execute simple commands, write expressions, or build scripts that will extend Maya software's existing functionality. The Script Editor displays commands and feedback generated by scripts and tools. Simple MEL commands can be typed in the Command Line, while more complex MEL scripts can be typed in the Script Editor.

Python® scripting is for programmers who would like to implement their tools using an alternate and popular scripting language. The implementation of Python scripting in Maya software provides the same access to native Maya commands as is provided through MEL. Note that only the built-in Maya commands are accessible through Python.

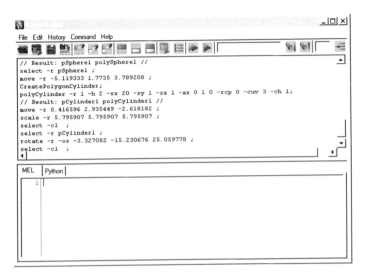

```
File  Edit  History  Command  Help

// Result: pSpherel polySpherel //
select -r pSpherel ;
move -r -5.119333 1.7735 3.789208 ;
CreatePolygonCylinder;
polyCylinder -r 1 -h 2 -sx 20 -sy 1 -sz 1 -ax 0 1 0 -rcp 0 -cuv 3 -ch 1;
// Result: pCylinderl polyCylinderl //
move -r 0.416596 2.935449 -2.618182 ;
scale -r 5.795907 5.795907 5.795907 ;
select -cl  ;
select -r pCylinderl ;
rotate -r -os -3.327082 -15.230676 25.059778 ;
select -cl  ;

MEL | Python |
    1|
```

The Script Editor

Scripting is the perfect tool for technical directors who are looking to customize Maya software to suit the needs of a particular production environment. Animators can also use scripting to create simple macros that will help speed up more difficult or tedious workflows.

Animation

When you animate, you bring objects to life. There are several different ways in which you can animate your scenes and the characters who inhabit them.

Animation is generally measured using frames that mimic the frames you would find on a film reel. You can play these frames at different speeds to achieve an animated effect. By default, Maya software plays at 24 frames per second, or 24FPS.

Keyframe animation

The most familiar method of animating is called keyframe animation. Using this technique, you determine how you want the parts of your objects to look at a particular frame, then you save the important attributes as keys. After you set several keys, the animation can be played back with Maya software filling motion in-between the keys.

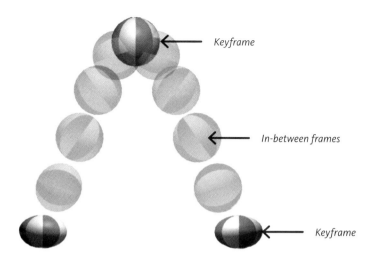

Keyframe

In-between frames

Keyframe

Keys and in-between frames

When keys are set on a particular attribute, the keyed values are stored in special nodes called animation curve nodes.

These curves are defined by the keys that map the value of the attribute against time.
The following is an example of several animation curve nodes connected to a transformation node.
One node is created for every attribute that is animated.

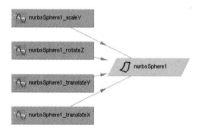

Dependency graph showing curve nodes

Once you have a curve, you can begin to control the tangency at each key to tweak the motion in between the main keys. You can make your objects speed up or slow down by editing the shape of these animation curves.

Generally, the slope of the graph curve tells you the speed of the motion. A steep slope in the curve means fast motion, while a flat curve equals no motion. Think of a skier going down a hill. Steep slopes increase speed while flatter sections slow things down.

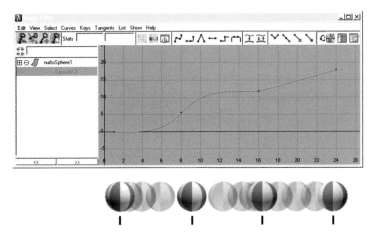

Graph Editor

Path animation

Path animation is already defined by its name. You can assign one or more objects so that they move along a path that has been drawn as a curve in 3D space. You can then use the shape of the curve and special path markers to edit and tweak the resulting motion.

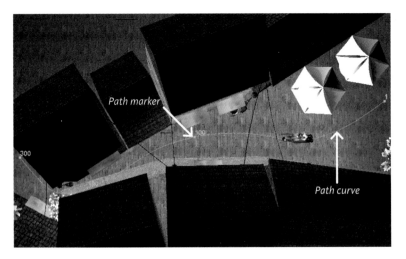

Path animation

Nonlinear animation

Nonlinear animation is a way to layer and mix character animation sequences independently of time. You can layer and blend any type of keyed animation, including motion capture and path animation. This is accomplished through the Trax Editor.

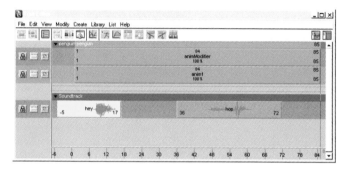

Trax Editor

Animation Layer Editor

The Animation Layer Editor lets you manipulate animation layers and change the way they blend together to create your result animation. Using this feature, you can modify a base animation easily. You can also isolate motions to specific layers, thus being able to modify the keyframed animation on its own.

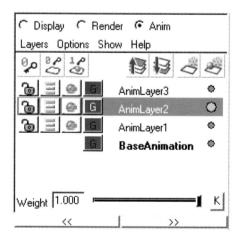

The Animation Layer Editor

Reactive animation

Reactive animation is a term used to describe animation in which one object's animation is based on the animation of another object.

An example of this technique would be moving gears when the rotation of one gear is linked to the rotation of other gears. You can set keys on the first gear and all the others will animate automatically. Later, when you want to edit or tweak the keys, only one object needs to be worked on and the others update reactively.

Animated gears

You can set up reactive animation using a number of tools including those outlined below:

Set Driven Key

This tool lets you interactively set up an attribute on one object to drive one or more attributes on another.

Expressions

Expressions are scripts that let you connect different attributes on different nodes.

Constraints

Constraints let you set up an object to point at, orient to, or look at another object.

Connections

Attributes can be directly linked to another attribute using dependency node connections. You can create this kind of direct connection using the Connection Editor.

Dynamics

Another animation technique is dynamics. You can set up objects in your scene that animate based on physical effects such as collisions, gravity, and wind. Different variables are bounciness, friction, or initial velocity. When you play back the scene, you run a simulation to see how all the parts react to the variables.

This technique gives you natural motion that would be difficult to keyframe. You can use dynamics with rigid body objects, particles, or soft body objects.

Rigid body objects are objects that do not deform. You can further edit the rigid body by setting it as either active or passive. Active bodies react to the dynamics, whereas passive bodies do not.

To simulate effects such as wind or gravity, you add fields to your dynamic objects.

Rigid body simulation of surfboard and house colliding

Particles are tiny points that can be used to create effects such as smoke, fire, or explosions. These points are emitted into the scene where they are also affected by the dynamic fields.

Particles

Soft bodies are surfaces that you deform during a simulation. To create a soft body, create an object and turn its points into particles. The particles react to the dynamic forces, which in turn deform the surface.

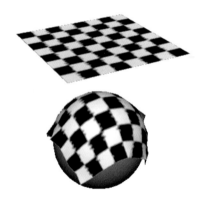

Soft bodies

Modeling

The objects you want to animate are usually built using either NURBS surfaces or polygonal meshes. Complementary to these two basic geometry types, subdivision surfaces (SubDs) mix the best features of both NURBS and polygons. Maya software offers you both of these geometry types so that you can choose the method best suited to your work.

NURBS curves

NURBS stands for nonuniform rational b-spline, which is a technical term for a spline curve. By modeling with NURBS curves, you lay down control points and smooth geometry will be created using the points as guides.

Shown below is a typical NURBS curve with important parts labeled:

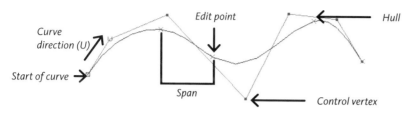

NURBS curve

These key components define important aspects of how a curve works. The flexibility and power of NURBS geometry comes from your ability to edit the shape of the geometry using these controls.

As your geometry becomes more complex, you may need more of these controls. For this reason, it is usually better to start out with simpler geometry so that you can more easily control the shape. If you need more complex geometry, then controls can be inserted later.

NURBS surfaces

Surfaces are defined using the same mathematics as curves, except now they are in two dimensions—U and V. You learned about this earlier when you learned about UV coordinate space.

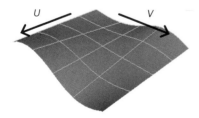

NURBS surface

Below are some of the component elements of a typical NURBS surface:

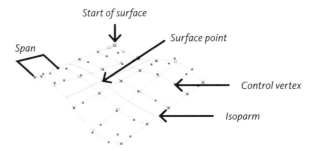

NURBS components

Complex shapes can be, in essence, sculpted using this surface type as you push and pull the controls to shape the surface.

Completed NURBS model

Polygons

Polygons are the most basic geometry type available. Whereas NURBS surfaces interpolate the shape of the geometry interactively, polygonal meshes draw the geometry directly to the control vertices.

Below are some of the components found on a polygonal mesh:

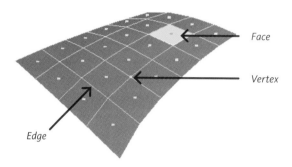

Polygon components

You can build up polymeshes by extruding, scaling, and positioning polygonal facets to build shapes. You can then smooth the shape to get a more organic look for your model.

Polygonal model before and after smoothing

Construction history

When you create models, the various steps are recorded as dependency nodes that remain connected to your surface.

In the example below, a curve has been used to create a revolved surface. Maya software keeps the history by creating dependencies between the curve, a revolve node, and the shape node. Edits made to the curve or the revolve node will update the final shape.

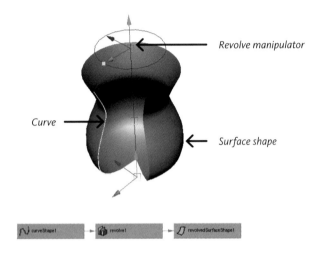

Revolve surface with dependencies

Many of these nodes come with special manipulators that make it easier to update the node attributes. In the case of the revolve, manipulators are available for the axis line and for the revolve's sweep angle.

It is possible to later delete history so that you are only working with the shape node. Do not forget though, that the dependency nodes have attributes that can be animated. Therefore, you lose some power if you delete history.

Deformations

Deformers are special object types that can be used to reshape other objects. By using deformers, you can model different shapes, or give animations more of a squash and stretch quality.

Deformers are a powerful Maya feature—they can even be layered for more subtle effects. You can also bind deformers into skeletons or affect them with soft body dynamics.

The following lists some basic deformer types available:

Sculpt objects

Sculpt objects lets you deform a surface by pushing it with the object. By animating the position of the sculpt object, you can achieve animated surface deformations.

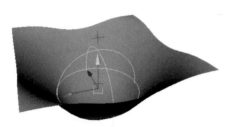

Sculpt object deformer

Lattices

Lattices are external frames that can be applied to your objects. If you then reshape the frame the object is deformed in response.

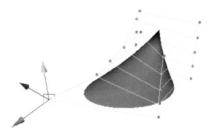

Lattice deformer

Clusters

Clusters are groups of CVs or lattice points that are built into a single set. The cluster is given its own pivot point and can be used to manipulate the clustered points. You can weight the CVs in a cluster for more control over a deformation.

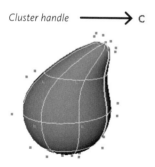

Cluster deformer

Character animation

Character animation typically involves the animation of surfaces using skeleton joint chains and inverse kinematic handles to help drive the motion.

Skeletons and joints

As you have already learned, skeleton joint chains are actually hierarchies. A skeleton is made of joint nodes that are connected visually by bone icons. Binding geometry to these hierarchies lets you create surface deformations when the joints are rotated.

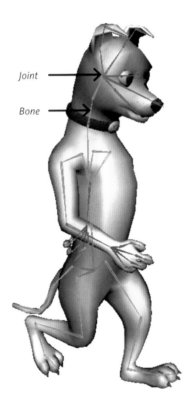

Joints and bones

Inverse kinematics

By default, joint hierarchies work like any other hierarchy—the rotation of one joint is transferred to the lower joint nodes. This is known as forward kinematics. While this method is powerful, it makes it hard to plant a character's feet or move a hand to control the arm.

Inverse kinematics lets you work with the hierarchy in the opposite direction. By placing an IK handle at the end of the joint chain, Maya software will solve all rotations within that joint chain. This is a lot quicker than animating every single joint in the hierarchy. There are three kinds of inverse kinematic solvers—the IK spline, the IK single chain, and the IK rotate plane.

Each of these solvers is designed to help you control the joint rotations with the use of an IK handle. As the IK handle is moved, the solver solves joint rotations that allow the end joint to properly move to the IK handle position.

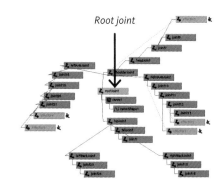

Character joint hierarchy

The individual solvers have their own unique controls. Some of these are outlined below:

Single chain solver

The single chain solver provides a straightforward mechanism for posing and animating a chain.

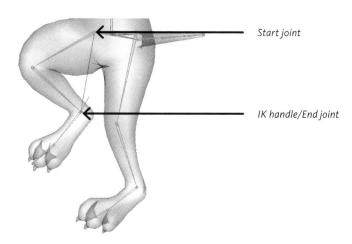

Start joint

IK handle/End joint

IK single chain solver

Rotate plane solver

The rotate plane solver gives you more control. With this solver, the plane that acts as the goal for all the joints can be moved by rotating the plane using a twist attribute or by moving the pole vector handle.

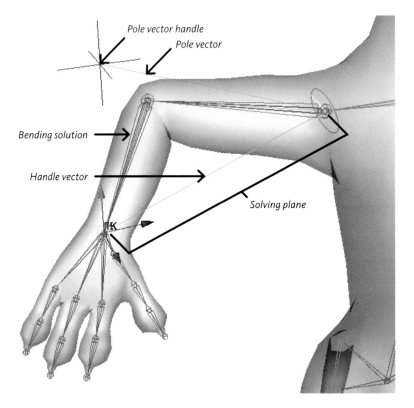

IK rotate plane solver

IK spline solver

The IK spline solver lets you control the chain using a spline curve. You can edit the CVs on the spline to influence the rotation of the joints in the chain.

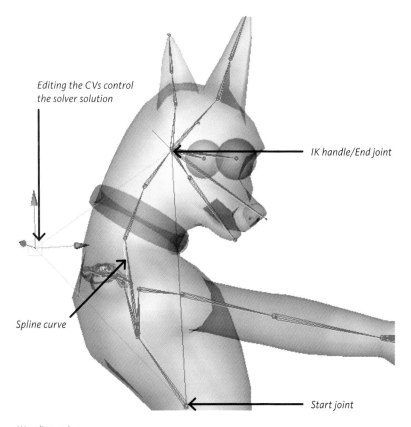

Editing the CVs control the solver solution

IK handle/End joint

Spline curve

Start joint

IK spline solver

Skinning your characters

Once you have a skeleton built, you can bind skin to the surfaces of your character so that they deform with the rotation of the joints. You can use either smooth skinning or rigid skinning. Smooth skinning uses weighted influences while rigid skinning does not.

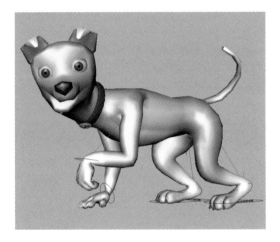

Flexors

In some cases, skinning a character does not yield realistic deformations in the character's joint areas. You can use flexors to add secondary level of deformations to help control the tucking and bulging of your character.

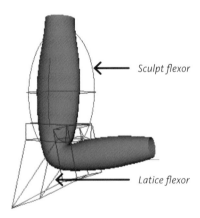

Sculpt flexor

Latice flexor

Flexors

Rendering

Once your characters are set up, you can apply color and texture, then render with realistic lighting.

Shading networks

Adding texture maps and other rendering nodes create shading networks. At the end of every shading network is a shading group node. This node has specific attributes such as displacement maps and mental ray® for Maya ports, but more importantly, it contains a list of objects that are to be shaded by that network at render time. Without this node at the end of the network, the shader will not render.

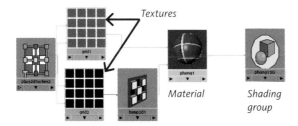

Shading group dependencies

You can think of a shading network as a bucket into which you place all the color, texture, and material qualities that you want for your surface. Add a light or two and your effect is achieved.

Texture maps

To add detail to your shading groups, you can texture map different attributes. Some of these include bump, transparency, and color.

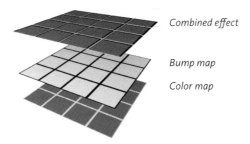

Texture map layers

Lighting

You can add light to your scenes using any number of lights. These lights let you add mood and atmosphere to a scene in much the same way as lighting is used by a photographer. You can preview your lights interactively as you model, or you can render to see the final effect.

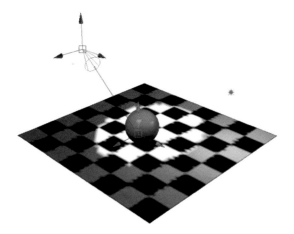

Light manipulator

Motion blur

When a real-life camera takes a shot of a moving object, the final image is often blurred. This motion blur adds to the animated look of a scene and can be simulated in Maya software. There are two types of motion blur: a 2 1/2 D solution and a 3D solution.

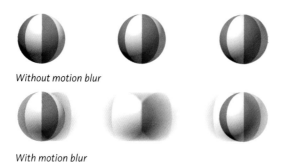

Without motion blur

With motion blur

Motion blur

Hardware rendering

Hardware rendering uses the power of your graphics card to render an image. This is a quick way to render as the quality can be very good or it can be used to preview animations. You will need to use the hardware renderer to render most particle effects. These effects can be composited in later with software rendered images of your geometry.

Hardware rendering

A-buffer rendering

The Maya rendering architecture is a hybrid renderer. It uses an Exact Area Sampling (EAS) or A-buffer algorithm for primary visibility from the eye (camera), and then raytraces any secondary rays.

A-buffer rendering

Ray-trace rendering

Raytracing lets you include reflections, refractions, and ray-trace shadows into your scenes. Only objects that have their ray-trace options turned on will use this renderer. Raytracing is slower than the A-buffer algorithm and should only be used when necessary.

Ray-trace rendering

Note: *Objects have raytracing turned On by default, but the renderer's raytracing is turned Off by default.*

How the renderer works

The Maya renderer works by looking through the camera at the scene. It then takes a section or tile and analyzes whether or not it can render that section. If it can, it will combine the information found in the shading group (geometry, lights, and shading network) with the Render Settings information, and the whole tile is rendered.

As the renderer moves on to the next section, it again analyzes the situation. If it hits a tile where there is more information than it wants to handle at one time, it breaks down the tile into a smaller tile and renders.

Rendering of A-buffer tiles in progress

When you use raytracing, each tile is first rendered with the A-buffer, then the renderer looks for items that require raytracing. If it finds any, it layers in the raytraced sections. When it finishes, you have your finished image, or if you are rendering an animation, a sequence of images.

Interactive Photorealistic Renderer

The Interactive Photorealistic Renderer (IPR) gives you fast feedback for texturing and lighting updates without needing to re-render.

IPR rendering in progress

Conclusion

Now that you have a basic understanding of what Maya software is designed to do, it is time for you to start working with the system directly. The concepts outlined in this introduction will be clearer when you experience them firsthand.

Project 01

In Project One, you are going to learn the basics of object creation, along with the fundamentals of animation, shaders, and textures. This will give you the chance to explore the Autodesk® Maya® workspace while building your scene.

You will start by creating an alley similar to the city alley found in the Roadside Romeo movie. You will then fill it with simple models in order to learn how to create, move, and modify objects. Then you will explore the rudiments of hierarchies and animation by creating a simple door. After that, you will experiment with shaders and textures, which will allow you to render your scene.

These lessons offer you a good look at some of the key concepts and workflows that drive Autodesk Maya software. Once this project is finalized, you will have a better understanding of the Maya user interface and its various modules.

Lesson 01
Primitives

This lesson teaches you how to build and transform primitives in 3D space in order to create a rudimentary environment, in which you will set up some animation shown in this book. You will explore the Autodesk® Maya® user interface (UI) as you learn how to build and develop your scene.

In this lesson, you will learn the following:

Setting up Maya software

The first step is to install the Autodesk Maya software. Once that is done, you should copy the Learning Maya support files to your *Maya projects* directory. The support files are found in the *support_files* directory on the DVD-ROM included with this book.

In order to find your *projects* directory, you need to launch Maya software at least once so that it creates your user directory structure. Here is where the *projects* directory is typically located on your machine:

Windows®: *Drive:\Documents and Settings\[username]\My Documents\maya\projects*
Mac® OS X: *Users/[username]/Documents/maya/projects*

Tip: *Ensure that the support files are not read-only after you copy them from the DVD-ROM.*

When Maya software is launched for the first time and you have other Maya versions installed, you will be asked if you want to copy your preferences or use the default preferences. In order to follow the course, you should be using default preferences. If you have been working with Maya software and have changed any of your user interface settings, you may want to delete or back up your preferences in order to start with the default Maya configuration.

Creating a new project

Maya software uses a project directory to store and organize all of the files (scenes, images, materials, textures, and so on) related to a particular scene. When building a scene, you create and work with a variety of file types and formats. The project directory allows you to keep these different file types in their unique subdirectory locations within the project directory.

1   **Launch Maya software**

2   **Set the project**

To manage your files, you can set a project directory that contains subdirectories for different types of files that relate to your project.

- Go to the **File** menu and select **Project** → **Set...**

  A window opens that directs you to the Maya projects directory.

- **Open** the folder *support_files*.

- Click the folder named *project1* to select it.

- Click the **OK** button.

  This sets project1 as your current project.

- Go to the **File** menu and select **Project → Edit Current...**

  Make sure that the project directories are set up as shown below. This ensures that Maya software is looking into the proper subdirectories when it opens scene files.

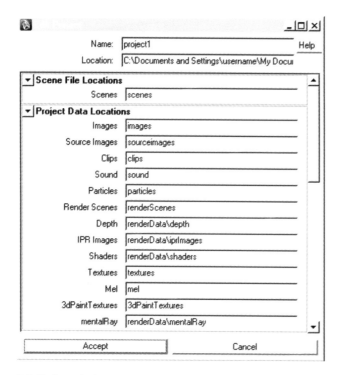

Edit Project window

- Click the **Accept** button when done.

3   **Make a new scene**

- Select **File → New Scene**.

  This will create a new scene in the current directory when you save it.

Build the environment

Every scene you create in Maya software will most likely contain objects such as surfaces, deformers, skeleton joints, or particle emitters. For this scene, you will build a dark alley, but first, you will need a large outdoor environment.

To start, you will build a ground plane surrounded by a large sky dome. These first objects will be a primitive polygonal plane and a primitive NURBS sphere. You can view the finished scene to get an idea of what you are about to create by opening the file called *01-alley_01.ma*.

1   **Launch Maya software**

2   **Change menu sets**

There are five main menu sets in Maya software: *Animation, Polygons, Surfaces, Dynamics,* and *Rendering.* These menu sets are used to access related tool sets.

- From the drop-down menu at the left edge of the Status Line (Toolbar), select **Polygons**.

  As you change menu sets, the first six menu items and the Help menu item along the top of the viewport remain the same while the remaining menu items change to reflect the chosen menu set.

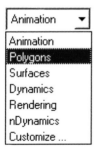

Menu set pop-up menu

3   **Create a polygonal plane**

A primitive plane will be used as a large ground plane on which you will build the house. It will be built using polygonal geometry. Throughout this lesson and in the next project, you will learn more about this geometry type.

- **Disable** the interactive creation mode of models (which is enabled by default) by selecting **Create → Polygon Primitives → Interactive Creation**.

- From the **Create** menu, select **Polygon Primitives** → **Plane**.

  A small plane is created at the origin.

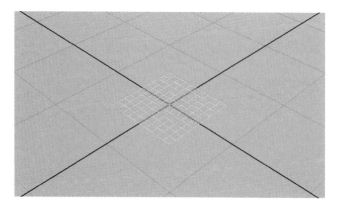

Perspective view of pPlane1

4   **Change the plane's dimensions**

The plane is a procedural model. This means that it is broken down into parts called *nodes*. One node contains its positioning information, one contains its shape information, and another contains input information that defines the plane's construction history using attributes such as width, height, and subdivisions. You can edit this Input node's attributes in the Channel Box in order to edit the plane's basic shape.

The Channel Box is found at the right side of the screen and lets you make changes to key attributes very easily.

Note: *If your Channel Box is not along the right side of the screen, you can access it by selecting* **Display** → **UI Elements** → **Channel Box/Layer Editor.**

- From the Channel Box's **Inputs** section, click *polyPlane1*.

  This will make several new attributes available for editing.

- Type **200** in the **Width** entry field and press the **Enter** key.

- Type **200** in the **Height** entry field and press the **Enter** key.

  Now the plane is very large in the Perspective view, but this is intended since you do not want to see any ground plane edges as you are working.

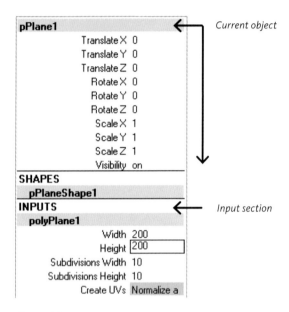

Channel Box

Note: *Another method for increasing the size of the plane would be to scale it. In Maya, you can often achieve the same visual results using many different methods. Over time, you will begin to choose the techniques that best suit a particular situation.*

5   **Rename the Plane node**

You should rename the existing Transform node to make it easier to find later.

- Click the *pPlane1* name at the top of the Channel Box to highlight it.

- **Type** the name *ground*, then press the **Enter** key.

```
Channels  Edit  Object  Show
ground
                   Translate X  0
                   Translate Y  0
                   Translate Z  0
```

Renaming the node in the Channel Box

6   **Create the sky**

You will now create another object to be used as a large sky dome.

- **Disable** the interactive creation mode of models by selecting **Create** →
  NURBS Primitives → **Interactive Creation**.

- Select **Create** → **NURBS Primitives** → **Sphere.**

7   **Modify the sphere**

- With the *pSphere1* still selected, set the **Scale X**, **Y,** and **Z** in the Channel Box to **100**.

  The sphere should now be as big as the ground plane.

Note: *You can dolly out in the Perspective view to see the entire scene by holding the Alt key and click+dragging the RMB.*

- Click the *makeNurbSphere1* node in the **Channel Box**.

- Set the following:

    End Sweep to **180**

    Sections to **4**

By changing the sphere's input, the sphere automatically updates. The sphere is now half a sphere with fewer sections.

8   Rotate the sphere

- With the *pSphere1* still selected, set **Rotate X** in the Channel Box to **-90** degrees.

  Doing this rotates the sphere so it covers the ground plane. You now have a closed environment in which you will create the rest of the scene.

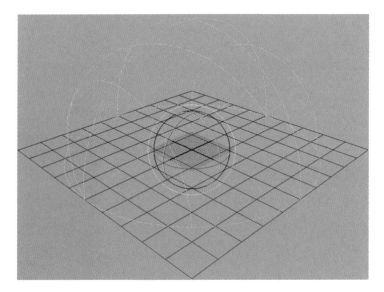

The ground plane with a sky dome

9   Rename the sphere

- **Rename** the *pSphere1 skydome*.

Viewing the scene

When you work in 3D space, it is important to see your work from different angles. The different view panels let you see your work from the front, top, side, and perspective views.

You can also use the view tools to change the views in order to reposition how you see your scene. In some cases, a view change is like panning a camera around a room, while in other cases a view change might be like rotating an object around in your hand to see all the sides. These view tools can be accessed using the **Alt** key in combination with various mouse buttons.

1   **Edit the Perspective view**

You can use the **Alt** key with your mouse buttons to tumble, track, and dolly in your Perspective view.

- Change your view using the following key combinations:

    Alt + LMB to tumble

    Alt + MMB to track

    Alt + LMB + MMB or **Alt + RMB** to dolly

    *You can also combine these with the **Ctrl** key to create a bounding box dolly where the view adjusts based on a bounding box. This is useful when you want to dolly on a precise section of the view or quickly dolly out to get the general look of the scene.*

    Ctrl + Alt + LMB to box dolly

    Click+drag from left to right to dolly in, and from right to left to dolly out

    You can also undo and redo view changes using the following keys:

    To **undo** views use **[**

    To **redo** views use **]**

- Alter your *Perspective* window until it appears as shown below:

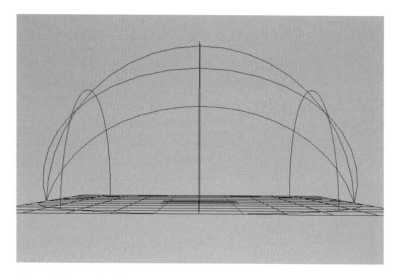

Changed Perspective view

2   **Four view panels**

By default, a single Perspective window is shown in the workspace. To see other views of the scene, you can change your panel layout.

- At the top of the Perspective view panel, go to the **Panels** menu and select **Saved Layouts** → **Four View**.

  You can now see the environment using three Orthographic views—top, side, and front—that show you the models from a projected view. You can also see them in a Perspective view that is more like the everyday 3D world. This multiple view setup is very useful when positioning objects in 3D space.

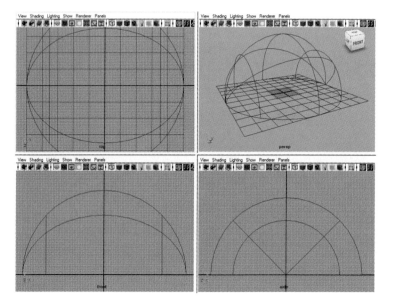

Four view panels

Tip: *Tapping the keyboard* **spacebar** *will switch from a single view panel to a four-view panel.*

3   **Edit the view in the side view**

Orthographic views use similar hotkeys, except that you cannot tumble by default in an Orthographic view.

- In the side view, change your view using the following key combinations:

    Alt + MMB to track;

    Alt + LMB + MMB or **Alt + RMB** to dolly.

- Keep working with the *Orthographic* views until they are set up as shown:

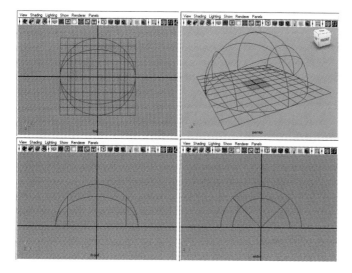

New Orthographic views

4   **Frame Selected and Frame All**

Another quick way to navigate in the different views is to use the Frame Selected or Frame All hotkeys for the active view.

- Select the *ground* plane.

- While in the *four-view* panels, move your mouse over a view.

- Press the **f** hotkey to frame the selected geometry in the view under your mouse.

- Press the **a** hotkey to frame everything visible in the view under your mouse cursor.

- Press the **Shift+a** hotkey to frame everything in all views at once.

Setting display options

The view panels let you interactively view your scene. By default, this means viewing your scene as a wireframe model. To better evaluate the form of your objects, you can activate hardware shading.

1   Turn on hardware shading

To help visualize your objects, you can use hardware shading to display a shaded view within any panel.

- From the Perspective view's **Shading** menu, select **Smooth Shade All**.

This setting affects all of the objects within the current view panel.

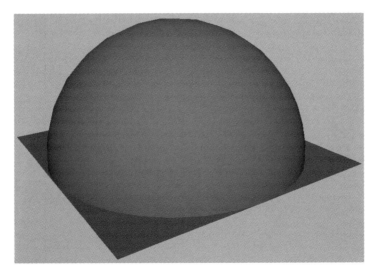

Smooth shaded view

Tip: *You can also turn on Smooth Shading by moving your cursor over the desired panel, clicking with your middle mouse button, and pressing the* **5** *key. The* **4** *key can be used to return the panel to a wireframe view.*

2 **Hide the grid**

You can hide the world grid to simplify your view using one of two options:

- From the view panel's **Show** menu, select **Grid** to hide the grid for that view only.

    OR

- From the **Display** menu, deselect **Grid** to hide the grid for all views.

Moving inside the environment

In order to have the feeling of being inside the environment in the Perspective view, you need to move the Perspective camera inside the sky dome geometry. You will soon realize that even if you can see inside the sky dome, sometimes its geometry will appear in front of the camera while moving, or it will prevent you from selecting some objects. The following actions are somewhat more advanced than what you will undertake in this project, but they will allow you to interact with you scene more easily.

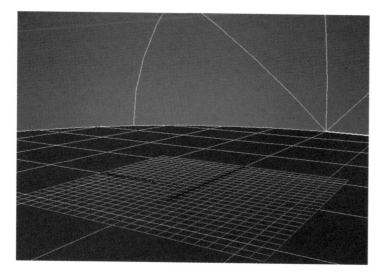

Perspective inside the environment

1 **Change the sky's display**

To simplify your scene interaction, there is a way of seeing inside the sky dome even when the camera is outside of it. To do so, you will have to change the way the geometry is displayed.

- Select the *skydome*.

- Select **Window** → **Attribute Editor**.

    The Attribute Editor is similar to the Channel Box, but with many more accessible attributes.

- **Expand** the **Render Stats** section by clicking the small arrow button.

    This section controls how the models are displayed in the viewports and render time.

- **Disable** the **Double-Sided** attribute.

    This tells Maya to hide the sides of the geometry facing away from the camera.

- **Enable** the **Opposite** attribute.

    This tells Maya that you want the geometry to be displayed inside out.

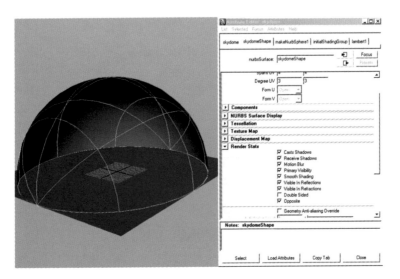

environment

2   **Change the sky's to block selection**

To simplify your scene interaction even further, there is a way preventing the sky dome from ever getting selected in the viewport. To do so, you will have to change the geometry state to be displayed as a reference only.

- Still in the Attribute Editor with the *skydome* selected, expand the **Object Display** category.

- Under the **Drawing Overrides** section, turn **On** the **Enable Overrides** option.

- Set the **Display Type** to **Reference**.

  You will not be able to select the object anymore from the viewports.

Note: *Later on in this project, when you will need to tweak the referenced object, you will be able to select it through the Outliner or by typing the MEL command* `select skydome` *in the Command Line.*

Create buildings

Now that you have established a proper sky dome and ground plane, you will create the alley by adding buildings to your scene. In this example, you will build the buildings only from primitives.

1 **Create a polygonal cube**

   Here, you will use the hotbox as an alternative method for accessing tools.

   - Press and hold the **spacebar** anywhere over the interface to display the hotbox.

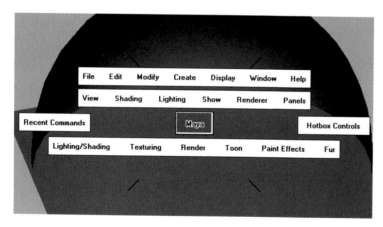

Hotbox access to menu items

- In the hotbox, select **Create** → **Polygon Primitives** → **Cube** → ❑.

- In the option window, set the **Normalize** option to **Off.**

  This option will make it easier for you to texture the building later in the project.

- Click the **Create** button.

  A small cube is placed at the origin.

Tip: *You can access all functions in Maya using either the main menus or the hotbox. As you become more familiar with the hotbox, you can use the UI options found in the **Display** menu to turn off the panel menus and, therefore, reduce screen clutter.*

2   **Rename the cube**

- Click the *pCube1* node's name at the top of the Channel Box and type the name *building*.

3   **Scale the building**

You can now use the **Scale Tool** to resize the building in the scene.

- Select the **Scale Tool** in the toolbox on the left of the interface, or press **r**.

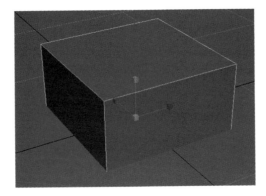

Toolbox   *Manipulator handle*

- **Click+drag** the center manipulator handle to scale the building along all axes to about **30** units.

- **Click+drag** the blue manipulator handle to **scale down** the building along the **Z-axis** until the building is about **15** units.

  You will notice that the manipulator handle turns yellow to indicate that it is active.

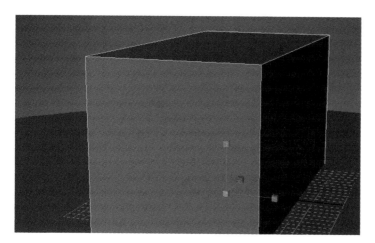

The building geometry

4   **Create the roof**

You will now use a polygonal cylinder to build the roof of the building.

- Select **Create → Polygonal Primitives → Cylinder**.

    The cylinder is create at the origin, but is hidden by the building.

- Select the **Move Tool** or press **w**, and then move the roof up on the **Y-axis** by about **17** units.

- **Rename** the cylinder *roof*.

- In the **Inputs** section of the Channel Box, set the following:

    Subdivisions Axis to **3**

    Subdivisions Caps to **0**

- Still in the Channel Box, set the **Rotate Z** attribute to **90** degrees.

- Select the **Scale Tool** or press **r**, and then scale the roof as follows:

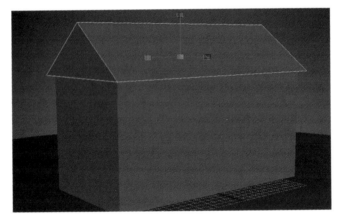

The roof geometry

5   **Move the building**

Since you need to create an alley, you will now translate aside the new building.

- Select both the *building* object, then hold down the **Shift** key and then select the *roof* object.

    Doing so will select both object at once so the next step affects then at the same time.

- Select the **Move Tool** in the toolbox on the left of the interface, or press **w**.

- **Click+drag** the blue manipulator handle to **translate** the building along the **Z-axis** to about **-15** units.

6   **Make more buildings**

Instead of always starting from a default primitive object, you can duplicate an existing one, preserving its position and shape.

- Select both the *building* and *roof* and select **Edit → Duplicate**.

When using the duplicate function, the new objects will be suffixed with a number such as building1 and roof1. Subsequent duplicates will get that number incremented.

Tip: *You can use the **Ctrl+d** hotkey to duplicate the selected geometry without going into the menu each time.*

- Using the **Move Tool** place the new geometry next to the first building.

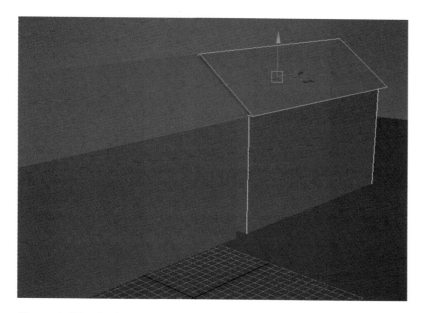

The new building in place

7   **Group the building parts**

Since you will be creating many buildings, it is a good idea to group the building and roof objects together so you can move them both at once.

- With both the *building* and *roof* object still selected, select **Edit** → **Group** → **o.**

- Set the **Group pivot** option to **Center**, and then click the **Group** button.

  The two objects are now grouped together and the group is currently selected. Notice the location of the Move Tool manipulator in the viewport. This is the group's pivot location, which is located at the center of the building as specified in above step.

- Rename the new group *buildingGroup***.**

- **Rotate** the new group to see the effect of grouping geometry.

Tip: *If you deselect the building group, you can get back to it by selecting any parts of the building, and then pressing the Up Arrow key.*

8   **More buildings**

- Still with the *buildingGroup* **selected, press Ctrl+d to duplicate the building again.**

- Use the **Move Tool** to translate the building group. You can also translate the building about the green **Y-axis** manipulator to make it taller or shorter.

- Switch to the **Rotate Tool** by pressing the **e** hotkey.

- Rotate the *buildingGroup* about the green **Y-axis** manipulator.

- Scale the *buildingGroup* to change the building size.

- Make a couple of copies of the buildings to create an alley similar to the following:

They alley is taking shape

9   Create a light post

You will use a cylinder to create the post of the light posts that will surround the alley.

- Select **Create** → **Polygonal Primitives** → **Cylinder**.

- **Rename** the cylinder *post*.

- **Click+drag** the **Scale Tool** handle to **scale up** the *post* along the **Y-axis** to about **6** units.

  Notice that your geometry is going through and underneath the ground plane.

Tip: *If any pieces of geometry get in the way when you select and modify objects, you can temporarily hide them. To do so, select the geometry to hide, then select* **Display** → **Hide** → **Hide Selection**. *To show the last hidden objects, select* **Display** → **Show** → **Show Last Hidden**. *To show all hidden objects, select* **Display** → **Show** → **All**.

- Press the **w** hotkey to select the **Move Tool**.

- **Click+drag** the green manipulator handle to **move** the *post* up on the **Y-axis** until the bottom of the cylinder touches the top of the ground.

- With the *post* still selected, highlight the *polyCylinder2* node in the Channel Box.

- Set the following:

    Radius to **0.2**

    Subdivisions Axis to **20**

    Subdivisions Height to **5**

    Subdivisions Caps to **0**

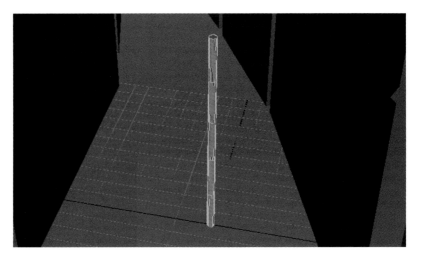

The light post geometry

10   **Change the shape of the post**

At this time, the post is boring and could use some details. Now that you are familiar with transforming an object, you will learn how to modify the shape of an object.

- With the *post* selected, press the **f** hotkey to frame it in the view.

- In the Status Line located at the top of the interface, click the **Component Mode** button.

The Component Mode button

Working in this mode will display the components of the currently selected geometry. You can then select and transform the points defining a surface's shape. Polygon points are called **vertex/vertices** and NURBS points are called **control vertices** or **CVs**.

- **Click+drag** around vertices in the viewport to select them.

- Select only the two bottom rings of vertices of the *post*.

> **Tip:** When selecting components, hold down **Shift** to toggle the new selection, hold down **Ctrl** to deselect the new selection, and hold down **Ctrl +Shift** to add the new selection to the currently selected group of components.

- Select the **Scale Tool**, then hold down the **Ctrl** key, and **click+drag** the **Y-axis**.

  Doing so will equally scale the vertices about the X and Z-axes.

- Shape the geometry as follows:

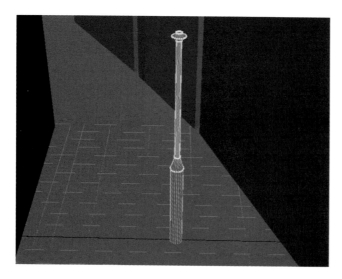

Shaped light post

- Click the **Object Mode** button in the Status Line to exit the Component mode.

Object mode

11   Create a decorative light

The light post is now only missing a light at the top of the post.

- Select **Create** → **Polygon Primitives** → **Prism**.

- In the Channel Box, set the following:

  Length to **2**

  Side Length to **0.5**

  Number Of Sides to **8**

  Subdivisions Height to **3**

  Subdivisions Cap to **1**

- **Rename** the *pPrism1 light*.

- Switch to **Component Mode**, and shape the light as follows:

The decorative light

12 Move the light post

In order to make it easier to move the light post, you will group them.

- Click one *post* to select it, then hold down the **Shift** key and click the *light* to get them both selected.

- Press **Ctrl+g** to group them together.

- **Rename** the group *lightPost*.

13 Repositioning the light posts

When moving an object in an Orthographic view, the move manipulator is limited to work in two axes. You can move an object in these two axes at once by dragging on the center of the manipulator or constraining the motion along a single axis using the handles.

- In the *top* view, **click+drag** the square center of the move manipulator to move the *lightPost* along both the **X** and **Y-axes**.

Note: *If you **click+drag** the center of the manipulator in the Perspective view, you will notice that it doesn't move along any particular axis. It is actually moving along the camera's view plane.*

- Place the *lightPost* next to a building, where the sidewalk would be.

- Press **Ctrl+d** to **duplicate** the *lightPost* and place a few copies around the alley.

Tip: *Be sure to always refer to more than a single view to verify that the object is positioned properly.*

14 Save your work

- From the **File** menu, select **Save Scene As...**

- Enter the name *01-alley_01.ma*.

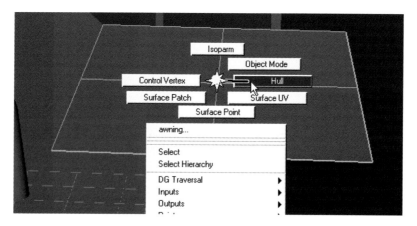

Windows Save As dialog box

- Click the **Save** button or press the **Enter** key.

More details

Now that you know how to place objects and interact with the Perspective view, you will add more details to the alley by making decorative awnings and adding electrical wires between the buildings.

1 Create a electrical wires

Now that you are getting familiar with the Component mode, you will use this knowledge to create a NURBS electrical wire.

- Select **Create** → **NURBS Primitives** → **Cylinder.**

- **Rename** the cylinder *wire***.**

- In the Channel Box, highlight the *makeNurbsCylinder1* node and set the following:

    Sections to **4**

    Spans to **4**

- Set the following for the *wire* object:

    Rotate X to **90**

    Rotate Z to **90**

    Scale X to **0.05**

    Scale Y to **10**

    Scale Z to **0.05**

- **Move** the *wire* up and place it so it interpenetrates with two of the buildings on either sides of the alley.

2   **Change the shape of the wire**

- Go into Component mode by pressing the **F8** hotkey.

    This is just another way of going into Component mode besides using the button in the Status Line.

- **Click+drag** to select groups of CVs and use the **Move Tool** to move them down on their **Y-axis**.

    Doing so will give a nice dangling look to the electrical wire.

The wire shape

Tip: *You might want to go into wireframe mode (hotkey 4), in order to select components more easily.*

- Pressing the **F8** hotkey to go back in Object Mode.

3   **Adjust NURBS smoothness**

The display of NURBS surfaces in a viewport can be adjusted by increasing or decreasing its smoothness.

- Select the *wire*.

- From the main **Display** menu, select **NURBS**.

- Select any of the menu items between **Hull**, **Rough**, **Medium**, **Fine,** or **Custom NURBS Smoothness**.

   These settings will affect how selected NURBS objects are displayed in all view panels.

Tip: *A NURBS object can have its smoothness set differently in each viewport using the following hotkeys:*
   1—rough
   2—medium
   3—fine

4   **Duplicate the wire**

- **Duplicate** and place a couple of wire copies.

Project 01

The duplicated wires

5   **Create an awning**

Even though you do not yet have windows and doors, you will now model a decorative awning using a NURBS plane.

- Select **Create** → **NURBS Primitives** → **Plane.**

- Rename the plane *awning*.

- Translate the *awning* up on the **Y-axis** to about **10** units.

- **Scale** the *awning* up by about **6** units on all axes.

- In the **Channel Box** under the *makeNurbsPlane* Input node, set the **Patches U** and **V** to **2.**

6   **Shape the awning**

You can now tweak the shape of the awning.

- Select the *awning*.

- **RMB** on the *awning* to pop up its contextual radial menu, and select **Hull**.

  Hulls define the curves of a NURBS surface. By using this type of component, you can modify all the CVs of a same line at once.

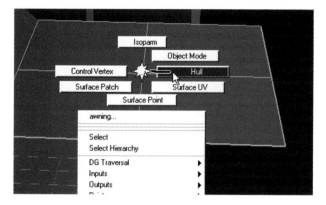

NURBS context menu

- Select the hull by clicking a purple line on the *awning*.

- Move the different hulls to get a shape as follows:

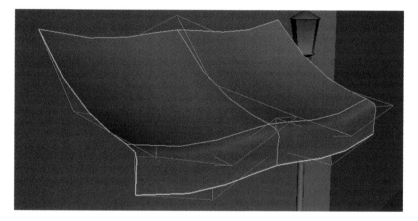

The NURBS awning

- To exit the Component mode, **RMB** on the *awning* to pop up its contextual radial menu, and select **Object Mode**.

- **Move** the *awning* at a proper location on a building.

- **Duplicate** it as you would like.

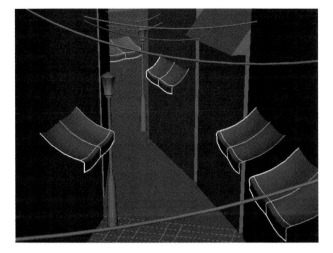

The final alley scene

7   **Save your work**

- From the **File** menu, select **Save Scene As...**

- Enter the name *01-alley_02.ma* and click the **Save** button.

   Make sure you save this file since you will be continuing with it in the next lesson.

Note: *Throughout this book, you will be using the final saved file from one lesson as the start file for the next, unless specified otherwise. Save your work at the end of each lesson to make sure that you have the start file ready. Othewise, you can use the scene files from the support files.*

Conclusion

Congratulations! You have completed your first exercise using Maya software. You should now be able to easily navigate the different views and change the basic hardware display settings. You should also be confident in creating, duplicating, transforming, and renaming objects, along with using the translation, rotation, and scale manipulators. At this point you should also understand the difference between Component mode and Object mode. As well, be careful to save scene files.

In the next lesson, you will explore in greater depth how to model objects and details.

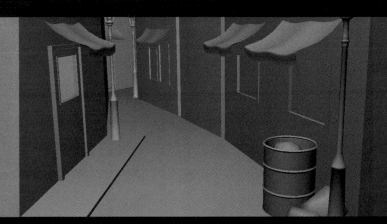

Lesson 02
Adding Details

In this lesson, you will modify existing models to enhance the richness of the scene. You will first build steps using a special modeling technique called revolve. You will then create an opening in the wall for a door and then you will build the throne. This is a good time to experiment with basic modeling tools and concepts.

In this lesson, you will learn the following:

- How to open a scene

- How hide objects

- How insert polygonal edges

- How to extrude and move polygonal faces

- How to delete a polygonal face

- How to draw and revolve a curve

- How to snap to grid

- How to combine polygonal objects

- How to move the pivot of an object

- About construction history

- How to delete construction history

- How to parent an object

Working with a good file

Use the scene that you saved in the previous lesson or use the one provided in your *scenes* directory, *01-alley_02.ma*.

1   Open a scene

There are several ways to open a scene in Autodesk® Maya® software. The following are three easy options:

• From the **File** menu, select **Open Scene**.

    OR

• Press **Ctrl+o**.

    OR

• Click the **Open** button located in the top menu bar.

File Open button

2   Find your scene

In the File Open dialog box, if you cannot immediately locate *01-alley_02.ma*, it might be because your project is not set correctly or that Maya did not direct you to the *scenes* directory.

• At the top of the dialog box, if the path is not pointing to the project created in the previous lesson, click the **Set Project...** button at the bottom of the window and browse to find the correct project directory. When you find it, click **OK**.

    *When you open a scene, it should now automatically take you to your current project's scenes directory. If it does not, open the combo box located at the top of the dialog in Windows and near the bottom of the dialog in Mac OS X and select **Current** scenes.*

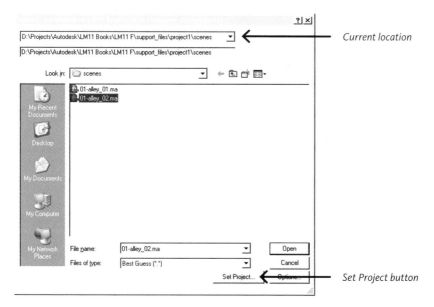

Current location

Set Project button

File Open dialog

- Select *01-alley_02.ma* and click **Open**.

3   **Save Scene As**

Since you will be modifying this scene, it is a good idea to save this file under a new name right away. Doing so will allow you to keep a copy of the previous lesson in case you would like to start this lesson over.

- Select **File → Save Scene As…**.

- Type *02-details_01* in the **File name** field.

- Select *MayaASCII (*.ma)* in the **Files of type** field.

    Maya software can save its files in two types of formats:

    Maya ASCII (.ma) saves your scene as a text file that is editable in a Text Editor. Though this format takes up more space on your drive, it is possible to review and modify its content without opening it in Maya. Experienced users find this very useful.

    Maya Binary (.mb) saves your scene as a binary file that is compiled as computer language. This format is faster to save and load, and takes up less space on your drive.

Door frame

In this exercise, you will modify one of the buildings by adding geometry components so it has a door frame. Doing so will introduce you to some important polygonal workflows.

1   Hide unselected objects

In order to facilitate modifying an object, you will hide most of the objects in the scene.

- Select the *ground*, and then **Shift** select the *building* and *awning* objects for which you would like to create a door.

- Select the **Display** → **Hide** → **Hide Unselected Objects or press the Alt+h hotkey.**

    Doing so will hide all the unselected objects, leaving visible only the important objects for the upcoming modifications.

The remaining visible objects

2 Insert edge loops

Inserting edge loops add lines on a polygonal surface. Doing so increases the number of vertices and thus allows you to further refine the shape of the object.

> **Note:**   *The number of vertices on an object can also be referred to as the **topology** of an object.*

- Select the *building* object.

- Press **F3** to select the **Polygon** menu set.

- Select **Edit Mesh** → **Insert Edge Loop Tool**.

  This tool allows you to insert a line of edges going all around the object.

- **Click+drag** the top horizontal edge to define the left frame border of the door, which should roughly align with the left edge of the awning.

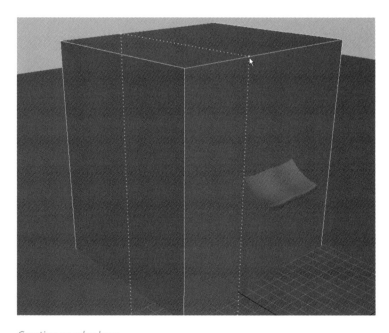

Creating an edge loop

As soon as you let go of the mouse button, the new defined edges are created.

- **Repeat** to create the right frame border of the door.

- **Click+drag** any vertical edge to create the top frame border of the door, which should be slightly below the top of the awning.

- **Repeat** to create the bottom frame border of the door, which should be below the ground surface.

3   **Select a polygonal face**

Now that the door frame borders are defined, you will need to select the door's face in order to extrude it.

- Press **q** to invoke the **Select Tool**.

- **RMB** on the *building* and select **Face**. You could also press the **F11** hotkey to go into Component mode with the polygonal faces enabled.

> **Tip:** *There are several hotkeys for going into Component and Object modes. The more you use Maya software, the better you will know the difference between these modes. The polygon-related hotkeys are listed here:*
> **F8** – *Toggle between Object mode and the last Component mode*
> **F9** – *Display vertices*
> **F10** – *Display edges*
> **F11** – *Display faces*
> **F12** – *Display UVs*

Notice as you hover the mouse cursor on the building that the face under the cursor turns red to inform you that this face is to be selected.

- **Click** to select the face under the *awning*.

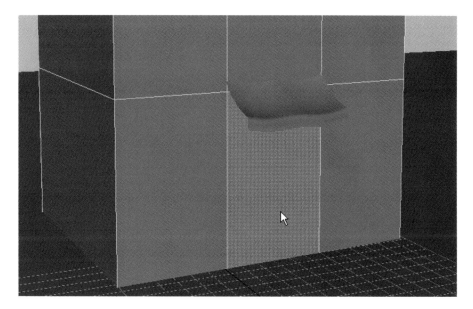

The door face

4   **Extrude a polygon**

You will now extrude the face to create moldings. Extruding polygons is a very common action. To do an extrusion, you first need to pick polygonal face components, and then execute the tool.

- Select **Edit Mesh** ⇢ **Extrude.**

  Notice a useful all-in-one manipulator displayed at the selection. This manipulator has all translation, rotation, and scale manipulators integrated.

    Click an arrow to display the translation manipulator.

    Click the outer circle to display the rotation manipulator.

    Click a square to display the scale manipulator.

    Toggle between local and global transformation by clicking the round icon.

- **Click+drag** the **Z-axis** arrow of the manipulator to create a small door border.

- Select **Edit Mesh** ⇢ **Extrude again.**

- **Click+drag** the **X-axis** cube and **Y-axis** cube of the manipulator to scale the door face inward.

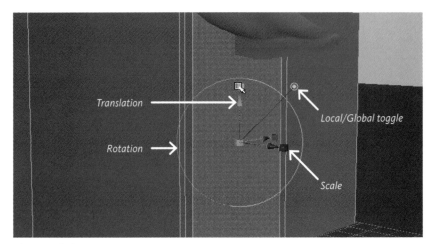

The extruded

- Select **Edit Mesh** → **Extrude one last time.**

- **Click+drag** the **Z-axis** arrow of the manipulator toward the inside to create the inside of the door border.

- With the door face still selected, press the **Delete** key on your keyboard to delete the face and reveal the building interior.

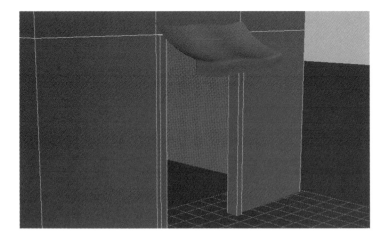

The deleted door face

Door

You will now create a simple door to fix in the door frame.

1 **Create the door**

- Select **Create** → **Polygon Primitives** → **Cube.**

- **Rename** the new cube *door*.

- **Scale** and **translate** *door* in place in the door opening.

- Press the **f** hotkey to frame the door geometry in the view.

- Use the **Edit Mesh** → **Insert Edge Loop Tool** to add a window to the door.

- Press **q** to exit the tool and invoke the Select Tool**.**

2 **Extrude a window**

- With the *door* is selected, press **F11** to enable the **face Component** mode.

- While in wireframe mode (**4** hotkey), select the appropriate faces to create a window in the door.

> **Tip:** You can also **click+drag** *faces to select them regardless of if the faces are facing you or behind the object. Combine this action with the* **Shift** *key to toggle, the* **Ctrl** *key to deselect, or the* **Shift+Ctrl** *keys to add faces to the current selection.*

- Go back into shaded mode (**5** hotkey), and select **Edit Mesh** → **Extrude.**

- **Click+drag** the blue arrow manipulator to translate the face slightly outward to create a small border.

- Select **Edit Mesh** → **Extrude** again.

> **Tip:** You can invoke the last command used (Extrude) by pressing the **g** hotkey rather than always going back into the menus.

- **LMB** on a square of the manipulator to enable its scale function.

- **LMB+drag** the central square to scale down the extruded faces.

- **LMB** on an arrow of the manipulator to use the translate function.

- Select **Edit Mesh** → **Extrude** again.

- **Translate** the faces on the **Z-axis** so the faces interpenetrate slightly.

- **Delete** the selected faces to create the window opening.

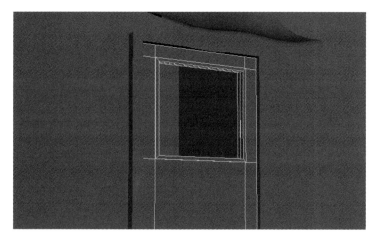

Door with a window opening

- Press **F8** to return in Object mode.

3   Save your scene

- **Save** your scene as *02-details_01.ma*.

Oil drum

In this exercise, you will use a different approach to create geometry that will introduce several new tools. Instead of starting from a primitive, you will draw a profile curve, which will then be revolved to create a round oil drum.

1   Draw a curve

The first step for modeling the oil drum is to draw a profile curve.

- Tap the **spacebar** to go into the *four-view* panel, and then tap it again with the mouse cursor placed over the *front* view.

- Select **Show** → **None** from the view's menu, then select **Show** → **NURBS Curves**.

  Doing so will clean the viewport so you can concentrate on you curve modeling.

- Select **Create** → **EP Curve Tool** → ❑.

- In the tool options, set **Curve degree** to **1 Linear**.

  By doing so, the curve will use linear interpolation between each point.

- Click the **Close** button.

- **Draw** the following curve:

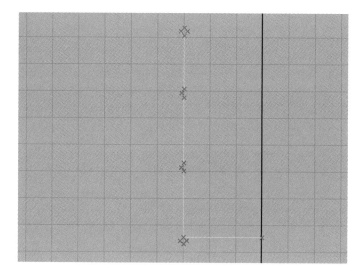

The oil drum's profile curve

Tip: *You can press the Delete key to delete the last drawn curve point.*

- Press **Enter** to complete the curve.

2   Refine the curve's shape

The CV located at the bottom center of the oil drum should be snapped to the thicker Y-axis grid line. Doing so will prevent the formation of a hole at the bottom of the oil drum when you will revolve the curve.

- Go in **Component mode** with the **NURBS Edit Points** component mask.

The NURBS Edit Points component mask

- Select the edit point located at the bottom center of the profile curve.

- Select the **Move Tool**.

- Hold down the **x** hotkey to **Snap to Grid** and **click+drag** the center of the manipulator on the thicker Y-axis grid line.

  The selected component will snap to the closest grid point.

- Let go of the **x** hotkey and **translate** the edit point on its **Y-axis** so the bottom line is horizontal.

- Fine-tune the curve's shape.

- Press **F8** to go into Object mode.

3   Revolve the oil drum

- **Go back into the** *Perspective* **view.**

- Press **F4** to select the **Surfaces** menu set.

- With the profile curve selected, select **Surfaces** → **Revolve.**

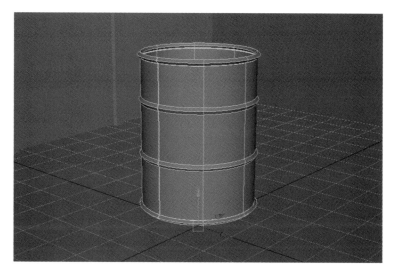

- **Rename** the new geometry *drum*.

4   Construction history

Many tools in Maya create hidden nodes called construction history that are present in the scene. For instance, because of the construction history, you can still tweak the shape of the oil drum by modifying the profile curve. Construction history nodes are also accessible through the Inputs section of the Channel Box. Changing nodes involved in the construction history will allow you to tweak action taken, without undoing and losing all of your work.

Note: *Construction history will be discussed in greater depth in Lesson 06.*

- With the *drum* selected, highlight the *revolve1* nodes in the **Inputs** section of the **Channel Box**.

- Try changing attribute values to see its effect on the geometry.

- Select the *profile* curve in the *front* view.

- Try to change the shape of the original curve to see its effect on the geometry.

- **Scale** down the original profile curve so the oil drum has proper sizing in the alley.

Note: *Construction history can be very handy, but it can also lead to unexpected results, especially with object topology changes. You will see how to delete the construction history later in this lesson.*

5   **The drum in the alley**

• Select **Display** → **Show All**.

• **Translate** the *drum* geometry to a location of your choice in the alley.

Be careful not to move the profile curve along with the drum geometry. Doing so would change the shape of the revolved surface in undesirable ways.

Details

Now that you have learned several ways of creating and modifying geometry, you should take some time to experiment and add your own details to the alley objects. Following are some general guidelines, but feel free to experiment.

1   **Light post refinements**

The light post could use some refinements. You can now use the existing geometry to make it prettier. To do so, add edge loops, tweak the positioning of vertices and extrude faces at will.

The modified light post

2   Combine polygonal objects

You might come across situations where you would like multiple polygonal objects to be treated as one single object. In the previous lesson you used grouping, but the objects were still independent. The **Combine** command will do that for you, so you will use it to combine the light post pieces together.

- Select all the light post pieces.

- Select **Mesh** → **Combine.**

  The light post is now combined into a single object.

- **Rename** the combined geometry *lightPost.*

3   Center pivot

Notice that when objects are combined together, the pivot of the new object is placed at the center of the world. There are different ways of placing the object's pivot at a better location.

- With the *lightPost* selected, select the **Move Tool** by pressing **w**.

- Zoom out and notice where the object's pivot is located.

- Press the **Insert** key on your keyboard (**Home** on Macintosh).

  *Doing so changes the current manipulator to the **Move Pivot Tool**. Alternatively, you could also hold down the **d** hotkey.*

- Using the different axes on the manipulator, place the pivot at the desired location.

- Press the **Insert** key again to recover the default manipulator.

  OR

- Select **Modify** → **Center Pivot**.

  Using this command automatically places the pivot at the center of its object.

4   Delete construction history

Construction history is always kept when doing certain operations. This history is sometimes not wanted as it increases file size and loading time. You will now delete the construction history from your scene.

- Select the *drum* object.

- To delete the construction history from the selected models, select **Edit** → **Delete by type** → **History**.

  The construction history is now gone from the Inputs section of the Channel Box.

- You can now **delete** the oil drum's profile curve.

- To delete all the history in the scene, select **Edit** → **Delete All by type** → **History**.

Tip: *Be careful when deleting an entire scene's history since history is sometimes required. For instance, character deformations are done via history. To delete only construction history, use* **Edit** → **Delete All by type** → **Non-Deformer History**.

5   Create a light bulb

You will now create a separate light bulb object and parent it to the light post object.

- Create a polygonal sphere and place at the top of the light post to use as a light bulb.

- **Rename** the sphere *lightBulb*.

- Select the *lightBulb* and then **Shift-select** the *lightPost* object.

- Select **Edit** → **Parent** or press the **p** hotkey to parent the *lightBulb* object to the *lightPost* object.

  Parenting object is similar to grouping objects, except that you are establishing a hierarchal relationship between the object. Thus, you can move the light post, which will also move the light bulb, but the light bulb can only be moved on its own.

6   Duplicate the lamp post

Now that you have modified one lamp post, it would be best to replace the other ones that are still the old shapes. You can now delete the old lamp posts and duplicate the new one to replace them.

7   Make your own refinements

Take some time to experiment and add more enhancements to the scene.

The final alley scenery

8   Save your scene

- **Save** your scene as *02-details_02.ma*.

Conclusion

You have begun to develop skills that you will use throughout your work with Maya. Both polygonal and NURBS modeling are entire subjects on their own. You will get to do more in-depth modeling in the next projects, but for now, you will continue experiencing different general Maya topics.

In the next lesson, you will bring colors into your scene by assigning shaders and textures to your objects.

Lesson 03
Shaders and Textures

Now that you have created an environment, you are ready to add colors and render your scene. The rendering process involves the preparation of materials and textures for objects.

Hiding the general UI

In the previous two lessons, you used menus, numeric input fields, and other UI elements to work with your scene. In this lesson, you will hide most of the user interface and rely more on the hotbox and other hotkeys to access the UI without actually seeing it onscreen.

1   Scene file

- Continue using the file you created from the previous lesson or open *02-details_02.ma* from the *support_files/scenes* directory.

2   Turn off all menus

- If you are in the *four-view* panel layout, position your cursor over the *Perspective* view panel, then tap the **spacebar** quickly to pop up this panel to full screen.

- Press and hold on the **spacebar** to open the hotbox.

Tip: *Tapping the spacebar can be used to toggle between window panes and holding down the spacebar can bring up the hotbox.*

- Click **Hotbox Controls**.

- From the marking menu, go down to **Window Options** and set the following:

    Show Main Menubar to **Off** (Windows only)

    Show Pane Menubars to **Off**

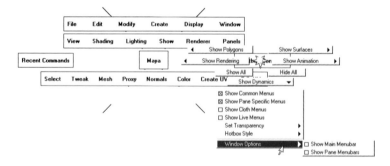

Marking menu

Now the various menus are hidden and you must rely on the hotbox to access tools.

3   Turn off all the workspace options

- From the hotbox, select **Display** → **UI Elements** → **Hide All UI Elements**.

Simplified UI

You now have a much larger working area that will let you focus more on your work.

- You can turn off the visibility of the panel toolbar by selecting **Windows** → **Settings/Preferences** → **Preferences** and then disable the Show panel toolbar under the Interface category.

- You can turn off the visibility of the ViewCube by selecting **Display** → **Heads Up Display** → **ViewCube.**

Tip: *You can also press the* **Ctrl+Spacebar** *hotkey to toggle between hiding all the main UI elements and restoring them.*

4   Change the panel organization

- Press and hold on the **spacebar** to evoke the hotbox.

- Click in the area above all the menus to apply the north marking menu.

- Select **Hypershade/Render/Persp** from this marking menu.

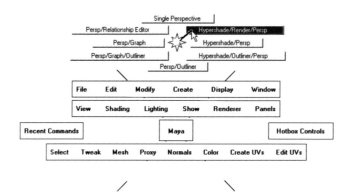

Hypershade/Render/Persp layout

Tip: *Each of the four quadrants surrounding the hotbox and the hotbox's center all contain their own marking menu sets. You can edit the contents of these menus using* **Window** → **Settings/Preferences** → **Marking Menu Editor.**

This saved layout puts a Hypershade panel above a Perspective panel and a Render View panel.

The Hypershade is where you will build shading networks, and the Render View is where you will test the results in your scene.

Tip: **Click+drag** *the pane divisions to change the width/height of the different windows in the layout.*

5   **Open the Attribute Editor**

- From the hotbox, select **Display** → **UI Elements** → **Attribute Editor**.

Now you also have an Attribute Editor panel on the right side of the workspace. This will make it easy to update shading network attributes.

New UI layout

Hotkeys

When working with a minimal UI, you will rely on the hotbox and hotkeys for your work. The following is a list of relevant hotkeys that you may need to use as you work:

spacebar	Hotbox/window popping
Ctrl + a	Show/hide Attribute Editor
f	Frame selected
a	Frame all
q	Pick Tool
w	Move Tool
e	Rotate Tool
r	Scale Tool
t	Show Manipulator Tool
y	Invoke last tool
g	Repeat last command
Alt + v	Start/stop playback
Alt + Shift + v	Go to first frame

Note: *For a complete listing of available hotkeys, go to* **Window →**
Settings/Preferences → Hotkey Editor.

Shading networks

To prepare the environment, and objects for rendering, you need to add color and texture. This is accomplished using *shading networks* that bring together material qualities, textures, lights, and geometry to define the desired look.

The Hypershade

The Hypershade panel is made up of three sections—the Create bar, the Hypershade tabs, and the work area. The Create bar allows you to create any rendering nodes required for your scene. The Hypershade tabs list all nodes that make up the current scene, while the work area allows you to look more closely and alter any part of the shading network's graph.

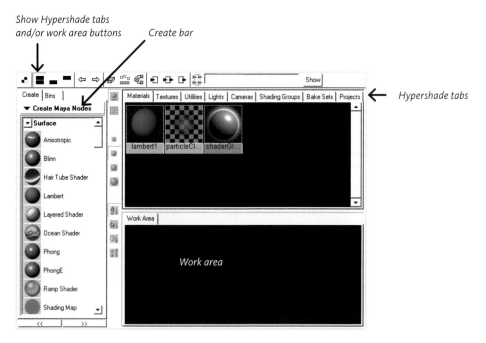

Close-up of Hypershade

Note: *The same mouse and key combinations that you use in the Orthographic viewports can be used for maneuvering in the Hypershade work area.*

Creating shading networks

A shading network consists of a series of nodes that input into a *shading group*. A shading group is a node that defines the various rendering attributes of its related objects, such as surface shading, volumetric shading, displacement shading, and so on.

In the following examples, you will create several nodes that define the material qualities of all the different objects, such as the buildings, awnings, ground, and so on.

1   **Light bulb material**

To build a material for the light bulbs, you will use the Hypershade and Attribute Editor.

- Click the **Show top and bottom tabs** button located at the top left of the Hypershade.

- At the top of the Create bar section, click the **Create tab**.

- Click the **down arrow** just below the **Create** tab, and make sure **Create Maya Nodes** is selected from the pop-up.

  This offers you a series of icons that represent new Maya nodes, such as surface materials.

- Click **Phong**.

  This adds a new Phong material under the materials' Hypershade tab and in the work area. You will also see the Attribute Editor update to show the new node information.

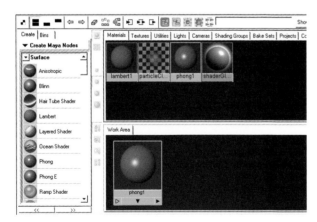

Phong is a particular type of shader that gives you control over the look of shiny materials.

2 Rename the Material node

- In the Attribute Editor, change the name of the Material node *lightM*.

  The M designation is to remind you that this node is a Material node.

Tip: *You can also hold down the **Ctrl** key and double-click the node in the Hypershade to rename it.*

3 Edit the material's color

To define how the material will render, you will need to set color attribute.

- In the Attribute Editor, click the color swatch next to the **Color** attribute.

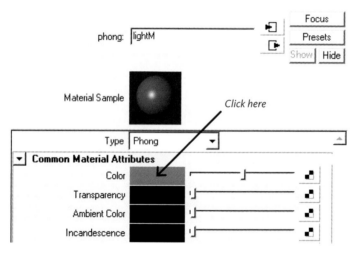

Color swatch in the Attribute Editor

This opens the Color Chooser. This window lets you set color by clicking a color wheel and editing HSV (hue, saturation, value) or RGB (red, green, blue) values.

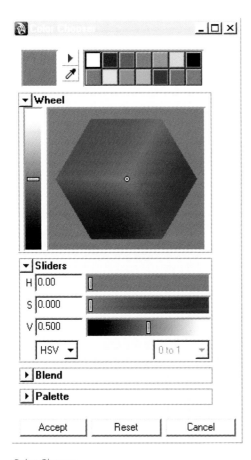

Color Chooser

- Choose a bright yellow color and click the **Accept** button.

4   **Edit the material's incandescence**

Since the light bulb is irradiating light, it should be self-lit. To further define how the material will render, you can set its incandescence attribute.

- In the Attribute Editor, click the color swatch next to the **Incandescence** attribute.

- Choose a dark yellow color and click the **Accept** button.

5   **Assign the material**

- Make sure one light bulb is clearly visible in the viewport.

- With your **MMB**, **click+drag** the *lightM* node, drag it from the Hypershade panel into the Perspective view and drop it on the *lightBulb* object.

   This assigns the material to the object.

- **Repeat** the previous steps for the other light bulbs.

Tip: *It is a good idea to be in Hardware Shading mode to ensure that the assignment is correct. The hotkey is **5** on your keyboard.*

Assigned shader

Creating a procedural texture map

To give the awnings a dirty worn out look, a fractal procedural texture will be added to the awning's material color. A procedural texture means the look of the texture is driven by attributes and drawn by mathematical functions. You will also experiment with the drag and drop capabilities of the Hypershade.

1   **Awning material**

- In the Hypershade, clear the work area by holding down the right mouse button and selecting **Graph** → **Clear Graph** or press the **Clear Graph** button at the top of the Hypershade.

The Clear Graph button

This clears the workspace so that you can begin working on a new shading network.

- From the Create bar section, create a **Lambert** material.

Lambert is a particular type of shader that gives you control over the look of flat materials without any shiny highlights.

- In the Attribute Editor, change the name of the Material node to *awningM*.

2   **Fractal texture**

The awnings look quite flat in shaded mode, and could use a dirty-like texture. Adding a fractal procedural texture will greatly help to create the effect of dirt.

- In the Create bar section of the Hypershade, scroll down to the **2D Textures** section.

This section allows you to create new textures.

- **MMB+drag** a **Fractal** from the Create bar anywhere into the work area.

- In the work area of the Hypershade, click with your **MMB** on the **Fractal** icon and drag it onto the *awningM* Material node.

When you release the mouse button, a pop-up menu appears offering you a number of attributes that can be mapped by the fractal texture.

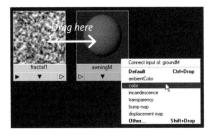

MMB+drag from the fractal onto the material

- Select **color** from the menu to map the *fractal* to the Material node's *color* attribute.

- Click the **Rearrange Graph** button at the top of the Hypergraph panel.

The Rearrange Graph button

Tip: *Rearranging the work area will organize the view so connections appear from left to right. This is very useful for following the flow of connections.*

3   **Assign the material**

- Select the *awning* objects, then **RMB** on your material *awningM* and select **Assign Material to Selection**.

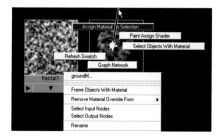

Assign to selection

Tip: *This method of assigning materials works better than the **click+drag** method when you want to assign a material to multiple objects.*

4   **View the texture**

In order to see the texture in the viewport, you will need to enable hardware texturing.

- Over the Perspective window, click with your **MMB** to make it the active window.

- Open the hotbox and select **Shading** → **Hardware Texturing**.

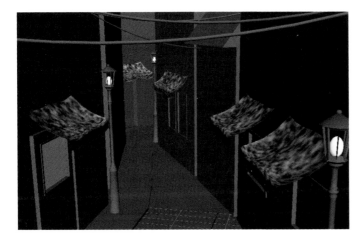

Hardware texturing

Tip: *You can also turn on hardware texturing by making the desired panel active and pressing the* **6** *key.*

5   **Edit the fractal attributes**

- In the Hypershade, click to select the *Fractal* node.

- In the Attribute Editor (**Ctrl+a** to show it if hidden), open the **Color Balance** section.

- Click the color swatch next to the **Color Gain** attribute.

- Choose any color you would like, such as **brown**, and click the **Accept** button.

- Click the color swatch next to the **Color Offset** attribute.

- Choose a **gray** and click the **Accept** button.

- Under the **Fractal Attributes** section, tweak the attributes to your liking, for instance:

    Amplitude to **0.8**

    Threshold to **0.3**

    Ratio to **0.6**

    The attributes found in this section control the way the fractal is being evaluated.

- At the top of the Attribute Editor, select the *place2dTexture* tab.

   This tab shows different placement options for the fractal texture.

- Change the fractal's placement attributes as shown below:

   Repeat U to **0.1**

   Repeat V to **0.1**

   The Attribute Editor allows you to easily update the look of a procedural texture to your liking.

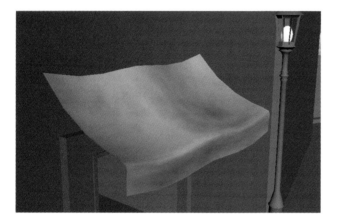

Ground texture

 Note: *The viewport texture shading is a representation of what your textures look like, but it might not reflect perfectly how your scene will render.*

6   **Display the whole shading group**

- With the *awningM* texture selected in the Hypershade, click **Input and Output Connections.**

Input and Output Connections button

   This displays some other nodes that help define this shading group.

- Press the **Alt** key and **click+drag** with your left and middle mouse buttons to zoom out.

- Press the **a** hotkey to frame everything in the view.

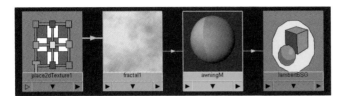

Complete shading network

Texture maps

You will create a material for objects using file textures instead of procedural textures. Many digital artists like to create textures in a 2D paint package. In this example, you will experiment with textures with and without transparency.

File texture

1   **Create a material for the street**

- From the Hypershade panel's work area, **RMB+click** and select **Graph → Clear Graph**.

- Scroll to the **Surface** section in the Create bar and select **Lambert**.

- **Rename** this node *streetM*.

2   Create a File Texture node

To load an external texture, you need to start with a File Texture node.

- **Double-click** *streetM*material to display its Attribute Editor (if hidden).

- In the Attribute Editor, click the **Map** button next to **Color**. The map button is shown with a small checkered icon.

Map button

> *This opens the Create Render Node window.*

- Click the **Textures** tab.

- In the **2D Textures** section, click **File**.

> *A File node is added to the Lambert material. The appropriate connections have already*

New File Texture node

3   Load the file texture

- In the Attribute Editor for the File node, click the **File folder** icon next to **Image name**.

- Select the file named *bricks.tif* from your project *sourceimages* directory, then click the **Open** button.

> *The file texture is now loaded into the shading network.*

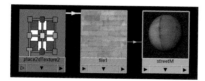

File Texture node

Note: *This file will be available only if you set up your project correctly from the support_files and if it is set to current.*

Note: *The file texture does not import the image into Maya. Instead, it keeps a path to the specified file and loads it on request from your drive.*

4   **Apply the textured material to the ground**

- Select the *ground* surface in the *Perspective* view.

- In the Hypershade, click the *streetM* node with your **RMB** and choose **Assign Material to Selection** from the pop-up menu.

   The texture is assigned to the ground surface.

5   **Texture tiling**

When a texture has a repeating pattern, such as bricks, you can tile multiple copies of the same texture side by side. The result is a larger texture with more definition that can make your geometry look good without the need of huge texture files. The following shows you how to tile a texture.

- In the Hypershade, select the *place2dTexture* node connected to the file texture node.

- Set **Repeat U** and **Repeat V** to **10.0**.

- If the bricks appear to be too big for your scene, try a bigger number such as **30** or **50**.

- Set the **Rotate Frame** attribute to **90**.

Ground with texture applied

6 Sky texture

You will now assign a star texture to the sky dome.

- In the Hypershade, **create** a **Surface Shader** material.

  Surface Shaders do not use any lighting information. They simply output the color or texture assigned to them, which is perfect for a night sky.

- **Rename** the shader *skyM*.

- In the Attribute Editor, click the **Map** button for the **Out Color** attribute.

- **Create** a **File** texture node and **assign** the image *stars.tif* to it.

- The *skydome* object is referenced, so you can either select it using the **Window** → **Outliner** or by typing `select skydome` in the **Command Line** at the bottom of the interface.

- With the *skydome* object selected, **RMB** on the *skyM* shader and select **Assign Material To Selection**.

- Select the *place2dTexture* node connected to the file texture node and set **Repeat U** and **Repeat V** to **5.0**.

Tip: *Try to hide the pole of the skydome so it is not visible at the end of the alley by rotating the sphere on its Y-axis. You should do so because the texture pinches at the pole of a NURBS sphere and is not dersirable in our particular example.*

7 Moon texture

You will now add a moon to your scene and assign a moon texture to it. You will use a texture with an *alpha channel*. This means that the texture contains the regular color channels, plus an alpha channel, which stores the transparency of the texture. This is perfect for the moon since you will be able to cut out the moon's shape without having to modify the actual geometry.

The texture and its alpha channel

- **Create** a **NURBS Plane**.

- **Rename** it *moon*.

- **Scale** and **move** the plane in the sky over the far end of the alley.

The moon plane

- Create a **Lambert** shader with a mapped **File texture**.

- **Rename** the shader *moonM*.

- Open the Attribute Editor for the new file texture, and then click the **Browse** button.

- Select the file named *moon.tif* from your project *sourceimages* directory, then click the **Open** button.

  Maya will automatically detect and connect the alpha channel to the **transparency** *attribute of the Lambert shader.*

- **Assign** the new *moonM* shader to the *moon* plane.

Moon with transparent texture

8   **Texturing polygons**

A good thing about polygon geometry is that you can assign different shaders onto different faces of the mesh. In this example, you will texture a building using two shaders.

- Create two **Lambert** shaders in the Hypergraph.

- Change the first shader to have the *wall.tif* texture and **rename** it *wallM*.

- Make the second shader a dark brown and **rename** it *frameM*.

- Select the *building*, and **assign** the *wallM* to it.

  Doing so assigns the material to the entire surface.

- Press the **F11** hotkey to go to Face Component mode.

- Select the faces making the door frame using the **Shift** key.

- **Assign** the *frameM* shader to the selected faces.

- Press **F8** to go back into Object mode.

9   **Texture color**

When loading a texture file, you might want to change the color slightly. In this example, you will change the color gain of a wood texture so you do not need to create a different texture for each slight color change you require.

- **Create** a new Lambert material and **map** a **texture file** to its color attribute.

- **Rename** the new material *woodM*.

- **Load** the texture file *wood.tif* from the *sourceimages* directory.

- **Assign** the shader to the *door* object.

  Notice how the wood texture appears too bright compared to the rest of the scene.

- With the texture node selected, open the **Color Balance** section.

- Change the **Color Gain** to **gray**.

  Doing so changes the color gain of the texture to be darker.

- With the *place2dTexture* node selected set **Repeat UV** to **3.0** and **3.0**.

The textured wooden door

10   Complete the scene

Before continuing with the next lesson, it is a good idea to assign materials to the remaining objects in your scene. Experiment with 2D procedural Texture nodes such as *Noise*, *Ramp*, and *Cloth*. You can also map some of the objects with file textures of your own or from those found in the support file directory. The following is an example of the completed room:

The completed scene

Test render

Now that you have materials and textures assigned, it is a good time to do a test render.

1   Display Resolution Gate

Your current view panel may not be displaying the actual proportions that will be rendered. You can display the camera's resolution gate to see how the scene will actually render.

- Make the Perspective view the active panel.

- Use the hotbox to select **View** → **Camera Settings** → **Resolution Gate**.

    The view is adjusted to show a bounding box that defines how the default render resolution of 640x480 pixels relates to the current view.

- Dolly into the view so that it is well composed within the resolution gate. Try to set up a view where you see every object.

  Keep in mind that only objects within the green surrounding line will be rendered.

The resolution gate displayed

Tip: *Select* **View** → **Camera Settings** → **Resolution Gate** *again to turn off the resolution gate.*

2   **Your first render**

- Select **Windows** → **Rendering Editors** → **Render View.**

- In the Render View panel, click with your **RMB** and select **Render** → **Render** → **persp** from the pop-up menu.

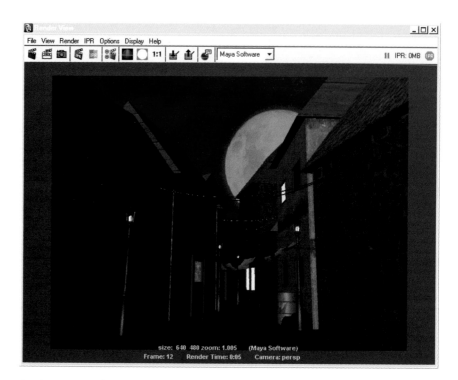

Render View panel

> You can now see a rendered image of your scene. However, because you have not created any lights, the image renders using a default light.

- Try adding lighting to your scene by creating lights from the **Create** → **Lights** menu, and then render your scene again.

 Note: *Lights are going to be covered later in this book.*

3   Zoom into the rendering

You can zoom in and out of the rendered image using the **Alt** key.

- Use the **Alt** key and the **LMB** and **RMB** to zoom in and out of the view.

  Now you can evaluate in more detail how your rendering looks at the pixel level.

Close-up of rendering

- In the Render View panel, click with your **RMB** and choose **View** → **Real Size**.

4   **Save your work**

- Through the hotbox, select **Save Scene As** from the **File** menu.

- Enter the name *03-textures_01.ma*, then click the **Save** button.

Conclusion

You have now been introduced to some of the basic concepts for texturing and rendering a 3D scene. The Maya shading networks offer a lot of depth for creating the look of your objects. You have learned how to create materials, procedural textures, and file textures, and assign them to objects and faces. Lastly, you rendered a single frame to preview the look of your shaders with default lighting.

In the next lesson, you will learn about animation basics by animating a door that is opening.

Lesson 04
Animation Basics

You have built a simple set using various primitive objects and then textured them. You will now learn about the basics of hierarchies and animate the door so that it opens.

In this lesson, you will learn the following:

- How to change and save preferences

- How to group and parent objects

- How to understand parent inheritance

- How to set keyframes

- How to use the Time Slider

- How to use the Graph Editor

- How to select animation curves and keyframes

- How to change keyframe tangents

- How to traverse a hierarchy

Preferences

You can now reset the interface to its default settings. Also, be sure to set your preferences to have an infinite undo queue.

1   Turn on all menus

- From the hotbox, click **Hotbox Controls**.

- From the marking menu, go down to **Window Options** and set the following:

    Show Main Menubar to **On** (Windows only);

    Show Pane Menubars to **On**.

    The menu bars are back to normal.

2   Turn on all of the workspace options

- Select **Display** → **UI Elements** → **Show All UI Elements**.

Tip: *You can press the* **Ctrl+spacebar** *hotkey to bring back the interface as it was before you hid everything.*

- If you turned off the ViewCube, select **Display** → **UI Elements** → **ViewCube**.

- If you turned off the panel toolbar, select **Windows** → **Settings/Preferences** → **Preferences**, and then enable the **Show panel toolbar** from the **Interface** category then click the **Save** button.

    You are now back to the default Autodesk® Maya® interface.

3   Change the Attribute Editor settings

You might want the Attribute Editor to open in its own window rather than in the Maya interface. The following will show you how to set your preference accordingly.

- Select **Window** → **Settings/Preferences** → **Preferences**.

- In the left **Categories** list, make sure **Interface** is highlighted.

- Set **Open Attribute Editor** to **In separate window**.

- You can do the same for **Open tool settings** and the **Open Layer Editor** if wanted.

  The different editors will now open in their own separate windows rather than cluttering the main interface.

4   **Infinite undo option**

By default, Maya has a limited amount of undo in order to reduce the memory usage of your computer. You will specify here if you want to keep an undo queue larger than the default setting.

- In the **Categories** list, highlight **Undo**.

- Make sure **Undo** is set to **On**.

- Set the **Queue size** to what you think is an appropriate value, such as **50**.

  OR

- Set the **Queue** to **Infinite**.

  The amount of undo is now defined to your liking.

5   **Save your preferences**

- In order to save these preferences, you must click the **Save** button in the Preferences window.

  The next time you open Maya, these settings will be used.

Note: *You can also save your preference by selecting* **File → Save Preferences.**

Organize your scene

Before animating objects, you need to make sure that the task will be as simple as possible. You will need to easily find the objects in your scene and animate them as intended. Placing objects logically into hierarchy is going to do just that. To do so, you will learn how to group and parent objects together as well as learn how to use the Outliner.

You can think of scene organization as having groups and subgroups. For instance, you can have an *environment* group that contains everything in the scene. Then you can have a *town* group, which will contain everything related to the town and in the *town* group, you can have a *building* group, and so forth.

Thus far you have modeled a bunch of objects, but you have not looked at how they were organized behind what you saw in the viewports.

1   **Hierarchy**

It is very important to understand the concept of a hierarchy. A hierarchy consists of the grouping of child nodes under parent nodes. When transforming a parent node, all of its children will inherit its transformation. The following steps explain how to create a hierarchy of objects:

- To better visualize what you are about to do, open the **Outliner** by selecting **Window → Outliner**.

    The Outliner lists all the nodes in your scene along with their hierarchies. Currently, in your scene, you can see the default Maya cameras, all of the prior lesson objects, every component of your environment and, at the very bottom, two default sets.

The Outliner

- Scroll in the Outliner to see the current organization of the scene.

    The first four nodes in the Outliner are always the default cameras. Following that are your scene contents, and then the different default object sets.

2   Groups

- Hold down the **Shift** key, and **select** all your scene's content from the Outliner starting from the *ground* down to *moon*.

    Doing so selects the geometry just like when selecting in a viewport.

- Select **Edit → Group**.

    The selected geometry is now all grouped under a Group node.

- **Double-click** the newly created *group* to enable the **rename** function directly in the Outliner.

- Enter the name *environmentGroup*, then press **Enter** to confirm the name change.

- **Expand** the group to see its content by clicking the **plus** (+) sign next to *environmentGroup*.

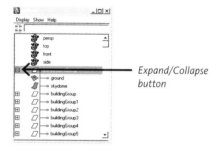   *Expand/Collapse button*

Hierarchy expanded

Note: *A new default group has its pivot at the origin and all of its attributes are set to their default values.*

3   Organizing the hierarchy

You will now create a group within the environment group.

- Select all the group objects called *buildingGroup* and all the *lightPost* groups.

- Press **Ctrl+g** to group them.

    A new group is created within the environmentGroup, containing only the building objects.

- **Rename** *group1 townGroup*.

- Select all the remaining objects that are not already in *townGroup*, except the *skydome*, *ground* and *moon* objects.

- Press and hold the **MMB** over the selection in the Outliner and drag them over the *townGroup*.

  As you can see in the following images, dragging and dropping a node onto another one will set it as the child of the object it was dragged onto.

 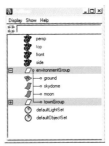

Drag   *Drop*

Note: *Notice the green highlight on the townGroup, which shows one or more of its children is currently selected.*

- Select *townGroup*.

- **MMB+drag** it in the Outliner just under the *environmentGroup* geometry and **drop** it when you see only a single black border highlight.

  Doing so reorders the scene hierarchy.

Tip: *Notice that when dragging objects in the Outliner, one black line shows that it will be placed between two nodes, while two black lines show that the objects will be parented.*

Project 01

4   **Parenting**

- Select the main building's walls (the one with the door) from the viewport.

  Take note of which buildingGroup is highlighted in green in the Outliner. This is the parent group of the building created in the first lesson.

- Press the **Up** arrow on your keyboard.

  Doing so will select the parent(s) of the currently selected object(s).

- **Rename** the main building group *mainBuildingGroup*.

- Select the *door* and *awning* objects of the same main building either from the Outliner or from the viewport.

- In the Outliner, hold **Ctrl,** then select the *mainBuildingGroup*.

  Make sure the mainBuildingGroup is selected last.

- From the **Edit** menu, select **Parent**.

  OR

- Press **p** on your keyboard.

  Doing so will parent the main objects to the main building group.

Tip: *Use **Shift+p** to unparent the selected objects.*

---

5   **Completing the hierarchy**

- If you did not delete the oil drum profile curve earlier, select it and delete it, since it is no longer required.

- Organize the hierarchy so that it looks like the following:

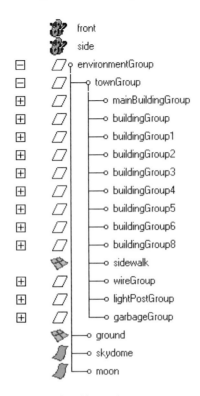

The completed hierarchy

 Tip: *To expand a hierarchy along with all the children, hold down the **Shift** key before clicking the **Expand** button in the **Outliner**.*

Display layers

In this exercise, you will sort your scene using display layers. A display layer is a grouping of objects that can be hidden, or displayed as reference templates, which makes them unselectable in the viewports.

Project 01

1　Create a display layer

The first display layer you will create will
contain the environment objects, such as
the ground and sky dome.

The Layer Editor

- In the Layer Editor, located below the
  Channel Box, select **Layers** → **Create
  Empty Layer.**

- **Double-click** the new layer, and enter
  envLayer as the name.

- Click the **Save** button.

2　Add objects to a display layer

- From the Outliner, select the *ground*,
  skydome and *moon* objects.

- **RMB** on the *envLayer*, and select **Add
  Selected Objects**.

3　Set the display of the layer

- Toggle the **V** button on the *envLayer* to set the visibility of the objects on that layer.

  Hidden layers are not to be rendered.

- Click in the empty square next to the V button to toggle the layer's display between
  Normal, **Template,** and **Reference.**

  *When templated, the layer objects are unselectable and displayed as dimmed wireframe. When
  referenced, the layer objects are unselectable, but displayed normally in the viewport.*

- Set the layer to be visible (**V**) and in reference (**R**).

4　Create another layer

In order to simplify any selection process in your scene even more, you will create another
layer and add any objects not intended for manipulation.

- **Create** a new layer and **rename** it *townLayer*.

- Add all the town objects that are child to the *townGroup* to the *townLayer*.

> **Tip:** *The display layers obey to the object's hierarchy. This means that if you hide a parent object using a layer, all the children will also be hidden.*

- Select the *mainBuildingGroup*.
- **RMB** on the *townLayer* and select **Remove Selected Objects**.
- Make the *townLayer* referenced.

  From now on, when selecting in the viewport, you will be able to select only a reduced amount of objects, which are not on the referenced layers.

Understanding inheritance

Hierarchies are useful to organize your scene, but they also play a role with animation. For instance, if you transform a parent object, all of its children and grandchildren will follow that transformation. Thus, it is essential to freeze transformations of objects to reset their transformation attributes to their default, without moving the object. You must also make sure that all objects' pivots are appropriately placed for your needs.

1 **Freezing transformations**

   At this time, most of your objects have some values in their translate, rotate, and scale attributes. When you animate your objects, those values will come into play and make your task more difficult. To make it easier, you can freeze an object's transformations.

   - Select the *environmentGroup*.
   - Select **Edit** → **Select Hierarchy**.
   - Select **Modify** → **Freeze Transformations**.

     Doing so resets all the selected objects' attributes to their default values.

> **Tip:** *If you do not want to freeze all the attributes of an object, you can open the commands option box to specify which attributes need freezing.*

Project 01

2   **Center pivots**

Since the groups and objects might not have their pivots at a centered location, it is a good idea to place all the pivots in one easy step.

- Select the *environmentGroup*.

- Select **Edit** → **Select Hierarchy**.

- Select **Modify** → **Center Pivot**.

  Every pivot is now located at the best centered location. When an object has children, the command takes into account the entire subhierarchy to position the pivot.

3   **Child values**

When you transform a parent object, none of its children's values change.

- Select the *townGroup*.

- **Rotate** and **translate** it to modify its positioning.

  Notice that all children are moving along.

- Select any of its children, and notice that all of their values are still zero.

- Select *mainBuildingGroup* and **move** it.

- Notice the *door* values did not change.

4   **Pivot placement**

You will now see how the pivot of an object, when well placed, can simplify your task when it comes to moving an object.

- Select the *townGroup* and set its **scale X**, **Y,** and **Z** to **1.5**.

  All of the group's children follow the parent scaling, but the town is moving away from the ground.

- **Undo** the previous action.

- Still with the *townGroup* selected, press the **Insert** key on your keyboard to bring up the **Move Pivot Tool**.

- From the *front* or *side* Orthographic view, place the pivot on the ground plane, near the origin.

 Tip: *You can snap it to the grid by holding down the **x** hotkey.*

- Press **Insert** again to exit the tool.

- Set the *townGroup* **scale X**, **Y,** and **Z** to **0.75**.

  Notice when scaling, you do not have to compensate for the floor moving up or down on the Y-axis.

5   **Save your work**

- **Save** your scene as *04-animation_01.ma*.

Animating the door

You now have enough knowledge of scene hierarchy and object inheritance to create your first simple animation.

1   **Door pivot**

Before animating the door, you must consider your needs in animation and make sure that you can achieve such animation with your scene setup. At this time, you need the pivot of that door to be located around the hinge area; otherwise, your door would rotate from its center, which is not ideal for animation.

- With the *door* selected, press the **Insert** key and move the pivot to where you think the hinges should be.

- Press **Insert** again to exit the **Move Pivot Tool**.

 Tip: *You can hold down the **d** hotkey to evoke the **Move Pivot Tool**.*

- Test your door by rotating it on its Y-axis.

Rotating the door open

- **Undo** the last move to reset the door to its default position.

2   **The timeline**

The first step with animation is to determine how long you would like your animation to be. By default, Maya software plays animation at a rate of 24 frames per seconds (FPS), which is a standard rate used for film. As such, if you want your animation to last one second, you need to animate 24 frames.

- In the Time Slider and Range Slider portion of the interface, change **Playback End Time** to **100**.

  The frames in the Time Slider now go from 1 to 100. One hundred frames is just above four seconds of animation in 24FPS.

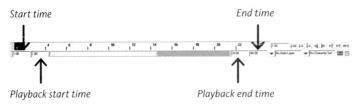

Start time   *End time*

Playback start time   *Playback end time*

Time Slider and Range Slider

3   Setting keyframes

Luckily, you do not need to animate every single frame in your animation. When you set keyframes, Maya will interpolate the values between the keyframes, giving you animation.

- Press the **First Frame** button from the playback controls to make the current frame **1**.

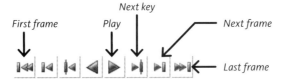

Next key

First frame   *Play*   *Next frame*

Last frame

Playback controls

- Select the *door*.

- Make sure all of its rotation and translation values are set to **0**.

- At the top of the interface, change the current menu sets for **Animation**.

Tip: *The Animation menu set hotkey is* **F2**.

- With the *door* still selected, select **Animate → Set Key**.

Tip: **Set Key** *can also be executed by pressing the* **s** *hotkey.*

- In the current frame field on the left of the rewind button, type **25** and press **Enter**.

  Notice the position of the current frame mark in the Time Slider.

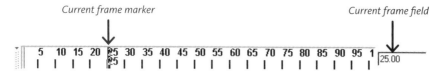

Current frame marker   Current frame field

The current frame mark

- Type **-125** in the **Rotate Y** field of the *door* and press **Enter**.

- Press the **Alt** key while your mouse cursor is over a viewport in order to remove focus from the Y-axis field, then press the **s** hotkey to **Set Key** at frame **25**.

4   **Play back preferences**

Before you play your animation, you need to set the Maya playback properly.

- Click the **Animation Preferences** button found at the far right side of the **Range Slider**.

The animation preferences button

> This opens the preferences window directly on the animation and playback options.

- In the **Time Slider** category, under the **Playback** section, make sure that **Playback Speed** is set to **Real-time (24FPS)**.

- Click the **Save** button.

- Press the **Rewind** button, then press the **Play** button in the playback controls area to see your animation.

- To stop the playback of the animation, press the **Play** button again or press **Esc**.

- You can also drag the current frame by **click+dragging** in the Time Slider area.

Dragging in the Time Slider

> Notice the red ticks at frame 1 and frame 25, specifying keyframes on the currently selected objects.

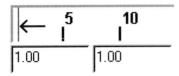

A keyframe tick in the Time Slider

5   Tweak the animation

You now have a partially animated door, but it is still missing refinement. Maybe you think the animation is too slow or too fast. In order to change the timing of the animation, you can drag keyframes directly in the Time Slider.

- With the *door* still selected, hold down the **Shift** key, then click on frame **25** in the Time Slider.

Doing so highlights frame 25 with a red zone. This zone is actually a manipulator that allows you to translate keyframes in the Time Slider.

- **Click+drag** the red zone to frame **15**.

The keyframe manipulator

The door animation now starts at frame 1 and stops at frame 15.

- Click anywhere in the Time Slider to remove the keyframe selection.

- Go to frame **35**.

- With the *door* still selected, set the **Rotate Y** attribute to **-140**.

- Click the **Rotate Y** attribute name in the Channel Box.

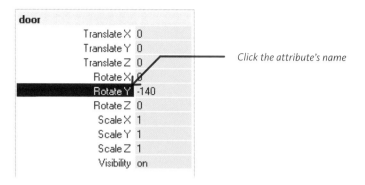

Click the attribute's name

Select only the Rotate Y attribute

- Click and hold the **RMB** over that same attribute.

  This will pop-up the attribute context menu.

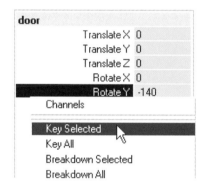

Select Key Selected from the attribute menu

- Select **Key Selected**.

  Doing so will set a keyframe on that attribute for every selected object.

Tip: You can use **Shift+w**, **Shift+e**, and **Shift+r** to keyframe only the translation, rotation, and scale attributes respectively.

- **Play back** your animation.

You will notice that the door is opening fast for the first 15 frames and then slows down up to frame 35.

Note: *To delete keyframes in the Time Slider, simply set the current time marker on a keyframe, then* **RMB** *and select* **Delete**. *To delete multiple keyframes at the same time, select the keyframes using the keyframe manipulator (using the* **Shift key**)*, then* **RMB** *and select* **Delete**.

6   **Graph Editor**

The Graph Editor is the place where you can look at all the keyframes on an object and see their interpolations as curves (function curves or fcurves).

- Select the *door*.

- Select **Window → Animation Editors → Graph Editor**.

- Select **View → Frame All** to frame the entire curve, or press the **a** hotkey.

- Press the **Alt** key and **click+drag** with the **LMB** and **MMB** to dolly in and out of the graph.

- Press the **Shift+Alt** keys and **click+drag** with the **LMB** and **MMB** to constrain the dolly along the dragged axis.

- Press the **Shift+Alt** keys and **click+drag** left and right with the **MMB** to constrain track along the dragged axis.

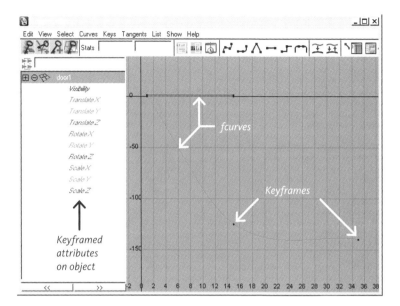

The fcurves on the door

> The keyframes you have set are represented by black dots. Animation curves of vector attributes are always color coded red, green, and blue for X, Y, and Z axes. The yellow animation curve shows a slope because you have keyframed the rotate Y attribute on the door. All other keyframes were set with their default value of o.

7   Selecting keyframes

- Experiment selecting animation curves and keyframes in the Graph Editor.

Note: *You can select an entire animation curve by click+dragging the curve itself. You can select keyframes by clicking them. You can also modify the selection using the* **Ctrl** *and* **Shift** *hotkeys.*

- With the **Move Tool** selected, **MMB+drag** keys around in the Graph Editor.

Tip: *Use* **Shift+MMB-dragging** *to constrain the axis of translation of the keyframe.*

---

8   Modifying keyframes

In order to modify only the Rotate Y keyframes without affecting other animation curves, you can display only the desired curve in the Graph Editor. You will now modify the animation so the door progressively gains speed when it is opening and loses speed once opened.

- In the Outliner section located on the left of the Graph Editor, highlight the **Rotate Y** attribute.

  Only this animation curve is now visible.

- Select the first and last keyframes of the animation curve.

- Select **Tangents → Flat**.

  This sets the keyframes to be flat, which causes a gradual acceleration and deceleration of the animation.

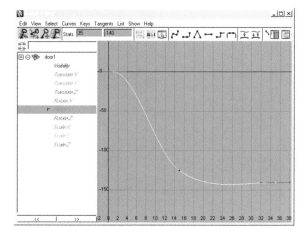

Flat tangents

Note: *Notice how the animation curve goes slightly above 140 around frame 25. This will cause the door to overshoot its animation and rotate a bit further than what was keyed. While this effect is desired in this example, you might want to correct the situation by moving up the keyframe at frame 15, or simply edit its tangent.*

- **Play back** your animation.

- Continue experimenting. Once you like your animation, **close** the Graph Editor.

9   Traversing a hierarchy

You can traverse hierarchies using the arrows on your keyboard. Traversing a hierarchy is useful for selecting objects without manually picking the object in the viewport or through the Outliner.

• Select the *door*.

• Open the Outliner to see the effect of the upcoming steps.

• Press the **Up arrow** to change the selection to the parent of the current selection (*mainBuildingGroup*).

• Press the **Up arrow** again to select the *townGroup*.

Tip: *You can use the following hotkeys to traverse a hierarchy:*
Up arrow—*Parent*
Down arrow—*First child*
Right arrow—*Next child*
Left arrow—*Previous child*

10   Save your work

• **Save** your scene as *04-animation_02.ma*.

Conclusion

You have now touched upon some of the basic concepts of hierarchies and animation. Maya utilizes more powerful tools than described here to help you bring your scenes to life, but these basic principles represent a great step forward. As well as learning how to group and parent objects together, you also learned about inheritance of transformation and animation and worked with two of the most useful editors—the Outliner and the Graph Editor.

The next lesson is a more in-depth look at most of the tools that you have been using since the beginning of this project. Once you have read this lesson, you will be able to make your own decisions about how to reach the different windows, menu items, and hotkeys.

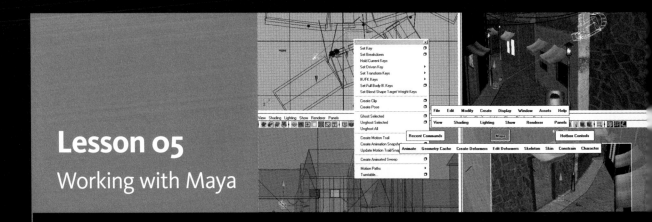

Lesson 05
Working with Maya

If you completed the first four lessons, you have worked with Autodesk® Maya® software from modeling and animation to shading and rendering. Now is a good time to review some of the UI concepts that you worked with and introduce new concepts in order to provide a more complete overview of how Maya works.

It is recommended that you work through this lesson before proceeding with the subsequent lessons in the book. This lesson explores the basic UI actions that you will use in your day-to-day work.

In this lesson, you will learn the following:

- About the Maya interface

- About the different UI parts

- About the view tools

- About the different hardware displays

- About menus and hotkeys

- About the manipulators and the Channel Box

- About selection and selection masks

- About the difference between tools and actions

The workspace

You have learned how to build and animate scenes using different view panels and UI tools. The panels offer various points of view for evaluating your work—such as Perspective views, Orthographic views, graphs, and Outliners—while the tools offer you different methods for interacting with the objects in your scene. Shown below is the workspace and its key elements:

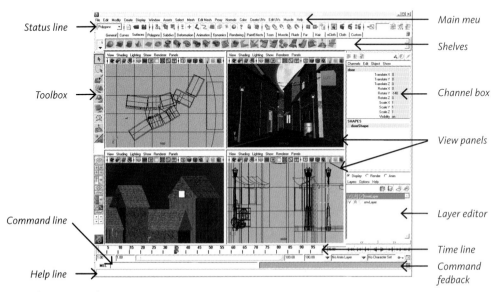

The Maya workspace

Layouts

When Maya is first launched, you are presented with a single Perspective view panel. As you work, you may want to change to other view layouts.

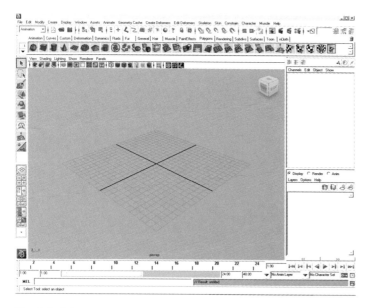

The default layout

1 **To change your view layouts**

• Go to the view panel's **Panels** menu and select a new layout option from the **Layouts** pop-up menu.

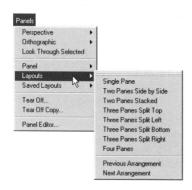

The Layouts pop-up menu

You can set up various types of layouts ranging from two to four panels.

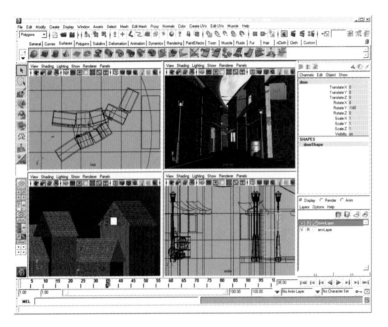

A four-view layout

Tip: *If you are looking at several view panels simultaneously and want to focus on one of them, put your cursor in that view and tap the spacebar. The view will become full-screen. Tap the spacebar again and the panels will return to the previous layout.*

View panels

As you begin to build and animate objects, you will want to view the results from various points of view. It is possible to place either Perspective or Orthographic views in each panel.

1 **To change the content of a view panel:**

- Go to the view panel's **Panels** menu and select a view type from either the **Perspective** or **Orthographic** pop-ups.

View tools

When you are working with Perspective and Orthographic views, you can change your view-point by using hotkey view tools. The following view tools allow you to quickly work in 3D space using simple hotkeys:

1   **To tumble in a Perspective view**

   - Press the **Alt** key and **click+drag** with the **LMB**.

> **Tip:**   The ability to tumble an Orthographic view is locked by default. To unlock this
> feature, you need to select the desired Orthographic view and under **View**, go to
> **Camera Tools** and unlock it in the **Tumble Tool** → ❏.

2   **To track in any view panel**

   - Press the **Alt** key and **click+drag** with the **MMB**.

3   **To dolly in or out of any view panel**

   - Press the **Alt** key and **click+drag** with both the **LMB** and **MMB** or only with the **RMB**.

> **Tip:**   You can also track and dolly in other view panels, such as the Hypergraph, the Graph
> Editor, Visor, Hypershade, and even the Render View window. The same view tools
> work for most panel types.

View Cube

The View Cube appears in the top right corner of any panel view and shows your current camera view.

The View Cube

You can move between views by clicking parts of the View Cube. Clicking any of the cube sections will rotate the current camera view to the selected view. Clicking the home icon will move the camera back to the default Perspective view.

1   **To hide the View Cube in a view**

  • Select **Show** → **Manipulators**.

2   **To turn the View Cube on and off**

  • Select **Window** → **Settings/Preferences** → **Preferences.**

  • In the **Categories** section, select **ViewCube** and choose your favorite settings.

Other panel types

As well, you can change the content of the view panel to display other types of information, such as the Hypershade or Graph Editor.

1   **To change the content of a view panel**

  • Go to the view panel's **Panels** menu and select a panel type from the **Panel** pop-up menu.

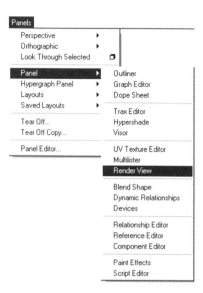

The Panels pop-up menu

In the workspace below, you can see a Hypergraph panel for helping select nodes, a Graph Editor for working with animation curves, and a Perspective view to see the results.

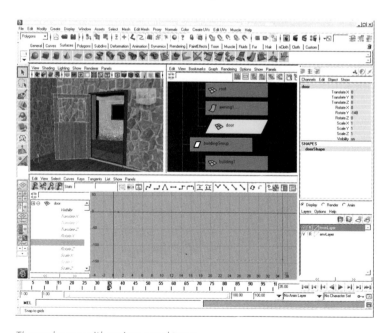

The workspace with various panel types

Saved layouts

As you become more familiar with Maya, you may want to set up an arrangement of panels to suit a particular workflow. For example, you may want a Dope Sheet, a Perspective view, a top view, and a Hypergraph view all set up in a certain manner.

1   To add a new layout of your own

- Go to the view panel's **Panels** menu and select **Saved Layouts** → **Edit Layouts...**

  In the Edit window, you can add a new saved layout and edit the various aspects of the layout.

2   To add a new layout to the list

- Select the **Layouts** tab and click **New Layout**.

- Select and edit the layout's name.

- Press the **Enter** key.

3   To edit the configuration of a saved layout

- Select the **Edit Layouts** tab.

- Choose a configuration, then **click+drag** the separator bars to edit the layout's composition.

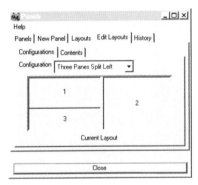

Layout Editor

- Select the **Contents** tab.

- Choose a panel type for each of the panels set up in the configuration section.

Tip: *There is a quicker access to preset layouts, panel types, and layout configuration through the toolbox on the left side of the Maya UI.*

Display options

Using the **Shading** menu on each view panel, you can choose which kind of display you want for your geometry.

1   **To change your panel display**

   • Go to the panel's **Shading** menu and select one of the options.

     OR

   • Click the appropriate buttons in the **Panel Toolbar** located under the panel's menu.

     OR

   • Click in a panel to set it as the active panel and use one of the following hotkeys to switch display types:

       4 for wireframe;

       5 for smooth shaded.

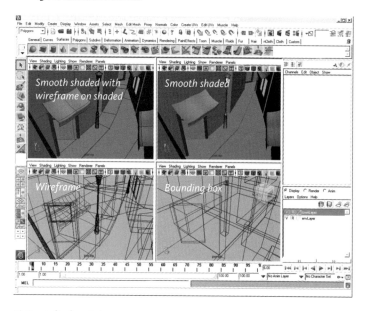

Various display styles

Texturing and lighting

Another important option found on this menu is hardware texturing. This option allows you to visualize textures and lighting interactively in the view panels.

1   To use hardware texturing

- Build a shader that uses textures.

- Go to the panel's **Shading** menu and select **Hardware Texturing**.

    OR

- Press the **6** hotkey.

2   To display different textures

It is possible to display different texture maps on your surface during hardware texturing. For example, you could display the color map or the bump map if those channels are mapped with a texture.

- Select the material that is assigned to your objects.

- In the Attribute Editor, scroll down to the **Hardware Texturing** section and set the **Textured channel** to the desired channel.

- You can also set the **Texture Resolution** in the Attribute Editor for each Material node so that you can see the texture more clearly in your viewport.

3   To add hardware lighting to your scene

- Add a light to your scene.

- Go to the panel's **Lighting** menu and select one of the options.

    OR

- Press the **7** hotkey for all lighting.

Hardware lighting and texturing

High quality rendering

When high quality interactive shading is turned on, the scene views are drawn in high quality by the hardware renderer. This lets you see a very good representation of the final render without having to software render the scene.

1   To turn on high quality rendering

• Go to the panel's **Renderer** menu and enable **High Quality Rendering**.

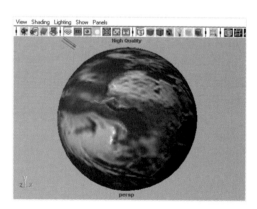

High Quality Rendering

Display smoothness

The viewport display of NURBS and polygonal objects can be changed in the viewport.

1   To change NURBS smoothness

By default, NURBS surfaces are displayed using a fine smoothness setting. If you want to enhance playback and interactivity, you can have the surfaces drawn in a lower quality.

- Go to the **Display** menu and under **NURBS** choose one of the smoothness options.

    OR

- Use one of the following hotkeys to switch display types:

    1 for rough;

    2 for medium;

    3 for fine.

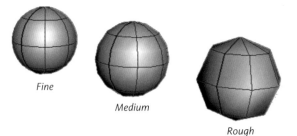

Fine

Medium

Rough

NURBS smoothness

Tip: *To speed up camera movement in a scene with heavy NURBS geometry, go to the* **Window** → **Settings/Preferences** → **Preferences**... *in the* **Display** *section to enable the* **Fast Interaction** *option. This option shows the rough NURBS smoothness any time a camera is moving.*

2   Smooth Mesh Preview

Use one of the following hotkeys to switch display types of polygonal objects:

1 for the polygon display;

2 for the polygon cage and smooth preview;

3 for the smooth preview only.

 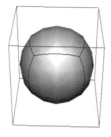 

Smooth Mesh Preview

> **Note:**   *When in smooth display, you can still go into Component mode and tweak the geometry's vertices.*

Show menu

The **Show** menu is an important tool found on each view panel's menu. This menu lets you restrict or filter what each panel can show on a panel-by-panel basis.

Restricting what each panel shows lets you display curves in one window and surfaces in another to help edit construction history. Or, you can hide curves when playing back a motion path animation while editing the same curve in another panel.

The Show menu

UI preferences

The Maya workspace is made up of various UI elements that assist you in your day-to-day work. The default workspace shows all of them on screen for easy access.

1   To reduce the UI to only view panels and menus

- Go to the **Display** menu and select **UI Elements** → **Hide All UI Elements**.

  With less UI clutter, you can rely more on hotkeys and other UI methods for accessing tools while conserving screen real estate.

2   To return to a full UI

- Go to the **Display** menu and select **UI Elements** → **Show All UI Elements**.

Tip: *You can use **Ctrl+Spacebar** to toggle between these UI settings.*

Menus

Most of the tools and actions you will use in Maya are found in the main menus. The first six menus are always visible, while the next few menus change depending on which UI mode you are in.

Menus and menu pop-ups that display a double line at the top can be *torn off* for easier access.

1   **To tear off a menu**

   • Open the desired menu, then select the double line at the top of the menu.

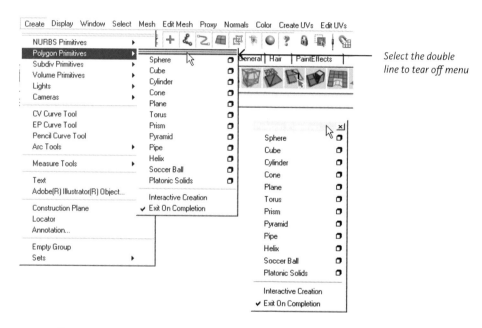

A tear-off menu

Menu sets

There are five menu sets in Maya Complete: *Animation, Polygons, Surfaces, Dynamics,* and *Rendering.* Each menu set allows you to focus on tools appropriate to a particular workflow.

1   **To choose a menu set:**

   • Select the menu set from the pop-up menu found at the left of the Status Line bar.

2   To choose a menu set using hotkeys

- While pressing the **h** key, **LMB+drag** over any viewport and choose the desired UI mode from the radial marking menu.

3   To choose a menu set using function keys

- Press **F1** to invoke **Help**

- Press **F2** for **Animation**

- Press **F3** for **Polygons**

- Press **F4** for **Surfaces**

- Press **F5** for **Dynamics**

- Press **F6** for **Rendering**

Shelves

Another way of accessing tools and actions is by using the shelves. You can move items from a menu to a shelf to begin combining tools into groups based on your personal workflow needs.

1   To add a menu item to a shelf

- Press **Ctrl+Shift** and select the menu item. It will appear on the active shelf.

2   To edit the shelf contents and tabs

- Go to the **Window** menu and select **Settings/Preferences** → **Shelf Editor.**
  OR
- Select the **Shelf Editor** from the arrow menu located to the left of the shelves.

3   To remove a menu item from a shelf

- **MMB+drag** the shelf icon to the trash icon located at the far right of the shelves.

Status Line

The Status Line, located just under the Maya main menu, provides feedback on settings that affect the way the tools behave. The display information consists of:

- The current menu set.

- Icons that allow you to create a new scene, open a saved one, or save the current one.

- The selection mode and selectable items.

- The snap modes.

- The history of the selected lead object (visible by pressing the input and output buttons).

- The construction history flag.

- The render into a new window and IPR buttons.

- The Quick Selection field and Numeric Input field.

1   **To collapse part of the shelf buttons**

- Press the small handle bar next to a button set.

Collapse handle

Select modes before collapsing

Select modes button collapsed

Hotbox

As you learned, tapping the spacebar quickly pops a pane between full screen and its regular size, but if you press and hold the spacebar, you gain access to the hotbox.

The hotbox is a UI tool that gives you access to as much or as little of the Maya UI as you want. It appears where your cursor is located and offers the fastest access to tools and actions.

1   To access the hotbox

- Press and hold the spacebar.

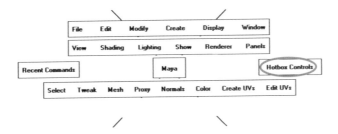

The hotbox with four quadrants marked

The hotbox offers a fully customizable UI element that provides you with access to all of the main menus as well as your own set of marking menus. Use the **Hotbox Controls** to display or show as many or as few menus as you need.

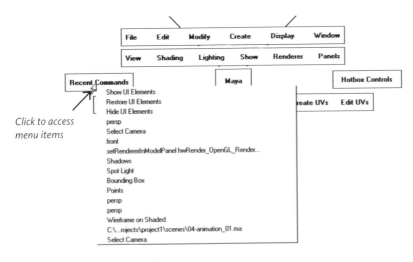

Accessing the recent commands menu

Hotbox marking menus

You can access marking menus in five areas of the hotbox. Since each of these areas can have a marking menu for each mouse button, it is possible to have fifteen menus in total. You can edit the content of the marking menus by going to the **Window** menu and selecting **Settings/Preferences** → **Marking Menu Editor.**

1   **To access the center marking menu**

   • Press the **spacebar**.

   • **Click+drag** in the center area to access the desired menu.

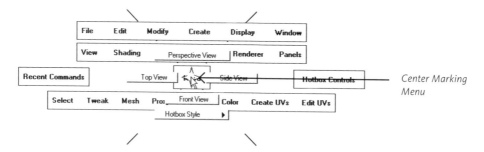

The center marking menu

2   **To access the edge marking menus**

   • Press the **spacebar**.

   • **Click+drag** in one of the north, south, east, or west quadrants to access the desired marking menu.

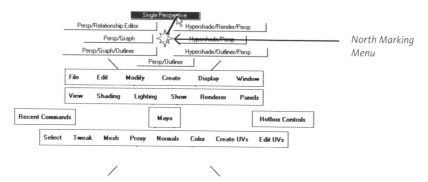

A quadrant-based marking menu

Customizing the hotbox

You can customize the hotbox to make it as simple or complex as you need. You can choose which menus are available and which are not.

If you want, you can reduce the hotbox to its essentials and focus on its marking menu capabilities.

A reduced hotbox layout

Alternatively, you could hide the other UI elements, such as panel menus, and use the hotbox to access everything. You get to choose which method works best for you.

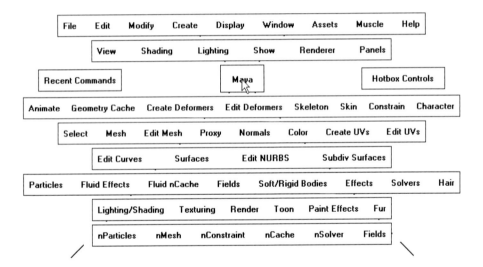

A complete hotbox layout

1 **To customize the hotbox**

- Use the **Hotbox Controls**.

   OR

- Use the center marking menu.

- Choose an option from the **Hotbox Styles** menu.

Tool manipulators

To the left of the workspace you have access to important tools. These include the **Select**, **Move**, **Rotate**, **Scale,** and **Show Manipulator** tools. Each of these is designed to correspond to a related hotkey that can be easily remembered using the QWERTY keys on your keyboard.

QWERTY tool layout

These tools will be used for your most common tool-based actions, such as selecting and transforming.

Note: *The Y key drives the last spot on the QWERTY palette, which is for the last tool used. The advantages of this will be discussed later in this lesson under the heading Tools and Actions.*

Universal Manipulator

The **Universal Manipulator** lets you transform geometry in translation, rotation, or scaling, both manually and numerically. A single click on any of the manipulators will display a numeric field allowing you to type in a specific value.

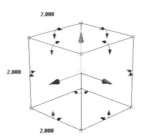

Universal manipulator

Soft Modification Tool

The **Soft Modification Tool** lets you push and pull geometry as a sculptor would on a sculpture. The amount of deformation is greatest at the center of the push/pull, and gradually falls off further away from the center. The corresponding action is **Deform → Soft Modification**.

Transform manipulators

One of the most basic Maya node types is the *Transform node*. This node contains attributes focused on the position, orientation, and scale of an object. To help you interactively manipulate these nodes, there are three transform manipulators that make it easy to constrain along the main axes.

Each of the manipulators uses a color to indicate their axes. RGB is used to correspond to X, Y, Z. Therefore, red is for X, green for Y, and blue for Z. Selected handles are displayed in yellow.

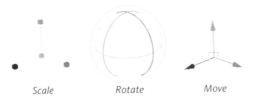

Scale   Rotate   Move

Transform manipulators

Project 01

To explore some of the options available with manipulators, you will use the transform manipulator.

1   **To use a transform manipulator in view plane**

    - **Click+drag** the center of the manipulator to move freely along all axes.

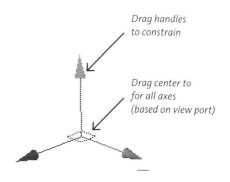

Drag handles to constrain

Drag center to for all axes (based on view port)

2   **To constrain a manipulator along one axis**

    - **Click+drag** one of the manipulator handles.

The move manipulator

3   **To constrain a manipulator along two axes**

    - Hold the **Ctrl** key and **click+drag** the axis that is aligned with the desired plane of motion.

    This now fixes the center on the desired plane, thereby letting you click+drag the center so that you can move along the two axes. The icon at the center of the manipulator changes to reflect the new state.

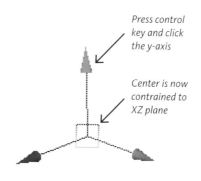

Press control key and click the y-axis

Center is now contrained to XZ plane

Working along two axes

4   **To go back to the default view plane center**

    - Press the **Ctrl** key and click the center of the transform manipulator.

Note: *The ability to constrain in two axes at one time is available for the move and scale manipulators.*

Using the mouse buttons

You can interact directly with manipulators by using the left mouse button (LMB) to select objects.

The middle mouse button (**MMB)** is for the active manipulator and lets you **click+drag** without direct manipulation.

1   **To select objects**

   • Set up selection masks.

   • Click with the **LMB**.

2   **To select multiple objects**

   • Use the **LMB** and **click+drag** a bounding box around objects.

3   **To add objects to the selection**

   • Press **Ctrl+Shift** while you select one or multiple objects.

4   **To manipulate objects directly**

   • **Click+drag** a manipulator handle.

5   **To manipulate objects indirectly**

   • Activate a manipulator handle;

   • **Click+drag** with the **MMB**.

Shift gesture

The manipulators allow you to work effectively in a Perspective view panel when transforming objects.

If you want to work more quickly when changing axes for your manipulators, there are several solutions available.

Project 01

1   To change axis focus using hotkeys

- Press and hold on the transform keys:

    w for move

    e for rotate

    r for scale

- Choose an axis handle for constraining from the marking menu.

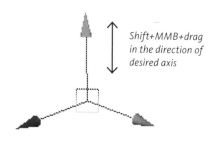

Shift+MMB+drag in the direction of desired axis

2   To change axis focus using the Shift key

- Press the **Shift** key.

- **Click+drag** with the **MMB** in the direction of the desired axis.

Transform manipulators

Set pivot

The ability to change the pivot location on a Transform node is very important for certain types of animation.

1   To change your pivot point

- Select one of the manipulator tools;

- Press the **Insert** key (**Home** on Macintosh);

- **Click+drag** the manipulator to move its pivot;

- Press **Insert** to return to the manipulator tool (**Home** on Macintosh).

Press Insert or Home　　*Click + drag manipulator*　　*Press Insert or Home*

Setting pivot using Insert / Home key

Tip: *You can also hold down the **d** hotkey to evoke the Move Pivot Tool.*

Channel Box

Another way of entering accurate values is through the Channel Box. This powerful panel gives you access to an object's Transform node and any associated Input nodes.

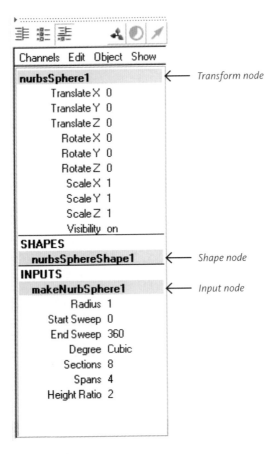

The Channel Box

If you have multiple objects selected, then your changes to a channel will affect every node sharing that attribute.

To put one of the selected objects at the top of the Channel Box so that it is visible, choose the desired node from the Channel Box's **Object** menu.

If you want to work with a particular channel, you can use the **Channels** menu to set keys, add expressions, and complete other useful tasks. You can also change the display of Channel Box names to short MEL-based names.

Project 01

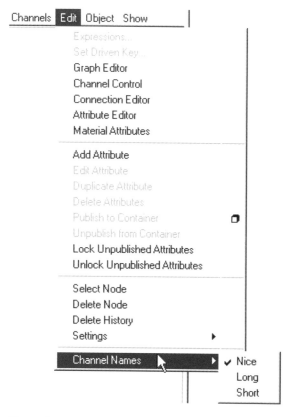

Channels Edit Object Show

Expressions...
Set Driven Key...
Graph Editor
Channel Control
Connection Editor
Attribute Editor
Material Attributes

Add Attribute
Edit Attribute
Duplicate Attribute
Delete Attributes
Publish to Container
Unpublish from Container
Lock Unpublished Attributes
Unlock Unpublished Attributes

Select Node
Delete Node
Delete History
Settings   ▶
Channel Names   ▶   ✓ Nice
                              Long
                              Short

Channel's menu

Note: *To control what channels are shown in the Channel Box, go to the* **Window** *menu,
and choose* **General Editors** → **Channel Control.**

Channel Box and manipulators

One of the features of the Channel Box is the way in which you can use it to access manipulators at the transform level.

By default, the Channel Box is set to show manipulators every time you tab into a new Channel Box field. You will notice that as you select the channel names such as *Translate Z* or *Rotate X*, the manipulator switches from translate to rotate.

One fast way to edit an attribute is to invoke the virtual slider by selecting the name of the desired channel in the Channel Box, then using the **MMB+drag** in a view panel to change its value.

There are three options for the Channel Box manipulator setting.

Default manipulator setting

This setting lets you activate the appropriate field in the Channel Box, and then modify the values with either the left or middle mouse button.

- Click the desired channel name or input field, then **click+drag** directly on the active manipulator with the **LMB**.

  OR

- Click the desired channel name or input field, then **click+drag** in open space with the **MMB**.

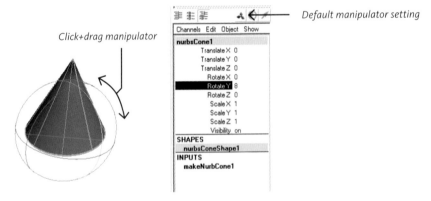

Click+drag manipulator

Default manipulator setting

Channel Box default manipulator setting

No-manipulator setting

You can click on the manipulator icon over the Channel Box to turn manipulation off, which leaves the Channel Box focused on coordinate input. With this setting, you cannot use the middle or left mouse buttons for manipulation.

- Click in the channel's entry field and type the exact value.

   OR

- Use one of the normal transform tools such as **Move**, **Rotate,** or **Scale**.

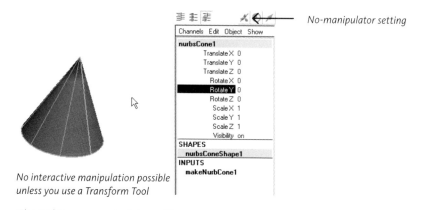

No-manipulator setting

No interactive manipulation possible unless you use a Transform Tool

Channel Box no-manipulator setting

No-visual manipulator setting

A third option found on this manipulator button returns manipulator capability to the Channel Box—but now you will not see the manipulator on the screen.

- Click the desired channel name or within the channel's input field.

- **Click+drag** in open space with the **MMB**.

   You can now use the two new buttons that let you edit the speed and drop-off of the manipulations.

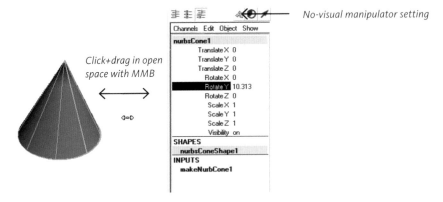

No-visual manipulator setting

Click+drag in open space with MMB

Channel Box no-visual manipulator setting

The first button that becomes available with the *No-visual* setting is the speed button which lets you **click+drag** with your **MMB** either slow, medium, or fast.

The second button is the drop-off button, which lets you choose between a linear motion as you **click+drag** with the **MMB**, or a **click+drag** that is slow at first and faster as you drag further.

Channel speed controls   *Channel drop-off options*

Attribute Editor

The Channel Box lets you focus on attributes that are keyable using **Set Key**, but the Attribute Editor gives you access to all the other attributes/channels.

The Attribute Editor is used for all nodes in Maya software. This means that shaders, textures, surfaces, lattices, Render Settings, and so on, can all be displayed in this one type of window.

1   **To open the Attribute Editor window**

   • Select a node.

   • Go to the **Window** menu and select **Attribute Editor**.

2   To open the Attribute Editor panel

- Select a node.

- Go to the **Display** menu and select **UI Elements** → **Attribute Editor**. The Channel Box is now replaced by an Attribute Editor panel.

When you open the Attribute Editor, you not only get the active node, but also related nodes based on dependency relationships. In the example below, a sphere's transform, shape, and *makeNurbSphere* nodes are all present. These are the same Input and Shape nodes shown in the Channel Box.

A typical Attribute Editor

Tip: *You can also press the **Ctrl + a** hotkey to open the Attribute Editor. You can set your preference for having the Attribute Editor in a panel or in its own window through* **Window** → **Settings/Preferences** → **Preferences** *and click the* **Interface** *section to modify the* **Open Attribute Editor** *option.*

Numeric input

To add specific values to your transformations, you can use the numeric input boxes. This allows you to apply absolute or relative values to the attributes associated with the current manipulator.

To enter absolute values

- Select the **Absolute Transform** option from the input field menu.

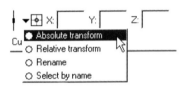

The input field menu

- Enter values and press **Enter** on your keyboard.

    The selected objects will be moved based on the input and the current manipulator.

To enter relative values

- Select the **Relative Transform** option from the input field menu.

- Enter values and press **Enter** on your keyboard.

 Note: *You are not required to enter zero values.*

Selecting

One of the most important tasks when using Maya software is your ability to select different types of nodes and their key components.

For instance, you may need to be able to select a sphere and move it, or to select the sphere's control vertices and move them. You may also need to distinguish between different types of objects so that you can select only surfaces or only deformers.

Selection masks

To make selecting work, you have a series of selection masks available to you. This allows you to have one Select Tool that is then *masked* so that it can only select certain kinds of objects and components.

The *selection mask* concept is very powerful because it allows you to create whatever combination of selection types that you desire. Sometimes, you only want to select joints and selection handles, or maybe you want to select anything but joints. With selection masks, you get to set up and choose the selected options.

The selection UI

The UI for selecting offers several types of access to the selection masks. You can learn all of them now and then choose which best suits your way of working down the line.

Grouping and parenting

When working with Transform nodes, you can create more complex structures by building hierarchies of these node types.

To build these structures, you can choose to *group* the nodes under a new Transform node, or you can *parent* one of the nodes under the other so that the lower node inherits the motion of the top node.

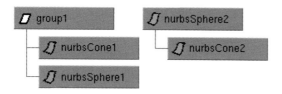

Grouped and parented nodes

Selection modes

At the top of the workspace, you have several selection mask tools available. These are all organized under three main types of select modes. Each type gives you access to either the hierarchy, object type, or components.

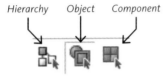

The select modes

Scene hierarchy mode

Hierarchy mode gives you access to different parts of the scene hierarchy structure. In the example shown below, the Leaf node and the Root node are highlighted. This mode lets you access each of these parts of the hierarchy. You can select Root nodes, Leaf nodes, and Template nodes using the selection masks.

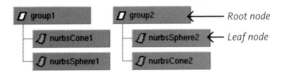

Hierarchy types

Object mode

Object mode lets you perform selections based on the object type. Selection masks are available as icons that encompass related types of objects.

With your **RMB**, you can access more detailed options that are listed under each mask group. If you create a partial list, the mask icon is highlighted in orange.

Object mode with selection masks

Tip: *Once you choose selection masks, Maya software gives priority to different object types. For instance, joints are selected before surfaces. You will need to use the* **Shift** *key to select these two object types together. To reset the priorities, select* **Window → Settings/Preferences → Preferences** *and click the* **Selection** *section to modify the* **Priority**.

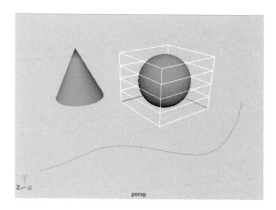

A lattice object and a curve object selected

Pop-up menu selection

When objects overlap in a view, the pop-up menu selection lets you display a pop-up list of the objects to select. **LMB+click** the overlap area to display the menu. Your selection is highlighted in the scene viewports as you select an item in the list.

- This option is disabled by default. To turn it on, select **Window → Settings/Preferences → Preferences** and click the **Selection** section to enable **Pick chooser**.

Selection pop-up menu

Component mode

The Shape nodes of an object contain various components such as control vertices or isoparms. To access these, you need to be in Component mode.

Component selection masks

When you select an object in this mode, it first highlights the object and shows you the chosen component type—you can then select the actual component.

Once you go back to Object mode, the object is selected and you can work with it. Toggling between Object and Component modes allows you to reshape and position objects quickly and easily.

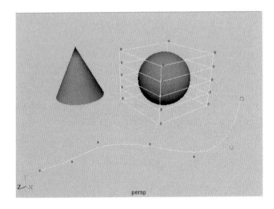

CV components and lattice point components

 Tip: *To toggle between Object and Component modes, press the **F8** key.*

RMB select

Another way of accessing the components of an object is to select an object, then click the right mouse button (**RMB**). This brings up a marking menu that lets you choose from the various components available for that object.

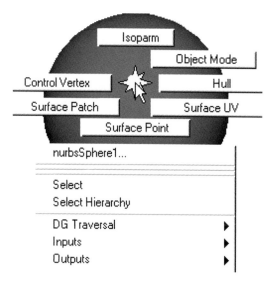

The RMB select menu

If you select another object, you return to your previous select mask selection. This is a very fast way of selecting components when in hierarchy mode, or for components that are not in the current selection mask.

Combined select modes

In front of the selection mask mode icons is a pop-up menu that gives you different preset mask options. These presets let you combine different object and component level select options.

An example would be the NURBS option. This allows you to select various NURBS-based mask types such as surfaces, curves, CVs, curve control points, and isoparms.

> **Note:** *In this mode, if you want to select CVs that are not visible by default, you must make them visible by going to the **Display** menu and selecting **NURBS → CVs**.*

When using a combined select mode, objects and components are selected differently. Objects are selected by **click+dragging** a select box around a part of the object, while components can be selected with direct clicking.

> **Note:** *If you have CVs shown on an object and the select box touches any of them, you will select these components instead of the object. To select the object, you must drag the select box over part of the surface where there are no CVs.*

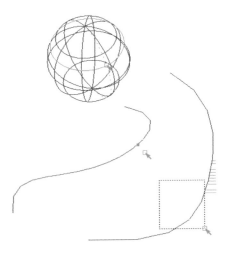

NURBS select options

Multiple component selection mode

Polygon objects have a multi-component selection mask that lets you select faces, vertices, and edges without having to change between selection modes. In this mode, you select components based on the mouse cursor's proximity to them.

- To turn on multi component selection mode for a single object, **RMB** a polygon object and then select **Multi** from the marking menu.

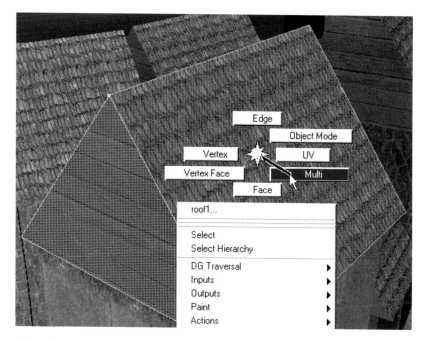

The multi component selection mode

Dragging a selection with multi component selection mode

When you perform a drag selection on an object in multi component selection mode and no components are initially selected, Maya will select all vertices in the selection zone.

If a component or multiple components of the same type are already selected, then Maya selects components of the same type within the selection zone.

If multiple components of different types are already selected, then Maya selects components based on a hierarchy of vertices, edges, and then faces. For example, if an edge and a face are already selected and you perform a drag selection on the object, Maya will select all edges in the selection zone.

Tools and actions

In Maya, a large group of menu items can be broken down into two types of commands: *tools* and *actions*, each working in their own particular manner. Almost every function can be set as a tool or action.

Tools

Tools are designed to remain active until you have finished using them. You select a tool, use it to complete a series of steps, then select another tool. In most cases, the Help Line at the bottom of the workspace can be used to prompt your actions when using the tool.

Earlier you were introduced to the **y** key on the QWERTY toolbox. By default, this button is blank because it represents the last tool used. When you choose a tool from the menus, its icon inserts itself into the QWERTY menu.

1 **As tool option**

- Choose a menu item and select its option box.

- Under the **Edit** menu, select **As Tool**.

  By default you will remain in this tool until you choose another tool. There is also an option that will deselect the tool after completion.

2 **To return to the last tool used**

- Press the **y** key.

Actions

Actions follow a selection-action paradigm. This means that you first have to choose something and then act on it. This allows you to choose an action, return to editing your work, and refine the results immediately.

Actions require that you have something selected before acting on it. This means that you must first find out what is required to complete the action.

1   **To find out selection requirements of an action**

   • Move your cursor over a menu item.

   • Look at the Help Line at the bottom-left of the interface.

   *If you have the Help Line UI element visible, the selection requirements are displayed. For instance, a **Loft** requires curves, isoparms, or curves on surfaces while **Insert Isoparm** requires isoparms to be chosen.*

2   **To complete the action**

   • If the tool is not already set as an action, select **Edit → As Action** from the menu item's options.

   • Use either the pick mode or the **RMB** pick menu to make the required selections.

   • Choose the action using the hotbox, shelf, or menus.

   The action is complete and the focus returns to your last transform tool.

Tip: *If a menu item contains the word "Tool" such as "Align Curves Tool," it uses tool interaction. If the word "Tool" is not mentioned, the menu item is set as an action. This dynamically updates according to your preferences.*

2D fillet as an action

A good example of a typical action is a 2D fillet. As with all actions, you must start with an understanding of what the tool needs before beginning to execute the action.

1   **Draw two curves**

   • Select **Create → CV Curve Tool**.

   • Place several points for one curve.

   • Press **Enter** to complete.

   • Press the **y** key to refocus on Curve Tool.

   • Draw the second curve so that it crosses the first.

- Press the **Enter** key to complete.

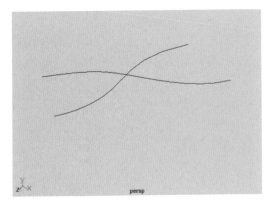

Two curves for filleting

2 **Find out 2D fillet requirements**

- In the **Surfaces** menu set, move your cursor over the **Edit Curves** → **Curve Fillet** menu item without executing it.

- Look in the Help Line to determine what kind of pick is required.

  The Help Line says: Select curve parameter points.

3 **Choose the first curve point**

- Click the first curve with the **RMB**.

- Choose **Curve Point** from the selection marking menu.

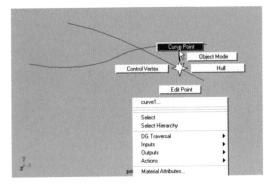

RMB pick of curve parameter point

- Click the curve to place the point on the side you want to keep.

4   **Choose the second curve point**

- Click the second curve with the **RMB**.

- Choose **Curve Point** from the selection marking menu.

- Press the **Shift** key and click the curve to place the point on the side of the curve you want to keep.

  *The **Shift** key lets you add a second point to the selection list without losing the first curve point.*

> **Note:** *You must first use the marking menu and then the **Shift** key to add a second point to the selection list, otherwise the selection menu will not appear.*

Two curve points in place

5   **Fillet the curves**

- Select **Edit Curves** → **Curve Fillet** → ❑ to open the tool options.

- Turn the **Trim** option **On**.

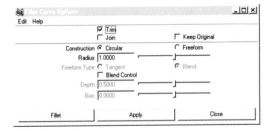

Fillet Tool options window

- Click the **Fillet** button.

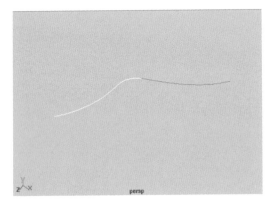

Final filleted curves

2D fillet as a tool

With this example you will use the menu item as a tool rather than an action.

1   **Draw two curves**

- In a new scene, draw two curves as in the previous example.

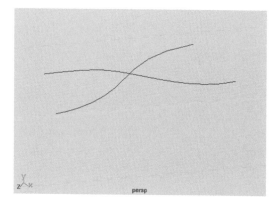

Two curves for filleting

2 **Change curve fillet to tool**

- Select **Edit Curves** → **Curve Fillet** → ❑.

- Select **Edit** → **As Tool** from the options window.

- Set **Trim** to **On**.

- Click the **Fillet Tool** button.

Note: *Notice the menu item now says Curve Fillet Tool.*

3 **Choose the first curve**

- Click with the **LMB** on the first curve.

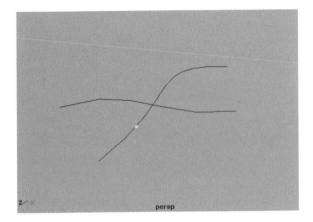

First curve selected

4   **Choose the second curve**

*   Click with the **LMB** on the second curve.

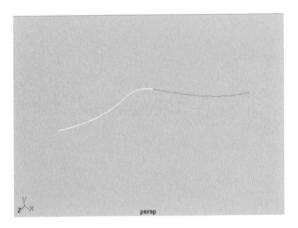

Final filleted curves

Project 01

Conclusion

You now know how to navigate the Maya UI and how tools and actions work. The skills you learned here will be applied throughout the rest of this book and in your career. You have the knowledge now to determine how you want to use the interface. Experiment with the different techniques taught here as you work through the Learning Maya projects.

The instructions for the following projects will not specify whether or not you should use the hotbox or menus to complete an action—the choice will be yours.

In the next lesson, you will explore the dependency graph. You will learn about the different nodes and how to build them into hierarchies and procedural animations.

Lesson 06

The Dependency
Graph

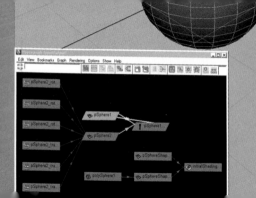

Maya architecture

The Maya architecture is defined by a node-based system, known as the *dependency graph*.
Each node contains attributes that can be connected to other nodes. If you wanted to reduce Maya
software to its bare essentials, you could describe it as *nodes with attributes that are connected*.
This node-based approach gives Maya software its open and flexible procedural characteristics.

Hierarchies and dependencies

If you understand the idea of *nodes with attributes that are connected,* you will understand
the dependency graph. Building a primitive sphere is a simple example involving the

3   View the Shape node

In the Hypergraph panel, you are currently looking at the scene view. The scene view is focused on *Transform nodes*. This type of node lets you set the position and orientation of your objects.

Right now, only a lone *nurbsSphere* node is visible. In fact, there are two nodes in this hierarchy, but the second is hidden by default. This hidden node is a *Shape node* which contains information about the object itself.

- In the Hypergraph, select **Options → Display → Shape nodes**.

You can now see the Transform node, which is the positioning node, and the Shape node, which contains information about the actual surface of the sphere. The Transform node defines the position of the shape below:

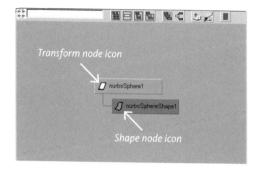

Transform and Shape nodes

- In the Hypergraph panel, select **Options → Display → Shape nodes** to turn these **Off**.

Notice that when these nodes are expanded, the Shape node and the Transform node have different icons.

When collapsed, the Transform node takes on the Shape node's icon to help you understand what is going on underneath.

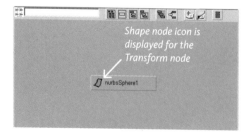

Transform node on its own

4   View the dependencies

To view the dependencies that exist with a primitive sphere, you need to take a look at the up and downstream connections.

- In the Hypergraph panel, click the **Input and output connections** button.

    The original Transform node is now separated from the Shape node. While the Transform node has a hierarchical relationship to the Shape node, their attributes are not dependent on each other.

    The Input node called makeNurbSphere is a result of the original creation of the sphere. The options set in the sphere's tool option window have been placed into a node that feeds into the Shape node. The Shape node is dependent on the Input node. Changing values for the Input node will affect the shape of the sphere.

    You will also see the initial shading group connected to the sphere. This is the default gray Lambert that is applied to all new objects.

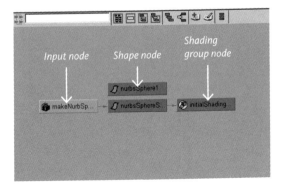

Sphere dependencies

 Tip: *In the previous image, the Orientation of the graph was changed to Horizontal.*

5   Edit attributes in the Channel Box

In the Channel Box, you can edit attributes belonging to the various nodes. Every node type can be found in the Channel Box. This lets you affect both hierarchical relationships and dependencies.

If you edit an attribute belonging to the *makeNurbSphere* node, then the shape of the sphere will be affected. If you change an attribute belonging to the *nurbsSphere* Transform node, then the positioning will be altered. Use the Channel Box to help you work with the nodes.

- For the Transform node, change the **Rotate Y** value to **45**.

- For the *makeNurbSphere* Input node, change the **Radius** to **3**.

> **Note:** *You can set attribute values to affect either the scene hierarchy or the dependency graph.*

Shading Group nodes

In earlier lessons, the word *node* was used a great deal when working with shading groups. In fact, Shading Group nodes create dependency networks that work the same way as Shape nodes.

1   **Create a shading network**

When you create a material, it automatically has a shading group connected to it.

- Select **Window → Rendering Editors → Hypershade.**

- In the Hypershade window, select **Create → Materials → Phong**.

- **Assign** this material to the sphere.

- Select the sphere in the Perspective panel and click the **Input and output connections** button.

   In the Hypergraph view, you will notice how the Input node is connected to the Shape node, which relates to the Phong shading group.

   A line is now drawn between the sphere's Shape node and Shading Group node. This is because the Shading Group is dependent on the surface in order to render.

   Every time you assign a shading network to an object, you make a dependency graph connection.

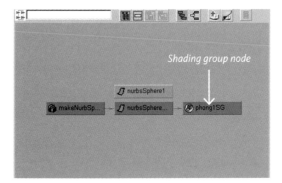

- Select the *nurbsSphere1* node and the *phong1SG* node in the Hypergraph.

- Again, click the **Input and output connections** button.

  You can now see how the phong Material node and the sphere's Shape node both feed the Shading Group. You can move your cursor over any of the connecting lines to see the attributes that are being connected.

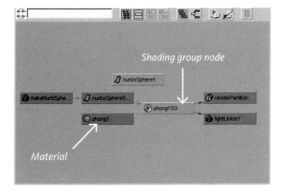

Assigned shading group

2   Open the Attribute Editor

You have seen how the nodes in the Hypergraph and Channel Box have been used to view and edit attributes on connected nodes. Now you will see how the Attribute Editor displays nodes, attributes, and connections.

- Click the **Scene Hierarchy** button in the Hypergraph panel to go back to a scene view.

- Select the *sphere*'s Transform node.

- Press **Ctrl+a** to open the Attribute Editor.

  In this integral window, you will see several tabs, each containing groups of attributes. Each tab represents a different node. All the tabs displayed represent parts of the selected node's dependency graph that are related to the chosen node. By bringing up several connected nodes, you have easier access to particular parts of the graph.

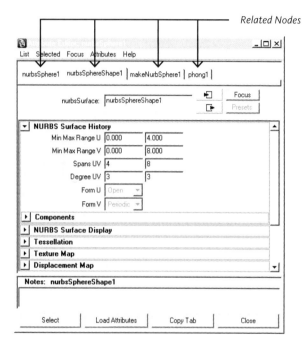

Nodes and attributes in the Attribute Editor

Note: *The Attribute Editor lets you focus on one part of the dependency graph at a time.*

Making connections

To help you understand exactly what a dependency graph connection is, you are going to make your own connection and see how it affects the graph.

1   Open the Connection Editor

- Select the *sphere*.

- Select **Window** → **General Editors** → **Connection Editor.**

- Click on the **Reload Left** button.

    The selected Transform node is loaded into the left column. All of the attributes belonging to this node are listed.

Note: *There are more attributes here than you see in the Channel Box. The Channel Box only shows attributes that have been set as keyable. Other attributes can be found in the Attribute Editor.*

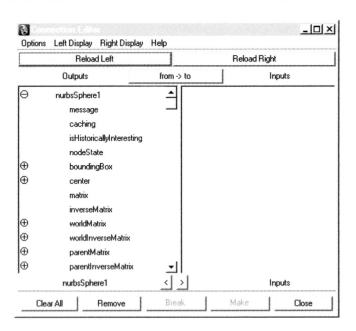

Transform node in the Connection Editor

2   Add phong as the Output node

- In the Hypergraph, select **Rendering** → **Show Materials**.

- Select the *phong1* Material node.

- In the Connection Editor, click the **Reload Right** button.

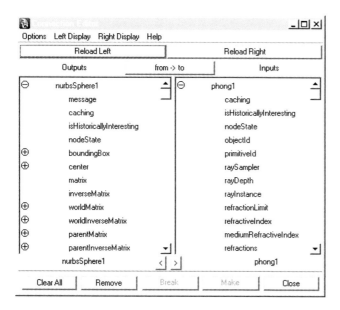

Material node in the Connection Editor

3   Make connections

You will now connect some attributes from the Transform node to the Material node.

- In the left column, scroll down until you find the *Translate* attributes.

- Click the plus (+) sign to expand this multiple attribute and see the *Translate X, Y,* and *Z* attributes.

- In the right column, scroll down until you find the *Color* attribute.

- Click the plus (+) sign to expand this multiple attribute and see the *Color R, G,* and *B* attributes.

- Click the **Translate X** attribute in the left column.

- Click the **Color R** in the right column.

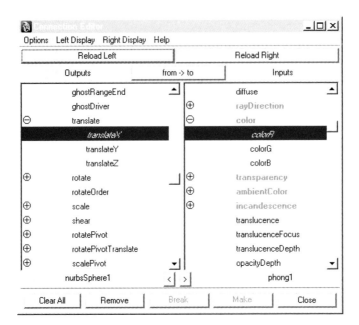

Connected attributes

- Use the same method to connect the following attributes:

  Translate Y to **Color G**;

  Translate Z to **Color B**.

4   **View the connections**

- In the Hypergraph panel, select the *Phong1* node and click the **Input and output connections** button.

- Move your cursor over the arrow connection between the Transform node and Material node.

The connection arrow is highlighted and the connected attributes are displayed. You now see the diagrammatic results of your action.

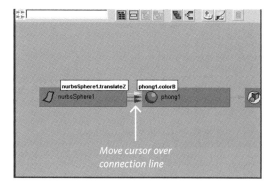

Viewing attribute connections

5   Move the sphere

You should see the effect of your connections when moving the sphere in the Perspective view.

• In the Perspective view, select the *sphere*.

• **Move** the sphere along the **X-axis**.

The color of the sphere changes to red. By increasing the value of the translation along X, you add red to the color.

• Try moving the sphere along each of the three main axes to see the colors change.

Adding a Texture node

While it is a fun and educational exercise to see the Material node's color dependent on the position of the ball, it may not be very realistic. You will now break the existing connections and map a Texture node in their place.

1   Delete connections

You can delete the connections in the Hypergraph view.

• In the Hypergraph view panel, select one of the three connection arrows between the Transform node and the Material node.

• Press the **Backspace** or **Delete** key to delete the connection.

- **Repeat** for the other two connections between these nodes.

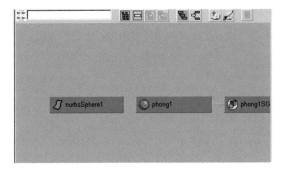

Broken connections

2   **Add a checkered texture map**

You will now use the Attribute Editor to help add a texture to the existing shading group.

- Click the *phong1* Material node.

- Press **Ctrl+a** to open the Attribute Editor.

- Click the **Map** button next to **Color**.

- Choose a **Checker** texture from the **Create Render Node** window.

- **MMB** in the Perspective view to make it active and press **6**.

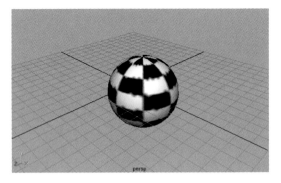

Textured sphere

In the Hypergraph, you can see the dependencies building up for the shading group. The texture is built using two nodes: the Checker node, which contains the procedural texture attributes, and the Placement node, which contains attributes that define the placement of the texture on the assigned surfaces.

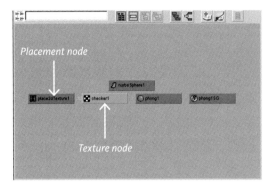

Shading group network

Animating the sphere

When you animate, you are changing the value of an attribute over time. You use keys to set these values at important points in time, then tangent properties to determine how the attribute value changes in between the keys.

The key and tangent information is placed in a separate Animation Curve node that is then connected to the animated attribute.

1   **Select the sphere**

• In the Hypergraph panel, click the **Scene Hierarchy** button.

• Select the *nurbsSphere* Transform node.

2   Return the sphere to the origin

Since you moved the sphere along the three axes earlier, it is a good time to set it back to the origin.

- Select the sphere's **Translate** attributes through the Channel Box by clicking the **Translate X** value and dragging to the **Translate Z** value.

  Doing so will highlight all three translate values, allowing you to enter a single value to change all of them at once.

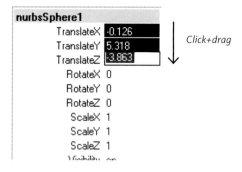

Click+drag the scale values

- In the Channel Box, type **0** and press **Enter**.

  Make sure all three translation values changed simultaneously.

- Make sure to also set all **Rotate** values to **0** and all **Scale** values to **1**.

3   Animate the sphere's rotation

- In the Time Slider, set the playback range to **120** frames.

- Go to frame **1**.

- Click the **Rotate Y** attribute name in the Channel Box.

- Click with your **RMB** and select **Key Selected** from the pop-up menu.

  This sets a key at the chosen time.

- Go to frame **120**.

- In the Channel Box, change the **Rotate Y** attribute to **720**.

- Click with your **RMB** and select **Key Selected** from the pop-up menu.

- **Playback** the results.

  The sphere is now spinning.

4   **View the dependencies**

- In the Hypergraph panel, click the **Input and output connections** button.

  You will see that an Animation Curve node has been created and then connected to the Transform node. The Transform node is shown as a trapezoid to indicate that it is now connected to the Animation Curve node. If you move the mouse cursor over the connection arrow, you will see that the connection is to Rotate Y.

  If you select the Animation Curve node and open the Attribute Editor, you will see that each key has been recorded along with value, time, and tangent information. You can actually edit this information here, or use the Graph Editor where you get more visual feedback.

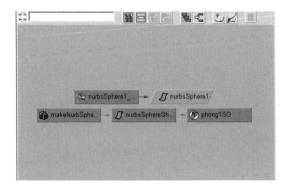

Connected Animation Curve node

Procedural animation

If the Maya procedural nature is defined as *nodes with attributes that are connected*, then a procedural animation would be set up by animating attributes at various levels of a dependency graph network.

You will now build a series of animated events that build on each other to create the final result.

1   **Create an edit point curve**

- Hide everything in your scene by selecting **Display → Hide → All**.

- Select **Create → EP Curve Tool**.

- Press and hold the **x** hotkey to turn on grid snap.

- Draw a curve as shown below:

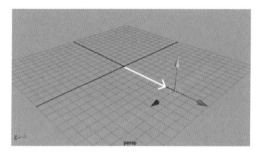

A new curve

- When you are finished, press **Enter** to finalize the curve.

- Select **Modify → Center Pivot**.

Note: *The pivot of a new curve is centered to the origin by default.*

2   **Duplicate the curve**

- Select **Edit → Duplicate**.

- **Move** the new curve to the opposite side of the grid.

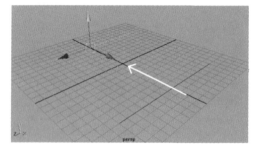

Moved curve

3 Create a lofted surface

A lofted surface can be created using two or more profile curves.

- **Click+drag** a selection box around both of the curves.

- Select **Surfaces** → **Loft**.

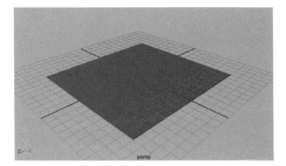

Lofted surface

4 Change your panel display

- In the Hypergraph panel, select **Panels** → **Perspective** → **persp**.

- In the new Perspective panel, select **Show** → **None and** then **Show** → **NURBS Curves**.

  Now you have two Perspective views. One shows the surface in shaded mode and the second shows only the curves. This makes it easier to pick and edit the curves in isolation from the surface itself.

5 Edit CVs on the original curves

- Select the first curve.

- Click with your **RMB** to bring up the selection marking menu and select **Control Vertex**.

- **Click+drag** a selection box over one of the CVs and **move** it down.

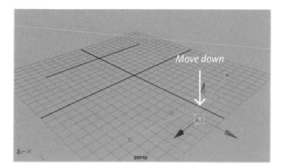

Edited profile curve

In the original Perspective view, you can see the effect on the lofted surface. Since the surface was dependent on the shape of the curve, you again took advantage of the dependency graph.

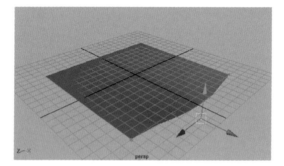

Resulting surface update

Note: The dependencies associated with models are sometimes referred to as construction history. By updating the input shape, you have updated the history of the lofted surface.

Curve on surface

You will now build a curve directly onto the surface. This curve will become dependent on the shape of the surface for its own shape.

The surface was built as a grid of surface lines called *isoparms*. These lines help define a separate coordinate system specific to each surface. Whereas world space coordinates are defined by X, Y, and Z, surface coordinates are defined by U and V.

1   Make the surface live

So far, you have drawn curves into the world space coordinate system. You can also make any surface into a *live* surface and draw into the UV space of the surface.

- Select the lofted surface.

  The CVs on the curve disappear and you are able to focus on the surface.

- Select **Modify** → **Make Live**.

  Live surface display changes to a green wireframe.

- Select **Display** → **Grid** to turn off the ground grid.

2   Draw a curve on the surface

- Select **Create** → **EP Curve Tool**.

- **Draw** a curve on the live surface.

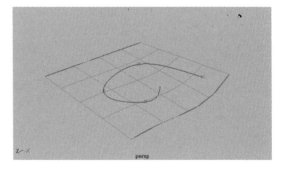

New curve-on-surface

3   Move the curve-on-surface

- Press the **Enter** key to complete the curve.

- Select the **Move Tool**.

  The move manipulator looks a little different this time. Rather than three manipulator handles, there are only two. One is for the U direction of the surface and the other is for the V direction.

- **Click+drag** the manipulator handles to move the curve around the surface space.

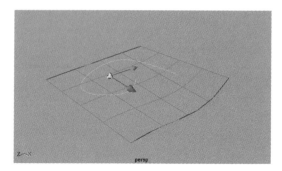

Moving the curve-on-surface

Tip: *This UV space is the same one used by texture maps when using 2D Placement nodes.*

4   Revert live surface

- Click in empty space to clear the selection.

- Select **Modify → Make Not Live**.

  With nothing selected, any live surfaces are reverted back to normal surfaces.

Tip: *You can also use the Make Live button on the right of the snap icons in the Status bar.*

Group hierarchy

You are now going to build a hierarchy by grouping two primitives, then animating the group along the curve-on-surface using path animation.

1   **Create a primitive cone**

   •   Select **Create** → **NURBS Primitives** → **Cone**.

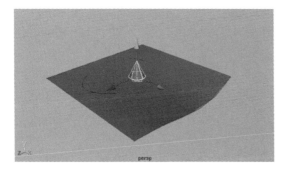

New primitive cone

2   **Create a primitive sphere**

   •   Select **Create** → **NURBS Primitives** → **Sphere**.

   •   **Move** the sphere above the cone.

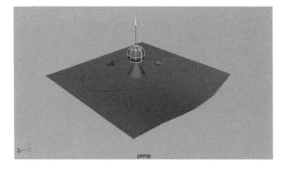

Second primitive object

3   **Group the two objects**

- Select the cone and the sphere.

- Select **Edit** → **Group** or use the **Ctrl+g** hotkey.

- Select **Display** → **Transform Display** → **Selection Handles**.

   The selection handle is a special marker that will make it easier to pick the group in Object selection mode.

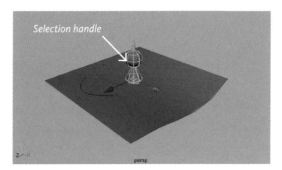

selection handle

Note: *Selection handles have higher selection priority than curves and surfaces.*

Path animation

To animate the new group, you will attach it to the curve-on-surface. You can use the curve-on-surface to define the group's position over time.

1   **Attach to the curve-on-surface**

- With the group still selected, press the **Shift** key and select the curve-on-surface.

- Go to the **Animation** menu set.

- Select **Animate** → **Motion Paths** → **Attach to Motion Path** → ❏.

- In the Option window, make sure that the **Follow** option is turned **Off**.

Project 01

- Click **Attach**.

- **Playback** the results.

As the group moves along the path curve, you will notice that it is always standing straight up.

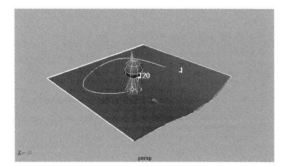

Path animation

2   **Constrain to the surface normal**

You will now constrain the orientation of the group to the normal direction of the lofted surface. The normal is like the third dimension of the surface's UV space.

- Click the loft surface to select it on its own.

- Press the **Shift** key and select the grouped primitives using the selection handle.

- Select **Constrain** → **Normal** → ❑.

- In the Option window, set the following:

    Aim Vector to **0, 1, 0**;

    Up Vector to **1, 0, 0**.

- Click **Add** to create the constraint.

- **Playback** the results.

> **Note:** *If your group is upside down, it could be because the surface normals are reversed. To fix this, select your plane and select* **Edit NURBS** → **Reverse Surface Direction**.

Now the group is orienting itself based on the normal direction of the surface. The group is dependent on the surface in two ways. First, its position is dependent on the path curve, which is dependent on the surface for its shape. Second, its orientation is directly dependent on the surface's shape.

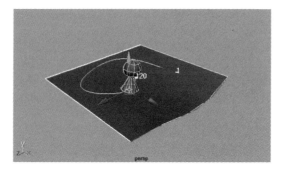

Constrained orientation

Layer the animation

The various parts of the dependency graph can all be animated to create exciting results. To see the dependency graph in motion, you will animate different nodes within the network to see how the dependencies react.

1   **Edit the loft curve shape**

    Since the shape of the surface is dependent on the original loft curves, you will start by animating the shape of the second curve.

    • Select the second loft curve.

   Tip: *You may want to use the second Perspective panel, which is only displaying curves.*

    • Click with your **RMB** to bring up the selection marking menu and select **Control Vertex**.

    Control vertices define the shape of the curve. By editing these, you are editing the curve's Shape node.

- **Click+drag** a selection box over one of the CVs and **move** it up to a new position.

  As you move the CV, the surface updates its shape, which in turn redefines the curve-on-surface and the orientation of the group. All the dependencies are being

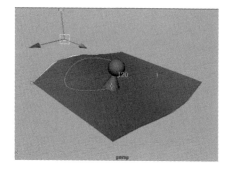

2   **Set keys on the CV position**

- Go to frame **1**.

Updating the dependencies

- Press **s** to set key.

- Go to frame **120**.

- Press **s** to set key.

- Go to frame **60**.

- **Move** the CV to a new position.

- Press **s** to set key.

- **Playback** the results.

  You can see how the dependency updates are maintained as the CV is animated. You are animating the construction history of the lofted surface and the connected path animation.

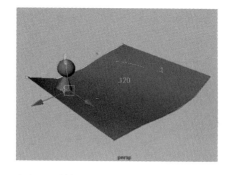

Animated history

3   **Animate the curve-on-surface**

To add another layer of animation, you will key the position of the curve-on-surface.

- Select the curve-on-surface.

- Go to frame **1**.

- Press **s** to set key.

- Go to frame **120**.

- **Move** the curve-on-surface to another position on the lofted surface.

  *Press **s** to set key.*

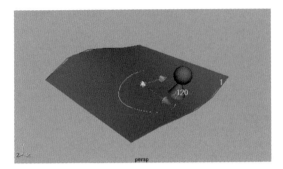

Animated curve on surface

4   **Assign the phong shading group**

To make it easier to see the animating objects, apply the checker shading group created earlier to the primitive group.

- Select the primitive group using its selection handle.

- Go to the **Rendering** menu set.

- Select **Lighting/Shading** → **Assign Existing Material** → **phong1**.

- **Playback** the scene.

5   **View the dependencies**

Of course, you can view the dependency network that results from all these connections in the Hypergraph view, which will probably be a bit more complex than anything you have seen so far.

- Select the primitive group that is attached to the motion path.

- Open the Hypergraph panel and click the **Input and Output Connections** button.

The resulting network contains the various dependencies that you built during this example.

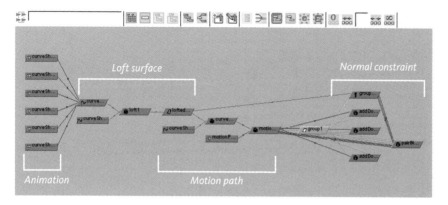

The dependency network

Conclusion

The procedural qualities of Maya software are tied to how the dependency graph uses nodes, attributes, and connections. You can see how deep these connections can go and how they are maintained throughout the animation process. Similar techniques can be used on other node types throughout Maya software.

Obviously, you do not have to use the Hypergraph and the Connection Editor to build, animate, and texture map your objects. In most cases, you will be thinking more about the motion of your character's walk or the color of their cheeks. It is still a good idea to know that the dependency graph supports everything you do and can always be used to your advantage.

In the next project, you will model, texture, set up, and animate the Romeo character.

Project 02

In this project, you will create a character named Romeo, one of the animals from the Walt Disney movie *Roadside Romeo*. You will begin by modeling and texturing his skin using several polygonal tools. Once that is done, you will set-up his skeleton and rig it so that you can fully animate him. You will then test the rig by keyframing a simple walk cycle.

Lesson 07
Polygonal Modeling

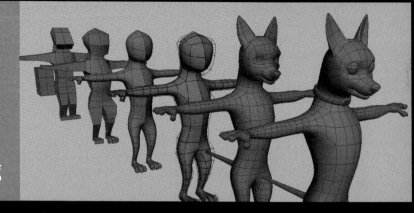

In this lesson, you will create Romeo, one of the animals from the Walt Disney movie *Roadside Romeo*. The character will be created starting from primitives. You will use many polygonal tools and deformers until the desired shape is achieved. As you learned in the first project, it will be possible to edit the construction history of modeling actions to update the model as you go. As well, you can edit the results throughout the lesson until you delete the history.

In this lesson, you will learn the following:

- How to model starting from a cube primitive

- How to model using smooth preview

- How to model with symmetry

- How to work with polygonal components

- How to edit the topology of a polygonal model

- How to work with procedural modeling attributes

- How to change edge normals

- How to use a lattice deformer

Set up your project

Since this is a new project, you must set a new directory as your current project directory. This will let you separate the files generated in this project from other projects. If you want to look at the final scene for this lesson, refer to the scene *07-polyModeling_06.ma*.

1   Set the project

As you have already learned, it is easier to manage your files if you set a project directory that contains subdirectories for different types of files that relate to your project.

- If you copied the support files onto your drive, go to the **File** menu and select
  Project → Set...
  A window opens, pointing you to the projects directory.

- Click the folder named *project2* to select it.

- Click the **OK** button.
  This sets the project2 directory as your current project.

  OR

- If you did not copy the support files on your drive, create a new project called *project2* with all the default directories.

2   Make a new scene

- Select **File → New Scene**.

Starting the character

You will build the character starting from a polygonal cube primitive. Facets will be extruded to create the more complex biped shape required and will then be refined to create the character shape.

It is important to understand what you will be doing throughout this lesson, so you must plan ahead and break down the task into simple stages. The following explains how you will approach the character modeling.

Torso

The cube primitive will be the pelvis area of the character. You will then extrude faces up to create the torso, neck, and head.

Legs

Starting from the pelvis geometry, you will extrude the polygon faces to create the legs.

Arms

Starting from the torso geometry, you will extrude polygon faces to create and refine the arms and hands.

Later in the lesson, you will ensure that your model is symmetrical by mirroring it.

Tip: *It is a good idea to look at reference images from this project and from the gallery in this book to give you an idea of the finished product.*

---

3   **Primitive cube**

- Select **Create → Polygon Primitives → Cube**.

- Press **5** to **Smooth Shade All**.

- **Rename** the cube *body*.

- From the **Inputs** section of the Channel Box, set the **Subdivisions Width** of the *polyCube1* node to **2**.

  Doing so will define polygonal edges going down the central line of the character.

Tip: *As a general convention, you should always model your characters facing the scene's positive Z-axis.*

- **Move** the cube up by about 8 units and **scale** it to roughly match the following, which represents the waist of the character:

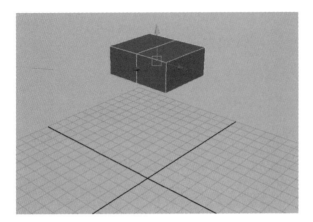

Start primitive cube

Tip: *When modeling, do not be afraid to model big. You do not want to be stuck working on a tiny model. Use the grid as a reference to represent the floor. You can always edit the proportions of your character later on.*

4   **Extrude faces**

Before extruding the faces, you need to make sure that the **Keep Faces Together** option is enabled. When this option is **On**, it extrudes chunks of facets instead of each facet individually. The following is an example of **Keep Faces Together** both **On** and **Off**:

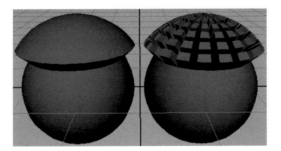

The Keep Faces Together effect

Note: *During the process of modeling the character, make sure that you do not accidentally select, deselect, or modify facets that are on the opposite side of the object. If you do, use Ctrl to deselect unwanted components.*

- Select the **Polygons** menu set by pressing **F3**.

- Make sure the option **Edit Mesh** → **Keep Faces Together** is set to **On**.

- Go into **Component** mode with faces displayed by pressing **F11,** or by setting the selection mask in the Status Bar as follows:

Component mode with faces enabled

Tip: *You can turn On or Off the preselection highlight in the preferences, under the Selection category. This book uses the option Select faces with: Center, which is also found under the Selection category. Feel free to use the selection method you prefer.*

- Select the two top faces on the cube, then select **Edit Mesh** → **Extrude**.

- **Move** the faces up in the **Y-axis**.

- **Scale** them down uniformly a little bit.

- **Repeat** the previous three steps to get geometry similar to the following:

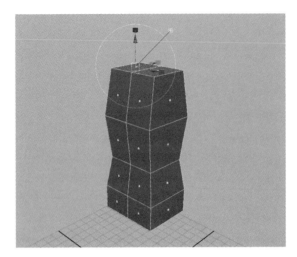

Waist and torso of the character

- **Extrude** four more times to make the neck, the chin, the middle of the head, and the top of the head of the character.

- As you are extruding, you can **rotate** the extruded faces on their **X-axis** by clicking the outer circle of the manipulator. By doing so, you can slightly tilt the head forward.

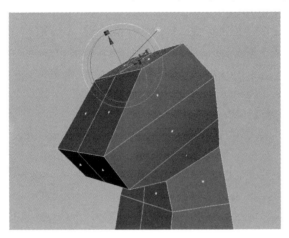

Neck and head of the character

Project 02

Smooth Mesh Preview

So far, you need a bit of imagination in order to see the character's shape. Smooth Mesh Preview is a simple tool that allows you to see a smoothed version of your model while still modeling on the cube from the previous steps.

- Go into **Object** mode.

- With the *body* selected, press the **2** hotkey.

  Doing so displays the original geometry, known as the cage, in wireframe and displays the smoothed resulting geometry within it. Whenever you update the cage geometry, the smoothed version will automatically update. Once you have refined the cage to your needs, you can either go back to the unsmoothed version, or convert the geometry to the smooth version using **Modify** → **Convert** → **Smooth Mesh Preview to Polygons**.

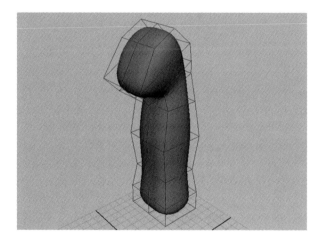

The cage and smoothed preview geometry

- With the *body* selected, press the **3** hotkey to display the smooth mesh only.

Tip: *You can tweak the smoothed version directly by pressing the **3** hotkey.*

- With the *body* selected, press the **1** hotkey to go back the normal display.

6   Extruding the legs

Now that you can see the rough shape of the character's body, you need to extrude the legs. Here, you will extrude both legs at the same time.

- Select the cage geometry and display its faces.

- Select the two faces from underneath the pelvis to start extruding the legs.

- Turn **Off** the **Edit Mesh** → **Keep Faces Together**.

  You will now be able to extrude both faces at the same time, still creating independent legs.

- Select **Edit Mesh** → **Extrude**.

- **Move** and **scale** the extruded faces down to the character's knees.

Note: *When you manipulate the handle associated with one face, the other face reacts equally. Extrusions work according to the normals of the original faces. Normals are lines that run perpendicular to the surface. To view polygon surface normals, select* **Display** → **Polygons** → **Face Normals**.

- **Extrude** again to create the ankles.

- **Extrude** and **move** the faces straight down to create the heels.

- Select the faces on the front of the last extrusion.

- **Extrude** to create the base of the toes.

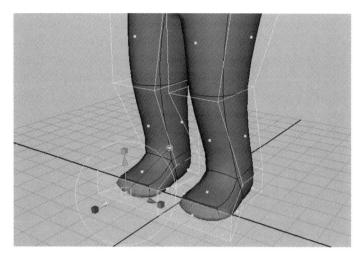

Leg and foot extrusions

7   Extruding the arms

Since you should be concentrating only on the basic shape of the character, you will stop refining the legs here and go into extruding the arms.

- Select the faces on either side of the top torso.

Tip: *While selecting, remember to use **Shift** to toggle the new selection, **Ctrl** to deselect, and **Ctrl+Shift** to add to the new selection.*

- **Extrude** once and **scale** the faces down so the arms start with small shoulders.

- **Extrude** the arms up to the elbows.

Note: *You may have to tweak one arm at a time in order to get the following result. Do not worry if the changes are not perfectly symmetrical; you will be mirroring the geometry later in this lesson.*

- **Extrude** again up to the wrists.

- **Extrude** one last time to create the palm of the hand.

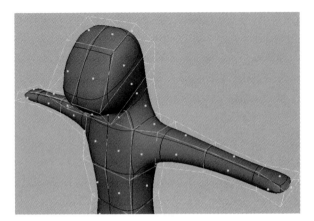

The extruded arms

8   **Save your work**

- **Save** your scene as *07-polyModeling_01.ma*.

Shaping the character

Now that the basic shape of the character is established, you can concentrate on moving polygonal vertices around to refine the general silhouette of the character.

Tip: *For a quick look at the silhouette of the character, you can press **7** on your keyboard. Without lights in your scene, this makes an instant black silhouette, allowing you to concentrate on contours.*

1   **Tweak the proxy**

In order to define the shape of the character a little better, you do not need to add geometry yet. Instead, you can edit the proxy geometry's vertices.

- Select the *body* geometry.

- Go into **Component** mode with **vertices** displayed.

Component mode with vertices enabled

- **Double-click** the **Move Tool** in the toolbox to bring up its options.

- In the Move Tool options, set the following:

    Reflection to **On**;

    Reflection space to **World**;

    Reflection axis to **X**;

    Tolerance to **0.1**.

- Click the **Close** button.

- Select a vertex on the proxy geometry and **move** its position.

    Because of the reflection option in the Move Tool, the corresponding symmetrical vertex is also moved.

Tip: *You should try to do symmetrical edits for this section of the lesson. It is not critical to always do so, but it will help you experience different tools and workflows. If you do not do symmetrical edits, try to always modify the same side of the model since you will eventually delete the other side to mirror the geometry.*

- **Tweak** the global shape of the character using the cage geometry, until you cannot improve it anymore unless by adding vertices.

Tip: *It is important to tweak the cage geometry so the smoothed geometry looks good and not the reverse.*

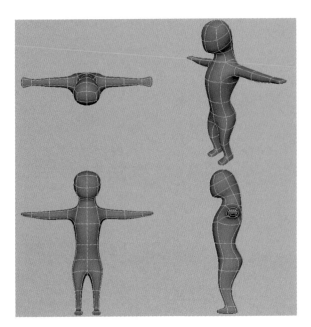

The refined shape

 Tip: *The wireframe lines on the smoothed mesh are excellent guidelines to place articulations.*

2 Modeling tips

- With vertices selected, you can press the arrows on your keyboard to traverse the geometry components.

- Make sure to always look through different views when modeling. You can stay in the Perspective view, but be sure to use the **View Cube** located in the upper right corner.

The View Cube

Project 02

- You can turn on the wireframe on shaded option by selecting **Shading** → **Wireframe on Shaded**. This will allow you to see the underlying geometry on the smoothed geometry.

- Try to not move the central line of vertices on their X-axis. This will make your work easier when you mirror the geometry.

Refine the character

You should now need more geometry to play with in order to get the character to the next level. Here, you will add to the existing geometry in order to better define key areas such as the arms, legs, feet, and hands. You will only refine one half of the model; you will then mirror the geometry to make both sides identical.

1   **Shape the bicep**

The arm is very simplistic and the first step is to add more geometry to play with. You will add several edge loops to define the muscles.

> **Note:**   *An edge loop is defined by a continuous line of connected edges. The edges perpendicular to an edge loop are called edge rings.*

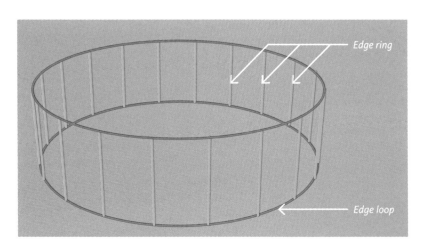

The difference between an edge loop and an edge ring

- With the *body* geometry selected, select **Edit Mesh → Insert Edge Loop Tool**.

- **Click+drag** any horizontal edge in the upper arm bicep area.

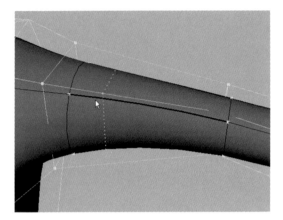

Insert an edge loop

- **Release** the mouse button to execute the tool.

- **Repeat** the previous step to insert another edge loop next to the one you just inserted.

Tip: *You can offset the edge loop by changing the Weight attribute for the polySplitRing node in the Channel Box.*

- **Tweak** the new vertices to shape the bicep.

2   **Shape the forearm**

- Insert a new edge loop in the middle of the forearm.

- Select **Edit Mesh → Offset Edge Loop Tool**.
  This tool allows you to simply add two edge loops on either side of an existing edge loop.

- **Click+drag** any edge from the edge loop you just inserted.

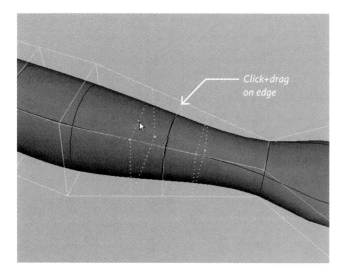

Click+drag
on edge

Offset edge loop

- **Release** the mouse button to execute the tool.

3   **Delete edges**

By inserting two new edge loops, you can now delete the edge loop in the middle of the forearm, which is no longer required.
If you need to delete edges, it is possible to simply select them and press the delete key on your keyboard. However, working this way leaves vertices on the perpendicular edges that are not wanted. In order to compensate for this, there is a specialized command that can be used to correctly delete edges and vertices.

- Press **F10** to go into Component mode with the edge mask.

- **Double-click** any of the vertical edge loops in the middle of the forearm.
  Doing so automatically selects the associated edge loop.

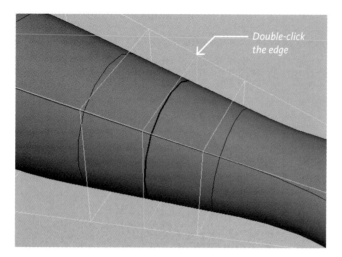

Double-click the edge

The edge loop to delete

- Select **Edit Mesh** → **Delete Edge/Vertex**.

  The entire edge loop is properly deleted.

- **Tweak** the new vertices to shape the forearm.

4   **Sliding edges**

At some point, you might want to offset edges or edge loops. The following shows a tool meant to do just that.

- **RMB** on the geometry and select **Edge**.

- **Double-click** the edge loop that you want to slide.

- Select **Edit Mesh** → **Slide Edge Tool**.

- With the edge loop still selected, **MMB+drag** in the viewport to slide the edges.

Tip: *Hold down the **Shift** key to slide the edges along their normals.*

5 Shape the leg

Using what you have just learned, shape the leg so it better defined. Note that this particular character does not have much muscle mass or great details, but think that you are still only looking to get a general shape for the leg.

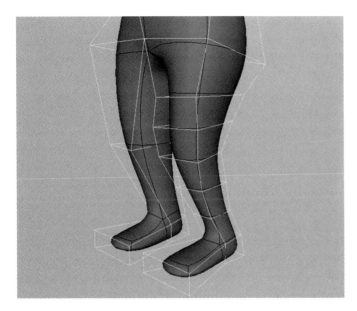

The shaped leg

Note: *Do not forget to tweak the leg on the same body side as the refined arm.*

6 Flatten the feet

As you can see, the smoothed character model does not have flat feet. This can be fixed by extruding an additional face underneath the foot.

- Select the faces under the foot.

- Enable the **Keep Faces Together** option.

- Select **Edit Mesh → Extrude**.

  Doing so forces the smoothed version of the geometry to be flatter in that area.

- Using the extrude manipulator, **scale** the face so it is a little smaller.

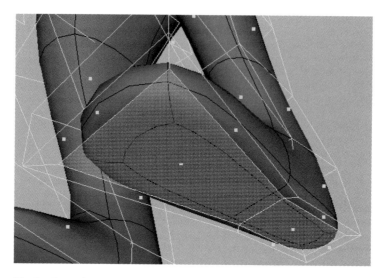

The flat foot sole

7   **Splitting polygons**

The Romeo character has three toes. In order to extract the toes, you will need to split polygonal faces at the front of the foot in order to create faces at specific locations to use for extrusions.

- Select **Edit Mesh** → **Split Polygon Tool**.

- **Click** the edge on the inner side of the foot and then drag up so the new edge starts at an already existing vertex.

- **Click+drag** the edge at the front of the foot to define a new vertex.

- **Click+drag** the edge at the bottom of the foot to define a new vertex.

- **Click+drag** the edge underneath the foot so the last edge ends at an already existing vertex.

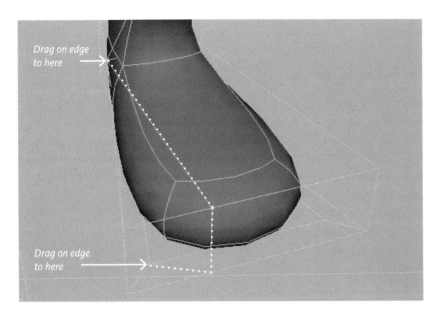

Drag on edge
to here

Drag on edge
to here

The toe split

- Click **Enter** to complete the action.

  Doing so inserts a new set of edges that will split in two the face at the front of the foot so you can extrude the toes.

- **Repeat** to insert a similar split on the other side of the foot.

  Doing so will create three faces on the front of the foot to use for extrusion.

8   **Toe extrusions**

- Select the three faces on the front of the foot where the toes should be extruded.

- Disable the **Keep Faces Together** option.

- **Extrude** twice to create the toes.

- **Tweak** the resulting vertices to your liking.

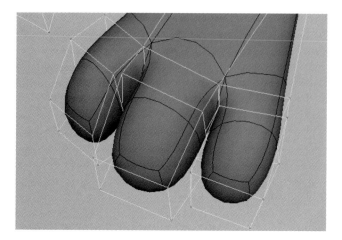

The extruded toes

9 **Shape the hand**

You can now take some time to extrude Romeo's three fingers and one thumb out of his palm.

• **Split** the palm three times as follows:

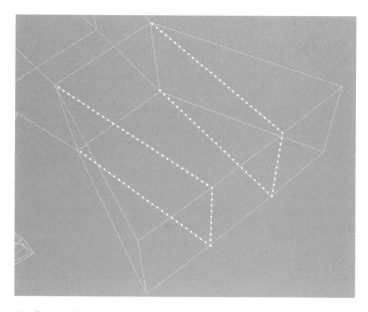

The finger splits

- **Extrude** the fingers two times.

  The second extrusion is not meant to be an articulation but rather to create a bulgy finger tip.

- **Extrude** the thumb three times out of the face on the side of the palm.

- **Tweak** the resulting geometry to your liking.

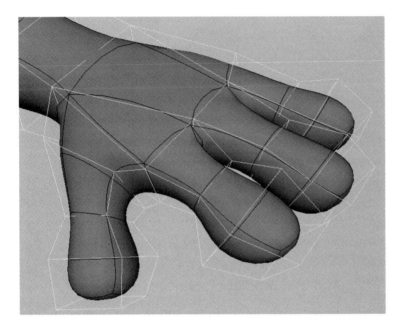

The refined hand

- **Extrude** the four faces on the inside of the palm, to create the palm pad.

- **Tweak** the resulting geometry to your liking.

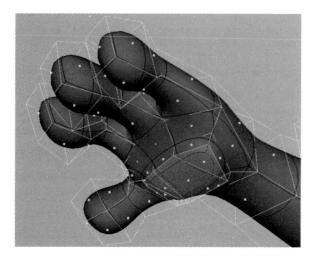

The refined palm

Note: *You will later cleanup and refine the hand edges so it consists of mostly quads rather than triangles.*

10 **Save your work**

• **Save** your scene as *07-polyModeling_02.ma*.

Mirror geometry

Mirroring geometry is a very important step when modeling since it saves you a lot of time when creating a symmetrical model.

The previous few steps were not reflected on the other half of the character, so rather than redoing all the work for the other side, it is simpler to create a mirrored version of your geometry. This will also simplify your work once you begin modeling the character's face.

1 **Delete one half**

You will now delete one half of the model and duplicate the remaining half using instance geometry.

• Display the original *body* geometry by pressing the **1** hotkey.

- From the *front* view, press **4** to display the model in wireframe.

- Select all the faces on the left side of the character as in the following image:

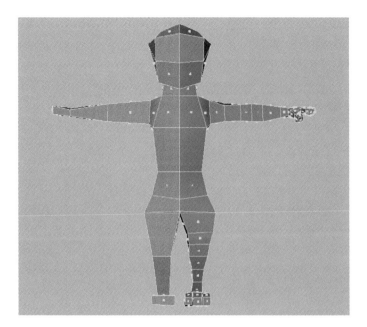

Half the body faces selected

Tip: *Be careful not to select faces that might be part of the other body half.*

- Press the **Delete** key on your keyboard.

2   Duplicate instance

- Go back into Object mode and select the *body* geometry.

- Select **Edit** → **Duplicate Special** → ❑.

- In the duplicate options, select **Edit** → **Reset Settings**, and then set the following:

    Geometry Type to **Instance**;

    Scale X to **-1**.

- Click the **Duplicate Special** button.

The model is duplicated as a mirrored instance. An instanced object uses the same geometry as the original object, except that it can have a different position, rotation, and scaling in space. Any adjustments done on one side will simultaneously be done on the other side.

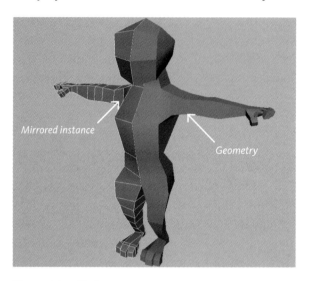

The model and its instance

Note: *It is normal that when you look at the cut geometry with the smooth preview, the central edges appear to be creased. This is because the smoothing of the geometry cannot occur between to separate polygonal shells. You will fix this later in the lesson.*

3   **Delete the history**

At this point, your model might start to be heavy because of all the construction history involved with your model. The construction history list for the model in the Channel Box is starting to look impressive, but it is useless. Now is a good time to delete the history on your model and from the entire scene in order to speed up your work.

- Select **Edit → Delete All by Type → History.**

4   **Save your work**

- **Save** your scene as *07-polyModeling_03.ma.*

Refine the head

Perhaps the most important part of the character is the face. This exercise will go through some steps in order to refine the head, but you will have to do most of the work by yourself, since this is an artistic task that cannot easily be explained step–by-step.

Several new tools will be explained here with some key examples that will require experimentation. If you would like to use the final scene of this exercise as a reference, look for the scene *07-polyModeling_04.ma* from the support files.

1 Split an edge ring

There are several ways to access the different modeling commands other than with the menus. If you like working with the menus, keep doing so, but the following is an alternative that involves a hotkey and a marking menu.

- **RMB** on the *body* and select **Edge**.

- **Choose** one of the horizontal edges on the side of the head.

- Hold down the **Ctrl** key and then **RMB** on the geometry.
  This brings up a polygonal modeling marking menu.

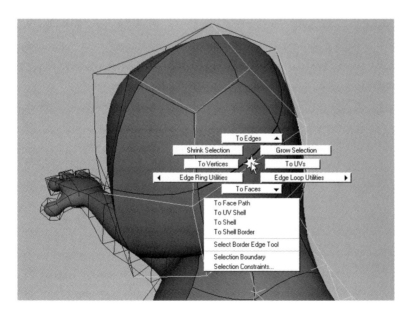

The modeling marking menu

- From the marking menu, select **Edge Ring Utilities**.

  Doing so automatically pops up a second marking menu related to edge rings.

- Select **To Edge Ring and Split**.

  The command automatically selects the related edge ring around the chosen edge, and then does a split on those edges.

  Notice that when inserting and splitting edge loops or rings, the tool keeps splitting across polygonal faces with four sides. If it encounters polygonal faces with more than or fewer than four sides, the tool stops splitting more edges. This can be very useful, but it can also go through your entire character before it stops splitting edges. In this example, notice how the edges split the middle finger and the toes, thus adding unwanted extra geometry.

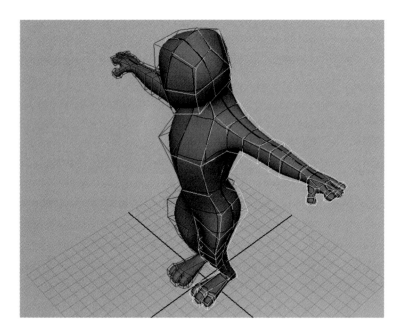

2   **Control splitting polygons**

In order for you to control how many edges are split as well as the path the tool is taking, there is an option that allows you to choose the edge to split. The following is an example of such an application.

- **Undo** the previous command.

- Select **Edit Mesh** → **Insert Edge Loop Tool** → ❑.

- In the shown window, turn **Off** the **Auto Complete** option.

- Click the **Close** button.

- **Choose** the central horizontal edge on the top of the head.

  The tool now requires you to choose subsequent edges in order to define an edge loop.

- **Choose** an edge on the wrist of the model.

  The tool displays the solved edge loop.

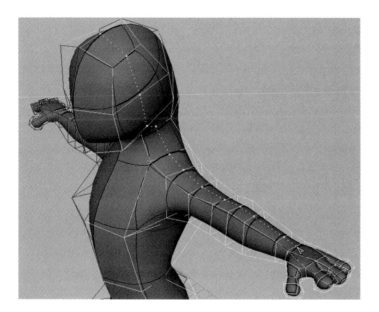

The solved edge loop

Note: *You can keep selecting other edges to define a longer edge loop. The edges do not need to be part of the same edge ring.*

- Press the **Enter** key when you are ready to insert the proposed edge loop.

- Select **Edit Mesh** → **Split Polygon Tool.**

- Split from the new vertex at the wrist to the vertex between the middle and pinky fingers.

- **Delete** the edge beside it to make a quad instead of two triangles.

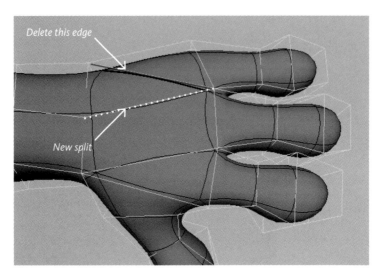

Delete this edge

New split

The new split and edge to delete

Tip: *When modeling, it is preferable to try building quad polygons rather than triangles.*

3   **Splitting the lower body**

You will now propagate a new edge loop split from the palm, along the side of the body, to the foot, and in between the legs.

- Select **Edit Mesh → Insert Edge Loop Tool.**

- **Choose** the central edge at the base of the palm.

- **Choose** the edge in the crotch between the legs.

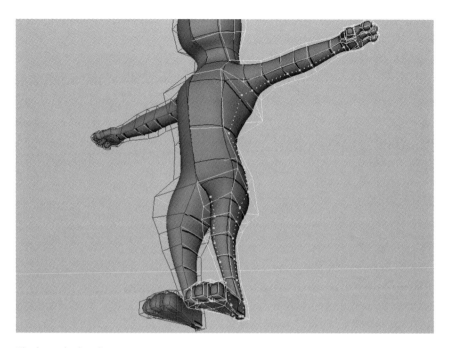

The lower body split

- Press the **Enter** key when you are ready to insert the proposed edge loop.

- Split from the new vertex in the palm to the vertex between the middle and pinky fingers.

- **Delete** the edge beside it to make a quad instead of two triangles.

4   **Tweak the inserted vertices**

There is now much more geometry to refine all over the character. The further you will get into the modeling, more and more artistic work comes into play. You must use your own judgment to define the geometry to your liking.

5   **Save your work**

- **Save** your scene as *07-polyModeling_04.ma*.

Keep on modeling

You now have a good understanding of polygonal modeling basics. By continuing to refine the character, you will see that the time spent experimenting will provide invaluable experience. Throughout the modeling process, you can explore trial and error processes that will eventually achieve great solutions. At some point, you will be able to visualize the different steps to take without ever touching the model.

The following are some general directions to finish modeling the character. To see the final scene of this exercise, look for the scene *07-polyModeling_05.ma* from the support files.

1   **Snap the central axis of the body**

The following will ensure that all the vertices on the central axis of the body are correctly aligned on the X-axis.

- Select the mirrored instance and then press the **Delete** key.

- With the *body* selected, select **Display** → **Polygons** → **Border Edges**.
  Doing so shows any edges that are located on borders in the geometry with thicker lines.

- From the *front* view, select all the vertices that are on a border.

 Tip: *Confirm in the Perspective view that you have selected all the required vertices.*

- **Double-click** the **Move Tool** to bring up its options.

- In the option window, scroll down and turn **Off** the **Retain component spacing** option.
  Doing so will allow you to snap the vertices to the X-axis all at once.

- Hold down the **x** hotkey to snap to grid, then **click+drag** the **X-axis** of the move manipulator to snap all the selected vertices to the central **X-axis**.

- Make sure that no vertex crosses the central X-axis. If so, translate them back on the left side of the *body*.

2   **Mirror the geometry**

You can now make the entire body a single polygonal mesh.

- While in Object mode with the *body* selected, select **Mesh → Mirror Cut.**
  A plane will be added to your scene, which is used as a mirror to make your model symmetrical.

- With the *mirrorCutPlane* selected, set its **Translate X** attribute to **0.0**.

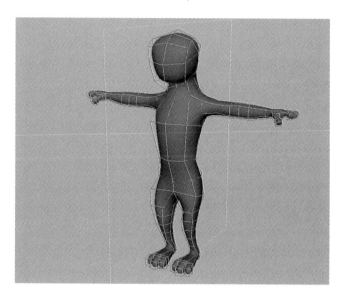

The mirrored geometry

- Select **Edit → Delete All by Type → History**.
  Doing so will allow you to finalize the geometry and delete the mirror plane.

- **Delete** the *mirrorCutPlane*.

3   **Smooth the geometry**

The Smooth Mesh Preview is a great way to create a general shape for your character, but at some point, you will need to tweak the smoothed geometry rather than continuing to work on the low resolution cage.
In the following, you will smooth the geometry to get a higher resolution and start refining the higher resolution model.

- Select the *body* geometry and press the **3** hotkey.

- Select **Modify** → **Convert** → **Smooth Mesh Preview to Polygons.**

   You now have a higher resolution model to work with, but the default smoothing value is higher than you require.

- Highlight the *polySmoothFace1* node in the Channel Box, and set **Divisions** to **1**.

   The geometry is now less dense, but perfect for your needs.

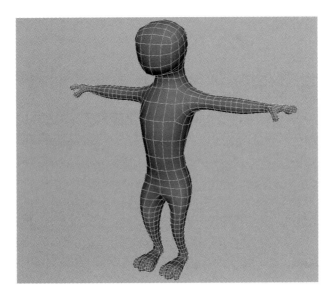

The high-resolution model

4   **Tweak the vertices**

Now that you have more vertices defining your character, you can play with the shape of the character.

- Make sure the **Reflection** option for the Move Tool is turned **On** so that any modifications are made on both sides of the model. Using this option will also prevent you from accidentally moving the central vertices away from the central axis.

Tip: *Do not be afraid of moving vertices one by one. You will most likely end up moving each vertex by hand for the entire model anyway.*

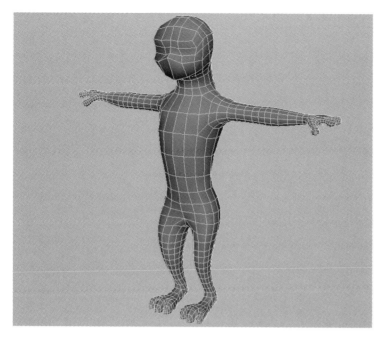

High resolution refinements

While you are tweaking the vertices around the eyes and the nose, try to define the different facial areas with edges. Doing so will help you see the different parts of the face, and it will also make it easier to split polygons to get even more resolution.

5   **Removing definition**

When working with a model that was automatically smoothed, you might end up with edge loops that are absolutely necessary to better define the model. For instance, the toes might have too much resolution for your needs. Here you will learn a quick way to delete edge loops.

- Identify an edge loop to be deleted.

- While in Component mode with the edge mask enabled, select a single edge of the edge loop to be deleted.

- Hold down the **Ctrl** key and click your **RMB** to select **Edge Loop Utilities** → **To Edge Loop and Delete.**
  The edge loop is automatically deleted.

- Experiment with other edge loop and edge ring utilities.

6   Add divisions

You must now concentrate on splitting and refining only one half of the model.

- **Delete** half the model and create a mirrored **instance** as previously shown.

- Use the **Split Polygon Tool** to insert new edges where required in order to better define certain areas.

- Use the **Delete Edge/Vertex** to remove unwanted edges where you will split new faces.

Tip: *As a rule, try to always create four-sided polygons when splitting geometry. Doing so will spare you problems later on.*

- **Extrude** the eye socket faces and **scale** them slightly toward the inside to add circular edges in the eye area.

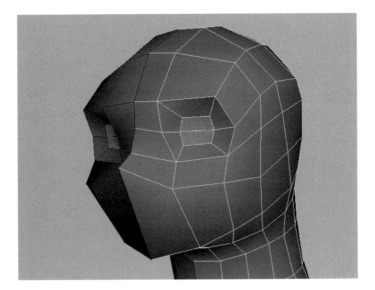

Edges inserted

- **Split** a horizontal edge loop going all around the head to split the mouth area.

- **Extrude** the nose's top and bottom parts.

Proportio

Sometimes
proportions
a lattice def
manipulatec
simply delet

1   **Create**

   • Sele

   • Fron

      A lar

T

The latti

N

Tip: *It is easier to extract faces when the Reflection option of the Move Tool is disabled.*

• **Extrude** the nose.

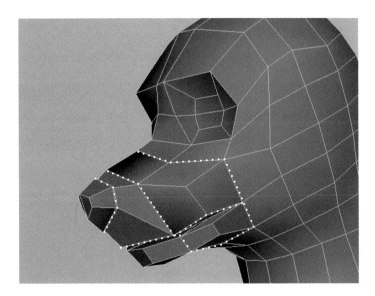

The extruded nose

Note: *To simplify your work, you will not see how to model the inner mouth in this lesson. Instead, concentrate on modeling the lips.*

7   **Interior faces**

When extruding faces touching the central axis of the character, you will get a polygon on the inside parallel to the central axis. You should delete these polygons.

• **Hide** the instance of the *body* by selecting it and pressing **Ctrl+h**.

• Locate and **delete** the faces parallel to the central axis on the inside of the mouth.

• Show the last hidden object by pressing **Ctrl+Shift+h**.

3   **Mirror the eyeball**

- Select the *eyeball* and *eyelid*.

- Press **Ctrl+g** to **group** them all together.

- With the new group selected, select **Edit → Duplicate Special.**
  Doing so will duplicate the required construction history on the eyelid, which will be needed later for eye blinking.

- In the Channel Box with the duplicated group still selected, set **Scale X** to **-1**.
  You now have eyes for both sides of the character.

Note: *From now on, do not delete the construction history for the entire scene since the eyelids require it for blinking. If you want to delete the history, do it only for the selected models.*

4   **Necklace**

You will now model Romeo's collar.

- **Create** the *collar* using a polygon **Torus**.

- Change the collar's **Input** to the following:
    Section Ration to **0.1**

    Subdivisions Axis to **24**

    Subdivisions Height to **12**

- **Create** the *jewel* using a **NURBS Sphere**.

- **Create** the letter *R* using **Create → Text → ❏**.

- Select a **Font** type by clicking the down arrow.

- Select the **Bevel** type and then choose the **Convex Out** type from the **Outer bevel style** list.

- Click the **Create** button.

- Place the resulting geometry as follows:

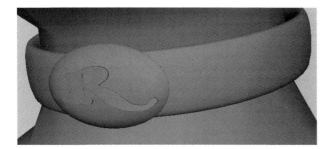

Romeo's collar

5   **Save your work**

- **Save** your scene as *07-polyModeling_06.ma*.

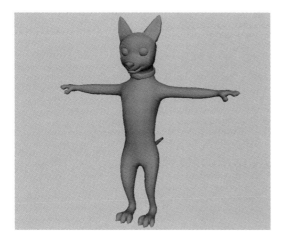

The final model

Conclusion

In this lesson, you learned how to model a complete character out of basic polygonal primitives. In the process, you used several polygonal modeling tools to create the shape and details. As you noticed, each tool created an Input node for which you were able to modify the construction history. You also used the lattice deformer, which is a great tool to know about.

In the next lesson, you will texture the character. This will allow you to experiment with polygonal texture tools and techniques.

Lesson 08
Polygonal Texturing

Texturing polygonal surfaces

The character will be textured using multiple shading groups and texture maps. You will start by positioning a texture on the main body geometry, which will be accomplished using constructive polygon texturing tools. Once that is done, you will texture the eyes of the character. Feel free to continue using your own file, or start with *07-Romeo_06.ma* from the previous lesson.

1   UV Texture Editor

The UV Texture Editor is where you can see the UVs of your model. UVs are similar to vertices except that they live in a flat 2D space. The UVs determine the coordinates of a point on a texture map. In order to properly assign a texture to a polygonal model, the UVs need to be unfolded somewhat like a tablecloth.

- Select the *body* geometry.

- Select **Window** → **UV Texture Editor**.

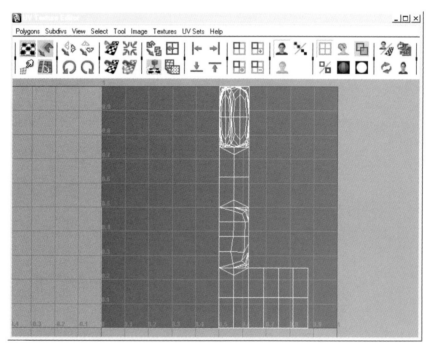

The UV Texture Editor

Displayed in the UV Texture Editor are the UVs for the selected geometry. Those UVs are now irregular and will result in a very poor texture mapping.

2   **Create and assign a body shader**

- **Open** the Hypershade window.

- **Create** a *Blinn* material node.
  Blinn is the simplest material that once properly set up can look like skin.

- **Rename** the Material node *bodyM*.

- **Assign** the *bodyM* material to the *body* geometry.

- To view the upcoming steps, press **6** on your keyboard to turn On the **Hardware Texturing** in the Perspective view.

3   **Map a checker to the color**

- Open the Attribute Editor for the *bodyM* material.

- **Map** the **Color** attribute with a **Checker** Texture node.

Irregular texture placement due to poor UVs

Note: *The checker texture is just a temporary texture in order to better see the UV placement on the model.*

4   Planar mapping

In order to start correcting the texture mapping of the character, you will use a
planar projection.

- With the *body* geometry selected, from the Polygons menu set, select **Create UVs** →
  Planar Mapping → ❏ In the option window, select **Project** from **X-axis**.

- Click the **Project** button.

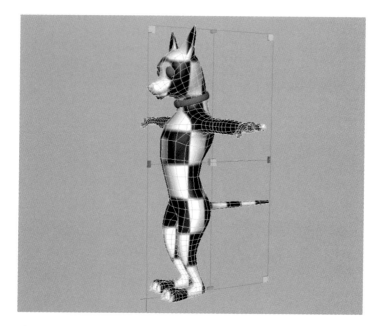

Planar projection

A large projection plane icon surrounds the object, which projects the texture map along the
*X-axis. You can see the texture mapped onto the surface with hardware texturing (**6** hotkey).*

5   Projection manipulators

The projection manipulator allows you to transform the projection to better suit
your geometry.

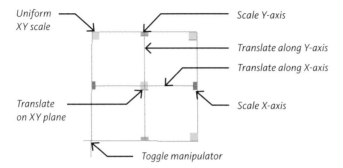

Planar projection manipulator

You can toggle the manipulator type for a conventional all-in-one manipulator by clicking the *red T*.

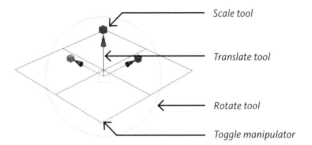

Other planar projection manipulator

> **Note:** *If the projection manipulator disappears, reselect the geometry, click the polyPlanProj Input node in the Channel Box, and select the Show Manipulator Tool, or press the **t** hotkey.*

6   **UV Texture Editor**

If you change the positioning of the manipulator from the previous step, you will see that the UVs of the model in the UV Texture Editor have been updated to be projected according to the manipulator in the viewport.

- In the UV Texture Editor menu bar, select **Image → Display Image** to toggle the display of the checker texture to **Off**.

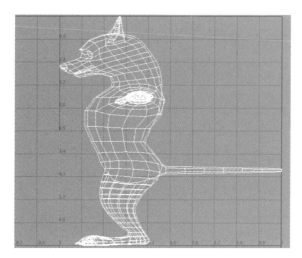

The projected UVs

> **Note:** *The view of the object and the loaded texture are both initially displayed in the Texture Editor with a square proportion—regardless of the proportion of the planar projection positioned in the 3D space of the model and the proportion of the texture image file.*

Modifying UVs

It is important to prevent overlapping of the UVs where it is not wanted. For instance, if you make a planar projection from the front of the model, the UVs would overlap on the front and back of the model. If you make the chest of the character another color, the back would also change. To prevent this, you need to split the different character sections by cutting the UVs.

1   **Projection for the nose**

The nose UVs will be projected from the front.

- **RMB** on the *body* geometry and select **Face**.

- Select the faces of the nose.

- Select **Create UVs** → **Planar Mapping** → ❑.

- In the option window, select **Project** from Z-axis.

- Click the **Project** button.

  Doing so will make the nose projection on the Z-axis.

2   **Moving the UVs**

- In the UV Texture Editor with the character's nose faces still selected, **RMB** and select **UV** from the context menu.

  Doing so sets the current selection mask to UVs only.

- **Click+drag** a selection rectangle over the entire nose.

  The UVs of the nose are now selected.

- **Scale** and **move** the UV shell to the upper right corner of the UV editor grid.

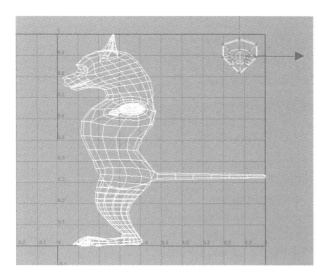

Tweaked UV shell

Note: *Individual UV groups are called UV shells.*

3   **Projection for the arms**

- Select the faces of the hands of the character in the Perspective view.

- From the main Maya interface, select **Select → Grow Selection Region**.
  The neighbor faces on the model are selected, which increases the current selection.

Tip: *You can press* **Shift+›** *to increase the selection and Shift+‹ to shrink the current selection.*

- Select **Select → Grow Selection Region,** or press **Shift+›** a few more times until you have the arm selected up to the shoulders.

- Select **Create UVs → Planar Mapping → ❑.**

- In the option window, select Project from Y-axis.

- Click the **Project** button.
  Doing so will make the arms symmetrical across the Y-axis.

- Select **Select → Convert Selection → To UVs.**

- **RMB** in the Texture Editor and select **UV** from the context menu.

- Place the **UV shells** in the **UV Texture Editor** like the following:

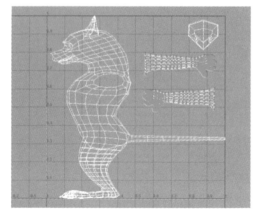

The arm UVs

4   **Separate overlapping UVs**

At this time, if you would texture the paws of the character, the top of the hand would also be texture because the top and bottom UVs of the arms are overlapping. You will now separate the overlapping UVs into separate UV shells.

• Select any UVs of the arms UV shells.

• Select **Select → Select Shell in the Texture Editor.**

• Select **Polygons → Layout → ❏.**
  Doing so will bring up the automatic UV layout tool options.

• In the options, set the following:

   Layout objects to **Per object (overlapping)**

   Separate shells to **Folds**

   Flip reversed to **Enabled**

   Scale mode to **None**

   Rotate to **None**

• Click the **Layout UVs** button.
  The selected UVs will automatically be separated and placed in the Texture Editor.

• Select **Select → Convert Selection → To UVs.**

• Place the UV shells as follows:

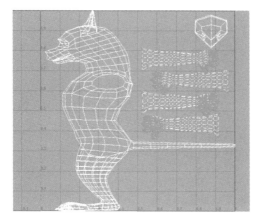

The new UV layout

5 Projection for the ears

- **Repeat** the previous two steps to create a projection across the **Z-axis** for the ears.

6 Layout UVs

Manually layout the UV shells to optimize the usage of the square texture space. The texture space corresponds to the coverage of a texture in UV space, which is represented by the grid in the Texture Editor.

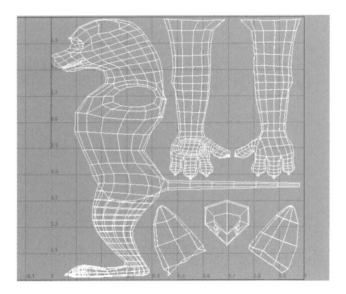

Final UV layout

Note: *The arms and ears were moved on top of each other so you only have to texture one of them in the next exercise.*

- Close the UV Texture Editor.

7 Save your work

- **Save** your scene as *08-polyTexturing_01.ma*.

3D Paint Tool

A great way to create custom texture is to paint a texture directly on a model in the viewport. The 3D Paint Tool allows you to paint using default paintbrushes or Paint Effects' brushes. You can use the tool to outline details to be painted in separate software, or to create a final texture directly in Autodesk® Maya® software.

Tip: *As you are working with the 3D Paint Tool, you might want to change the way the UVs are laid out to minimize texture stretching and overlapping.*

1   **Open the 3D Paint Tool**

- Select the *body* geometry.

- Select the **Rendering** menu set by pressing **F6.**

- Select **Texturing** → **3D Paint Tool** → ❑.
  This will open the tool's option window.

- Scroll down to the **File Textures** section.

- Make sure **Attribute to Paint** is set to **Color**.

- Click the **Assign/Edit Textures** button.
  This will open the new texture creation options.

- Set **Image Format** to **Tiff (tif)**.

- Set both the **Size X** and **Size Y** to **512**.

Tip: *For more definition in your textures (if your computer can handle it), you might want to boost up the texture resolution to 1,024x1,024 or even 2,048x2,048.*

- Click the **Assign/Edit Textures** button.
  Doing so will duplicate the currently assigned texture and save it in your project in the 3dpainttextures folder. As you paint on the geometry, only this new texture will be automatically updated.

2   **Set the initial color**

You will now paint a color over the old checkered pattern.

- In the 3D Paint Tool settings, change the **Flood Color** attribute in the **Flood** section to be **golden brown**.

- Click the **Flood Paint** button.

  The character is now totally brown.

3   **Set erase image**

To make sure that you can erase your drawing and come back to the original texture, you need to set the erase image as the current texture.

- Scroll to the **Paint Operations** section and click the **Set Erase Image** button.

4   **Paint on geometry**

- Under the **File Textures** section, turn **On** the **Extend Seam Color** option.

  This option will make sure that there are no seams visible when painting.

- Scroll at the top of the 3D Paint Tool and make sure the second **Artisan** brush is enabled in the **Brush** section.

- When you put your mouse cursor over the geometry in the viewport, if the brush size is too big or too small for painting, set its **Radius (U)** in the option window, or hold the **b** hotkey and **drag** the radius of the brush in the viewport.

- Change the **Color** attribute from the **Color** section to **beige**.

- **Paint** directly on the geometry to define the character's chest.

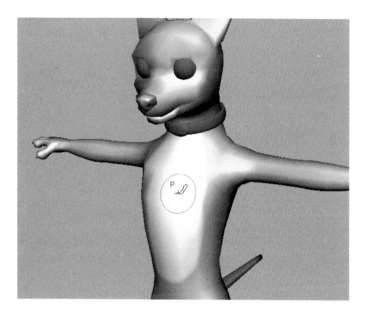

The painted chest

Both sides of the body are updated symmetrically because the chest UVs are overlapping.

> **Tip:** Undoes are supported when painting strokes, or you can erase them by setting the Paint Operation to Erase. When erasing, you are reverting to the texture saved when you clicked the Set Erase Image button in the previous step.

5   **Reflection**

Since the model is to be symmetrical, it is a good idea to turn on the reflection capability of the 3D Paint Tool.

• Under the **Stroke** section, turn **On** the **Reflection** option, and make sure the **Reflection axis** is set to **X**.

6   Paint options

Under the **Paint Operations** section, you can set various paint operations like Paint, Erase, Clone, Smear, and Blur. You can also set the Blend Mode, which affects the way new strokes are painted on your texture. Those options can be very useful for tweaking your texture.

- Continue painting the character with different colors on the different parts of his body such as the nose, ears, hands, feet, and tail.

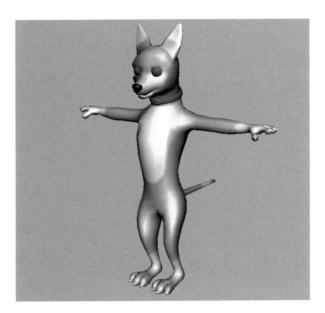

Fully painted character

Note: *Sometimes, painting directly on the geometry creates artifacts due to things such as seams, color, texture resolution, UV placement, UV overlapping, and so on. One way of correcting this is by editing the texture later in a paint program.*

7   Paint Effects

- Scroll to the **Brush** section of the tool and enable the first **Paint Effects** brush.

- To choose a template brush, click the **Get Brush** button to pull up the Visor.

Paint Effects:

Get Brush button

- In the Visor, scroll to the **Pencils** directory and choose the brush called *pencilSmooth.mel*.

- Experiment by painting on Romeo's nose to give it some whiskers.

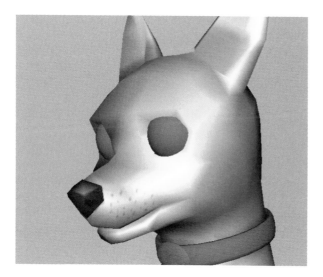

Paint Effects' strokes

8   Screen projection

When painting with a Paint Effects brush, you will notice that the brush icon in the viewport looks stretched. This is because the brush bases itself on the object's UVs, which are stretched. To correct the problem, you need to enable the screen projection option.

Stretched brush

- Expand the **Stroke** section in the 3D Paint Tool window.

- Turn **On** the **Screen Projection** attribute.

- **Paint** on geometry.

Note: *When painting with Screen Projection, you are painting using the current camera view. This can be very useful in some cases, but can also create stretched textures when painting on geometry parallel to the view.*

9   **Reference strokes**

You might find it easier to draw only reference strokes in Maya and then use a paint program to refine the look of the texture. To do so, you will draw where you want to add texture details on the object, and then open the texture in a paint program. Once you are finished with the texture, you can reload it in the Maya software.

10   **Save textures**

You have not yet saved to disk the texture just drawn, making it inaccessible to another program.

- To save the texture manually, click the **Save Textures** button in the **File Textures** section.

   OR

- To save the texture automatically on each stroke, turn **On** the **Save Texture on Stroke** checkbox in the **File Textures** section.

11   **Edit the texture**

You can now edit your texture from the *3dpainttextures* directory in a paint program. When you have finished modifying the texture, save the new image.

The final texture

- Back in Maya, in the texture's Attribute Editor, click the **Reload File Textures** button to update the skin texture for the new version.

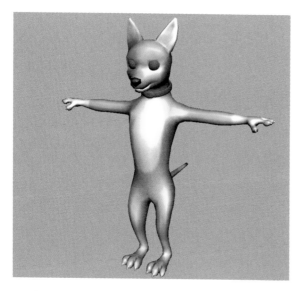

The final texture on the model

Tip: *If you saved the file under a different name or in a different location, browse to get the modified texture.*

Final touches

In order to finish texturing the character, you must texture the eyeballs and eyelids. Note that the eyes were made out of NURBS surfaces, so they will not require extra UV steps. The texturing of NURBS surfaces will be shown in more detail in the third project.

1 **Create and assign an eye shader**

- **Open** the Hypershade window.

- **Create** a *phong* Material node.

  Phong is the material that suits the shiny eyes best.

- **Rename** the Material node *eyeM*.

- **Assign** the *eyeM* material to both *eyeballs*.

2   **Map a ramp to the color**

- Open the Attribute Editor for the *eyeM* material.

- **Map** the **Color** attribute with a **Ramp** Texture node.

Tip: *Make sure that the Normal option is selected at the top of the Create Render Node window.*

- **Rename** the Ramp node *eyeColor*.

3   **Tweak the ramp**

- In the Attribute Editor for the *eyeColor*, set **Type** to **U Ramp**.

- **Tweak** the ramp's colors as in the following image:

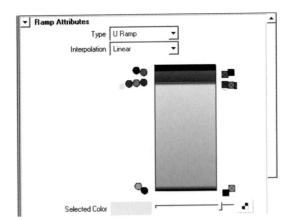

The eye color Ramp Texture

4   Create and assign an eyelid shader

- **Create** a B*linn* material and **rename** it *eyelidM*.

- Set the **Color** of the material to be a color similar to the surrounding eye color of the character.

Tip: *Use the Teardrop Tool in the Color Picker window to directly select the color you need on the model.*

- **Assign** the *eyelidM* to the *eyelid* objects.

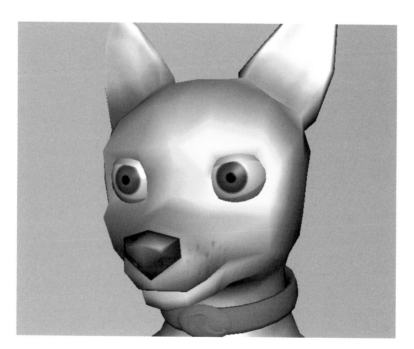

The textured eyes

5   **Texture the collar**

Texture the collar to your liking. You can use the textures *belt.tif* and *gold.tif* from the *support_files* directory.

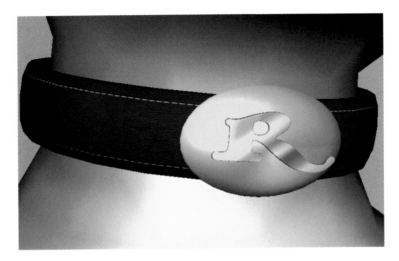

Romeo's collar

6   **Nails**

- **Assign** a dark gray **phong** shader to the nail faces.

Optimizing the scene

To maintain a good workflow, you should clean up your scene once texturing is complete. For instance, you might want to delete all unused shading networks in the scene.

1   **Delete unused nodes**

- From the Hypershade window, select **Edit → Delete Unused Nodes**.
  Maya will go through the list of Render nodes and delete anything that is not assigned to a piece of geometry in the scene.

2   **Optimize scene size**

•   Select **File** → **Optimize Scene Size**.

Maya software will go through the entire scene and remove any unused nodes.

3   **Delete the history**

•   Select all the objects except the *eyelids*.

•   Select **Edit** → **Delete by Type** → **History**.

4   **Save your work**

•   The final scene, *08-polyTexturing_02.ma*, can be found in the support files.

Conclusion

You now have a good understanding of texturing polygons. You have experimented with a projection and some polygonal tools and actions. There is much more to learn concerning polygonal texturing, so feel free to experiment on your own.

In the next lesson, you will learn about creating joint chains, which is the first step for animating a character.

Lesson 09
Skeleton

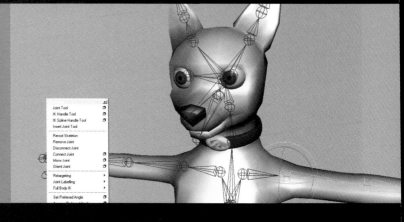

In this lesson, you will create the skeleton hierarchy to be used to bind the geometry and to animate Romeo. In order to create a skeleton, you need to draw joints to match the shape of your character. The geometry is then bound to the skeleton and deformations are applied.

In this lesson, you will learn the following:

- How to create skeleton joints

- How to navigate around a joint hierarchy

- How to edit joint pivots

- How to mirror joints

- How to reorient joints

- How to edit the joint rotation axis

Drawing a skeleton chain

In this exercise, you will draw skeleton chains. Even if this operation appears to be simple, there are several things to be aware of as you create a joint chain.

1   **Joint Tool**

- Open a new scene and change the view to the *side* Orthographic view.

- From the **Animation** menu set, select **Skeleton** → **Joint Tool** → ❏.
  The tool's option window is displayed.

- Change the **Orientation** attribute to **None**.

 Note: *This attribute will be explained later in this exercise.*

- Click the **Close** button to close the tool window.

- In the side view, **LMB+click** two times to create a joint chain.

- Press **Enter** to exit the tool.

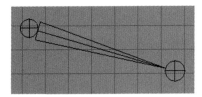

A simple joint chain

2   **Joint Hierarchy**

- Open the Hypergraph.
  Notice the joint hierarchy, which is composed of two nodes.

Joint hierarchy

3 **Adding joints**

- Click the **Joint Tool** icon in the toolbox or press the **y** hotkey to access the last tool used.

- **LMB** on the end joint of your previous chain.
  The tool will highlight the end joint.

- **LMB+click** two times to create a Z-like joint chain.
  The new joints are children of the joint selected in the previous step.

- You can **MMB+drag** to change the last joint placement.

- Press **Enter** to exit the tool.

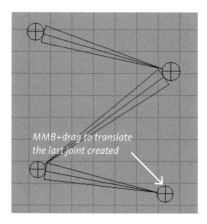

New joint chain

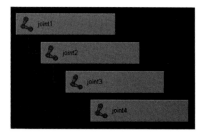

Joint hierarchy

4   Automatic joint orientation

When using the automatic orientation, all three joint axes are aligned according to the right-hand rule. For example, if you select an orientation of XYZ, the positive X-axis points into the joint's bone and toward the joint's first child joint, the Y-axis points at right angles to the X-axis and Z-axis, and the Z-axis points sideways from the joint and its bone.

 Note: *If you look closely at the joints in the Perspective view, you can see these axes and where they are pointing.*

- **Double-click** the **Joint Tool** icon in the toolbox.
  The tool's option window is displayed.

- Change the **Orientation** attribute to **XYZ**.

- **Close** the tool window.

- Create a second joint chain similar to the first one.
  Notice that as you draw the joints, they are automatically oriented toward their child.

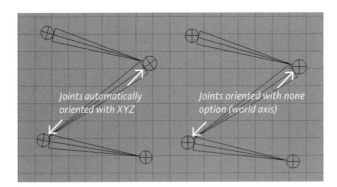

Joint orientation

5   Joint rotation axis

To better understand the effect of the joint orientation, you need to rotate in local mode and compare the two chains you have created.

- **Double-click** the **Rotate Tool** icon in the toolbox.
  The tool's option window is displayed.

- Select **Local** as the **Rotation Mode**.

  This specifies that you want to rotate nodes based on their local orientation rather than using the global world axis.

- **Close** the tool window.

- Select the second joint of both chains and see the difference between their rotation axes as you rotate them.

  Notice that when the joint is properly oriented, it moves in a more natural way.

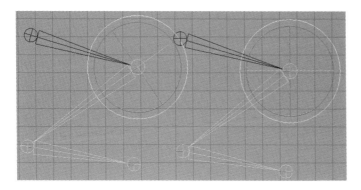

Joint rotation axis

Complex joint chain

When you create a complex joint chain, you can use some features intended to simplify your work. For instance, you can navigate in a hierarchy of joints as you create them. You can also use a command to reorient all the joints automatically.

1   **Navigate in joint hierarchy**

- **Delete** all the joint chains in your scene.

- Make the *top* view active.

- Press the **y** hotkey to access the **Joint Tool**.

Note: *Make sure the tool* **Orientation** *is set to* **XYZ**.

- **Draw** three joints as follows:

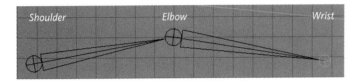

Arm chain

- **Draw** a thumb made of two joints.

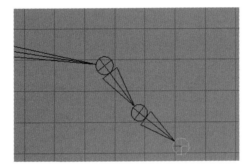

Thumb joints

- Press the **up arrow** twice on your keyboard to put the selection on the wrist joint.
  The arrows let you navigate in the hierarchy without exiting the Joint Tool.

- **Draw** the index joints and press the **up arrow** again.

- **Draw** the remaining fingers as follows:

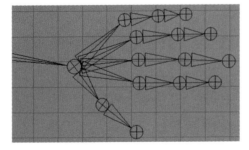

Completed hand

2 Snap to grid

- Press the **up arrow** until the selection is on the shoulder joint.

- Hold down the **x** hotkey to snap to grid and add a spine bone.

- Press **Enter** to exit the Joint Tool.

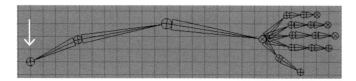

Spine bone

3 Reroot a skeleton

In the previous step, you created a spine bone that is the child of the shoulder bone. This is not a proper hierarchy since the spine should be the parent of the shoulder. There is a command that allows you to quickly reroot a joint chain.

- Select the *spine* bone, which was the last joint created.

- Select **Skeleton → Reroot Skeleton**.

  The spine is now the root of the hierarchy.

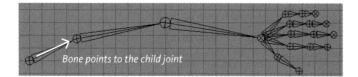

Spine joint as root

4 Mirror joints

Another very useful feature is the ability to mirror a joint chain automatically.

- Select the *shoulder* bone.

- Select **Skeleton → Mirror Joint → ❑**.

- In the option window, specify **Mirror Across** the **YZ** plane.

- Click the **Mirror** button.

Both arms

Skeleton

You are now ready to create a skeleton for the character from the previous lesson. To do so, you need to determine the proper placement of each joint. Once that is done, you will need to set a proper joint orientation so that when you rotate a joint, it rotates in an intuitive manner. If you do not take great care for placement and orientation, you will have difficulty animating the character later.

1   **Open scene**

- **Open** the file *08-PolyTexturing_02.ma*.

- While in Hardware Texturing mode, select **Shading → X-Ray Joints** from the panel menu.
  This shading mode shows the joints on top of the geometry, helping you place the joints accurately.

2   **Character spine**

In this step, you need to determine a good placement for the pelvis bone, which will be the root of the hierarchy. Once that is done, it will be easy to create the rest of the spine bones.

- Select **Skeleton → Joint Tool**.

- Make the *side* view active.

- **LMB** to create the *pelvis* joint.
  It is recommended that the pelvis joint be aligned with the hips.

- **LMB** to draw three equally spaced joints, which will represent the *spine, spine1,* and *neck* joints.

- **LMB** to draw two equally spaced joints, which will represent the *neck1* and *head* joints.

- Lastly, **LMB** to draw the *nose* joint.

- Press **Enter** to complete the joint chain.

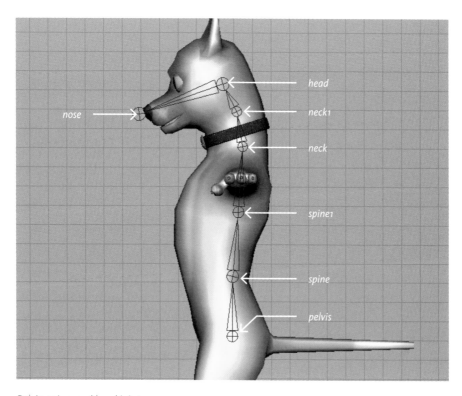

Pelvis, spine, and head joints

Tip: *If you find the displayed joints to be too big or too small, this is a visual represen-tation that can be changed by* **setting Display** → **Animation** → **Joint Size** *to your liking. You cal also chage the Radius attribute in the Channel Box for each joints.*

- **Rename** each joint properly.

Note: *A spine could be made of more bones, but this is not required in this example. The nose joint would normally be used only to get a visual representation of the head when the geometry is hidden, but you might as well use it to deform the nose to create a cartoon-y animation.*

3   **Create a leg**

You now need to create the legs of the character. The new joint chain will be in a separate hierarchy, but you will connect it to the pelvis later on.

- Select **Skeleton → Joint Tool**.

- **Click+drag** the *hip* joint to its proper location.

  You are click+dragging the first joint because if you click the pelvis joint, the tool will assume that you want to draw a joint chain starting from the pelvis. The hip joint should be centered on the hip geometry, very close to the pelvis joint.

- **Draw** the remaining *knee*, *ankle*, and *toe* joints, and create an extra joint on the tip of the foot, which should be called *toesEnd*.

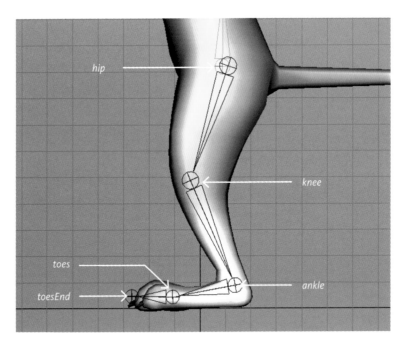

Leg joints

- Press **Enter** to exit the tool.

- Change to the *front* view.

  Notice that all the bones you created were drawn centered on the X-axis. That was correct for the spine, but not for the leg.

- On the *hip* joint, **Translate** on the X-axis and **rotate** on the Y-axis to fit the geometry as follows:

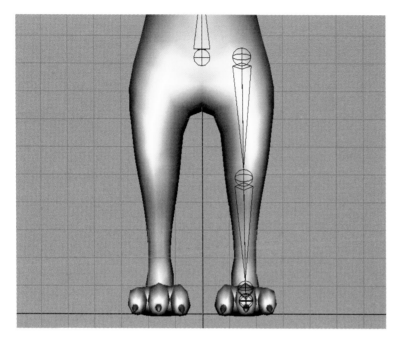

Front view

4   **Connect and mirror the leg**

- Select the *hip* joint, then **Shift-select** the *pelvis* joint.

- Select **Skeleton → Connect Joint → ❏**.

- Change the **Mode** option to **Parent Joint**.

- Press the **Connect** button.

  The leg is now parented to the pelvis.

Note: *You could also parent using the **p** hotkey.*

- Select the *hip* joint.

- Select **Skeleton** → **Mirror Joint** → ❑.

- Set the following:

  Mirror across to **YZ**;

  Mirror function to **Orientation**.

  This option will cause the legs to rotate in a similar way when rotating both at a same time.

- Click the **Mirror** button.

  If your character was modeled symmetrically, it should now have two legs properly placed.

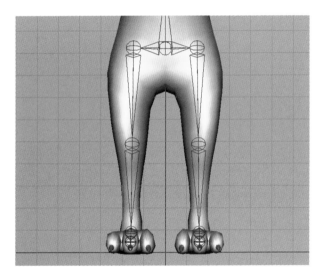

Completed lower body

- **Rename** all the joints appropriately.

Tip: *Make sure to prefix the joints on the left side with **l**, and the ones on the right side with **r**. For example, if you name the ankle, you may want to call it lAnkle.*

5   **Arm and hand joints**

- Select **Display** → **Animation** → **Joint Size...**

- Set the **Joint Size** to **0.25**.

  Doing so will reduce the display size of the joints in the viewport, making it easier to place joints close together, such as the finger joints.

- From the *front* view, **draw** a joint to represent the *clavicle* between the *spine1* and *neck* joints, then **draw** the *shoulder* joint.

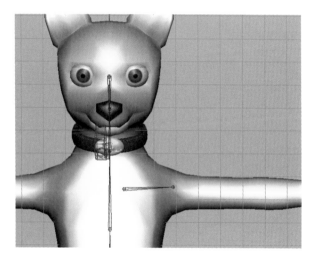

The clavicle and shoulder joints

- Change to the *top* view.

- **Move** the *clavicle* on the **Z-axis** to better fit the geometry.

- With the Joint Tool active, click the shoulder joint to highlight it.

  By doing so, you are specifying that the next joint chain should start from the position of the shoulder joint.

- **Draw** the character's *elbow* and *wrist* joints.

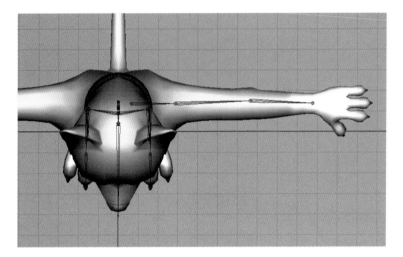

The arm and hand joints

- Change to the *front* view.

- **Rotate** down the shoulder joint on the **Z-axis** to better fit the geometry.

Tip: *It is a better workflow for joint placement to rotate the joints rather than translating them.*

- From the *top* view, **draw** the finger and thumb joints.

- Make sure the joints are properly positioned in the *Perspective* view.

- **Rename** all the joints correctly.

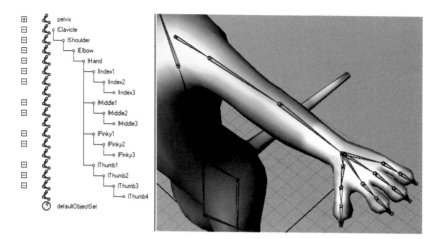

```
⊞      pelvis
⊟      lClavicle
⊟        lShoulder
⊟          lElbow
⊟            lHand
⊟              lIndex1
⊟                lIndex2
⊟                  lIndex3
⊟              lMiddle1
⊟                lMiddle2
                   lMiddle3
⊟              lPinky1
⊟                lPinky2
                   lPinky3
⊟              lThumb1
⊟                lThumb2
⊟                  lThumb3
                     lThumb4
       defaultObjectSet
```

Joints correctly placed and named

> **Tip:** It might be easier to set the display in the viewport as X-Ray Joints with Wireframe
> on Shaded.

6   Joint pivot

In some cases, you might want to adjust the position of a joint without moving all of its
children. You can use the **Insert** key (**Home** key on Macintosh) to move a joint on its own, or
hold down the **d** hotkey.

For instance, if the angle defined by the shoulder, elbow, and wrist joints is not appropriate,
you can correct the problem by moving a joint on its own.

• Select the *elbow* joint.

• Select the **Move Tool**.

• Press the **Insert** key (**Home** on Macintosh).

• **Move** the pivot of the *elbow* joint.

• Press the key again and exit the Move Pivot manipulator.

7   **Connect and mirror the arm**

- Select the *clavicle* joint, then **Shift-select** the *spine1* joint.

- Press **p** to parent the joints.

  The arm is now parented to the spine1 joint.

- Select the *clavicle* joint.

- Select **Skeleton → Mirror Joint → ❑.**

- In the option window, set the following:

  Mirror function to **Behavior**

  Search for *l*

  Replace with *r*

This option will cause the arms to have mirrored behavior when rotated both at a same time. Also, the search and replace fields will automatically replace the left prefix with a right prefix.

Note: *Be careful when using the serach and replace option, since it will replace all the matching cases of the name.*

- Click the **Mirror** button.

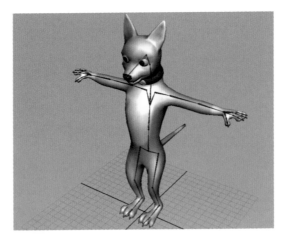

Proper arms

8   **Details**

- Press the **4** hotkey in the *side* view to display the wireframe model.

- Select the **Joint Tool**.

- Click the *head* joint to highlight it.

- **Draw** one joint for the *eye* and two for the *jaw* as follows:

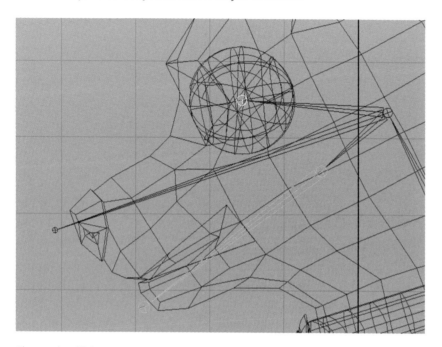

The new head joints

- **Rename** and **translate** the new joints as needed.

- **Mirror** the *lEye* joint with the **Orientation** option enabled.

> **Tip:**   When mirroring the eye joint, the Mirror function should be set to Orientation so the eyes move together and not in a mirrored way.

9   **Ears and tail**

Using what you have learned so far, create the joint chains for the ears and the tail.

10   **Save your work**

- **Save** your scene as *09-skeleton_01.ma*.

Joint orientation

Now that the character has a skeleton, you need to double-check all the joint orientations using the Rotate Tool. In this case, most of the joint orientations will be correct by default, but there will be times when you will need to change some orientations to perfect your skeleton.

1   **Hide the geometry**

- From the *Perspective* view, select **Show → Polygons** and **Show → NURBS Surfaces** to hide them.

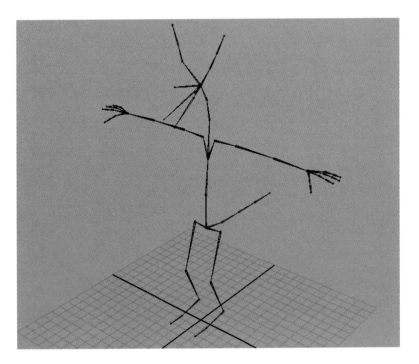

Complete skeleton

2   Default rotation values

It is recommended that all rotations of a joint hierarchy be zeroed out. This means that when the skeleton is in the current default position, all the joint rotations are zero.

• Select the *pelvis* joint.

• Select **Modify → Freeze Transformations**.

If you rotated bones in previous steps, their rotations are now zeroed out.

Note: *Unlike geometry, joint translations cannot be zeroed or else they would all be at the origin.*

3   Reorient all joints

You can reorient all the joints in a hierarchy automatically to your preferred orientation, such as XYZ.

• Select the *pelvis* joint.

• Select **Skeleton → Orient Joint → ❑**.

• Make sure the **Orientation** is set to **XYZ**, then click the **Orient** button.

All the joints are now reoriented to have their X-axis pointing toward their first children.

Note: *When reorienting joints, you might lose inserted mirrored behavior when mirroring the joints. A good workflow is to mirror the joints only after making sure half the skeleton was perfectly created with proper local rotation axes.*

4   Local rotation axes

The automatic orientation of the joints is not always perfect. Depending on how your skeleton was built, it can flip certain local rotation axes and you need to manually fix those pivots.

• Select the *pelvis* joint.

- Press **F8** to go into Component mode and enable the **?** mask button.

Local rotation axes mask

All the local rotation axes are displayed in the viewport for the selected hierarchy.

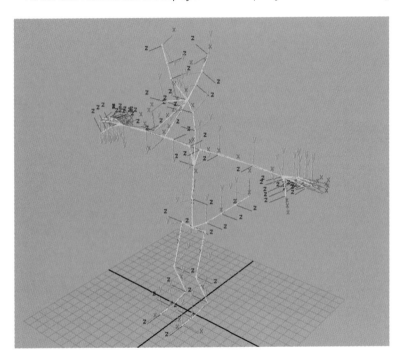

Local rotation axes in the viewport

5   Manually set the local rotation axes

It might seem confusing at the moment, but changing the local rotation axes is quite easy. There is one axis per joint, and if you dolly closer to a joint, you will see that the axis respects the left-hand rule, where the X-axis points toward the first child joint.

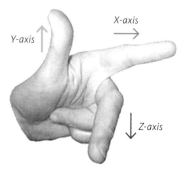

X-axis

Y-axis

Z-axis

The left-hand rule

In certain cases, you will not want the automatic orientation setting. Problems usually arise when you select multiple bones and rotate them at the same time. For instance, if you selected all of the spine and neck joints, you would notice an odd rotation shaped like an accordion, since their Z rotation axes point in different directions.

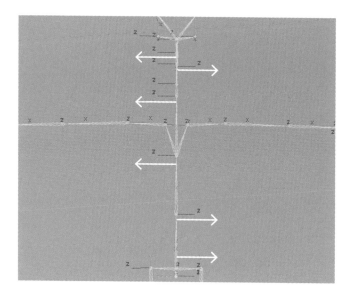

Bad rotation axes

To fix the problem, manually select an incorrect local rotation axis and rotate it into a good position.

• Still in Component mode with the local rotation axis displayed, select the *pelvis*, *spine*, and *neck1* local rotation axes (in this case), by clicking on them and holding down the **Shift** key.

• **Double-click** the **Rotate Tool**.

- In the tool's options, set **Discreet rotate** to **On** and **Step size** to **90**.

- **Rotate** on the **X-axis** by **180 degrees**.

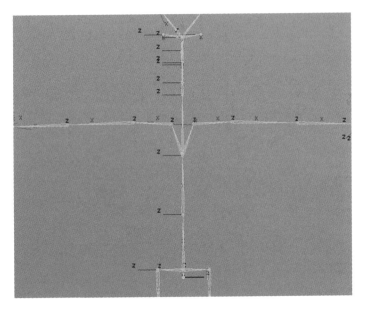

The corrected rotation axis

- In the **Rotate Tool**'s options, set **Discreet rotate** to **Off**.

- Go back into Object mode and try rotating the hips, spine, neck, and head together. *The problem seen earlier is now solved.*

Note: *It is normal that mirrored joints have an inverted local rotation axis. This is a welcome behavior set in the Mirror Joint command, which allows animation to be mirrored from one limb to another.*

6 Test the skeleton

You should now test your skeleton to see if everything is rotating as expected. If you notice incorrect local rotation axes, attempt to correct them manually by following the steps outlined above. Typical problematic areas are the knees and ankles, since the joint chains are made in a Z shape, and any joints with multiple child joints such as the wrists.

> **Note:** *The end joint's local rotation axis usually is not important since it might not be intended for animation.*

7 Save your work

- **Save** your work as *09-skeleton_02.ma*.

Conclusion

You now have greater experience creating skeleton chains and navigating skeleton hierarchies. You have learned how to move and rotate joints, and how to use joint commands such as reroot, connect, mirror, and orient. Finally, you have manually changed local rotation axes, which is the key to creating a good skeleton for animation.

In the next lesson, you will bind the character geometry to the skeleton and explore different techniques and tools used for character rigging.

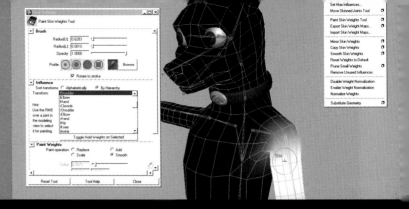

Lesson 10
Skinning

To get your character's geometry to deform as you move joints, you must bind it to the skeleton. There are many skinning techniques to bind a surface. In this lesson, you will first experiment with basic examples, which will help you to understand the various types of skinning. You will then use this understanding to bind the Romeo character.

In this lesson, you will learn the following:

- How to bind using parenting

- How to use rigid binding

- How to use the Edit Membership Tool

- How to edit rigid bind membership

- How to use flexors

- How to use lattice binding

- How to use smooth binding

- How to access skin influences

- How to set and assume a preferred angle

- How to set joint degrees of freedom and limits

Parent binding

Perhaps the simplest type of binding is to parent geometry to joints. This type of binding is very fast and needs no tweaking, but requires the pieces of a model to be separate. For instance, an arm would need to be split into two parts: an upper arm and a lower arm. There are other scenarios where parenting is appropriate, for example, a ring on a finger, or the eyes of a character.

1 **Create a simple scene**

- Open a new scene and change the view to the *top* Orthographic view.

- **Draw** three joints defining an arm.

- Change the view to the *Perspective* view.

- Create two polygonal cylinders and place them over the bones, as follows:

Basic parenting setup

2 **Parent the geometry**

- Select the *left cylinder*, then **Shift-select** the *left bone*.

- Press the **p** hotkey to parent the cylinder to the bone.

- Repeat the previous two steps to parent the *right cylinder* to the *right bone*.

Note: *Notice that the geometry is now a child of the joints in the Outliner.*

3 **Test joint rotations**

- Select the bones and rotate them to see the result of the parenting.

Joints' rotation

Note: *Notice that when selecting, bones have a higher selection priority than geometry. To select a bone, simply make a bounding box selection over the bone and geometry.*

Rigid binding

Rigid binding works like the parenting method, except that it affects the geometry's components. By rigid binding geometry on bones, the vertices closer to a certain bone will be instructed to follow that bone. This type of binding usually looks good on low-resolution polygonal geometry or NURBS surfaces, but can cause cracking on dense geometry. The following are two examples using rigid binding:

1   **Create a simple scene**

- Open a new scene and change the view to the *top* Orthographic view.

- **Draw** three joints to define an arm.

- Select the first joint and press **Ctrl+d** to duplicate the joint chain.

- **Move** the joint chains side by side.

- From the *Perspective* view, create a *polygonal cylinder* and a *NURBS cylinder*.

- Place each cylinder so it entirely covers a joint chain.

- Set the polygonal cylinders **Subdivisions Height** to **10**.

- Set the NURBS cylinder's **Spans** to **10**.

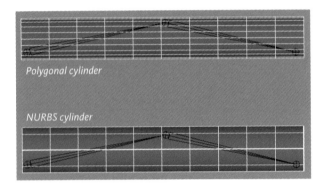

Example scene setup

2   **Rigid bind**

- Select the *first joint chain*, then **Shift-select** the *polygonal cylinder*.

- Select **Skin → Bind Skin → Rigid Bind**.

- Select the *second joint chain*, then **Shift-select** the *NURBS cylinder*.

- Select **Skin → Bind Skin → Rigid Bind**.

3   **Test joint rotations**

- Select the bones and rotate them to see the result of the rigid binding on both geometry types.

  The polygonal object appears to fold in on itself, since a vertex can only be assigned to one bone. The NURBS object seems much smoother because the curves of the surface are defined by the CVs, which are bound to the bones just like the polygonal object.

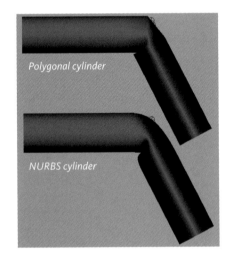

Rigid binding

Note: *Notice in the Outliner that the geometry is not parented. The binding connects the geometry's vertices to the joints.*

4 Edit Membership Tool

When using rigid bind, you might want to change the default binding so that certain points follow a different bone. The Edit Membership Tool allows you to specify the cluster of points affected by a certain bone.

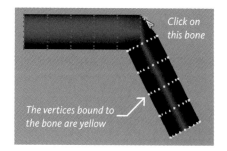

Click on this bone

The vertices bound to the bone are yellow

The Edit Membership Tool

- Select **Edit Deformers → Edit Membership Tool**.

- Click the *middle bone* of the first joint chain.

  You should see all the vertices affected by that joint highlighted in yellow. Vertices affected by other bones are highlighted using different colors to distinguish them.

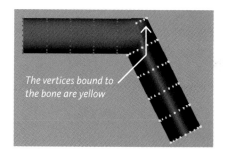

The vertices bound to the bone are yellow

Added polygon vertices

- Using the same hotkeys as when you select objects, toggle points from the cluster using **Shift**, remove points from the cluster using **Ctrl** and add points to the cluster using **Shift+Ctrl**.

- **Repeat** the same steps for the NURBS geometry to achieve a better deformation.

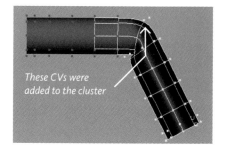

These CVs were added to the cluster

Added NURBS vertices

Flexors

Flexors are a type of deformer designed to be used with rigid bound surfaces. By creating a flexor for a joint, you can smooth out the binding region between two bones, thus preventing geometry from cracking. Flexor points can also be driven by Set Driven Keys to modify their positions as the bone rotates. For instance, you can refine an elbow shape when the elbow is folded.

1 **Creating flexors**

- From the previous scene, reset the rotations of the bones to their default positions.

- Select the *middle joint* for the first joint chain.

- Select **Skin** → **Edit Rigid Skin** → **Create Flexor...**.
  An option window is displayed.

- Make sure the **Flexor Type** is set to **Lattice**.

- Turn **On** the **Position the Flexor** checkbox.

- Click the **Create** button.
  A flexor is created at the joint's position and is selected so that you can position it correctly.

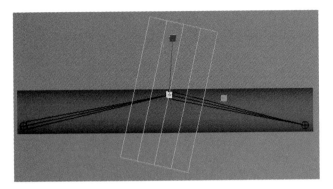

The flexor deformer

- **Translate** and **scale** the flexor to cover the bending region.

2 **Test joint rotations**

- Select the *middle bone* and rotate it to see the result of the flexor on the geometry.
  Notice that the bending area of the polygonal geometry is now much smoother.

3 **Set Driven Keys**

- **Zero** the rotation of the bones.

- Select **Animate** → **Set Driven Key** → **Set...**

- In the **Driver** section, load the *middle joint* and select the **Rotate Y** attribute.

- Select the *flexor* and press **F8** to display its points.

- Select all the flexor's lattice points and click the **Load Driven** button in the Set Driven Key window.

- Highlight all the driven objects in the **Driven** section and highlight the **XYZ values** on the right side.

- Click the **Key** button to set the normal position.

- Go back into Object mode and **rotate** the *middle joint* on the **Y-axis** by about **80** degrees.

- Select the *flexor* and press **F8** to display its points.

- **Move** the flexor points to confer a nice elbow shape on the cylinder.

- Click the **Key** button to set the bent position.

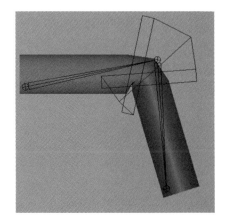

The bent geometry using a flexor

4   **Test joint rotations**

- Select the *middle bone* and rotate it to see the result of the driven flexor on the geometry.

  Notice that you can achieve a much better crease by using a driven flexor.

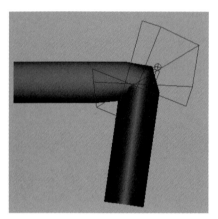

Driven flexor

Lattice binding

Another way to achieve nice skinning using rigid bind is to create a lattice deformer on the geometry and rigid binding the lattice to the bones. This technique can achieve a very smooth binding, using the simplicity of the rigid binding to your advantage.

1   **Detach a skin**

- Select the *polygonal cylinder* from the previous exercise.

- Select **Skin → Detach Skin**.

  The geometry returns to the original shape and position it was in before being bound.

- Select the *middle joint* and zero its rotation.

- Select the *flexor* and press **Delete** on your keyboard, as it is no longer required.

2   **Create a lattice**

- Select the *polygonal cylinder*, then select **Deform → Create Lattice**.

  A lattice is created and fits the geometry perfectly.

- Increase the number of lattice subdivisions by going to the **Shapes** section in the Channel Box and setting its **T Divisions** attribute to **9**.

3   **Rigid bind the lattice**

- With the lattice still selected, **Shift-select** the *first bone* of the joint chain.

- Select **Skin** → **Bind Skin** → **Rigid Bind**.

4   **Test joint rotations**

- Select the *middle bone* and rotate it to see the result of the lattice on the geometry.
  At this time, the binding is not much different than a normal rigid binding.

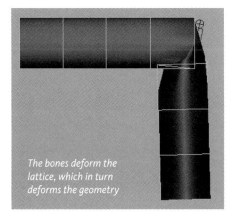

The bones deform the
lattice, which in turn
deforms the geometry

The bound lattice

5   **Adjust the lattice**

- Select the *lattice* object.

- In the **Outputs** section of the Channel Box, highlight the *ffd1* node.

- Set the following:

  Local Influence S to **4**;

  Local Influence T to **4**;

  Local Influence U to **4**.

  The deformation of the geometry is now much smoother.

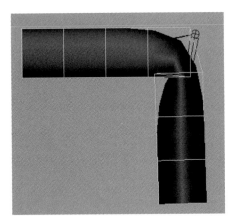

The smoothed influences of the lattice

6 Edit membership

It is now much easier to edit the membership of the lattice points rather than the dense geometry vertices.

7 Driven lattice

If the Edit Membership Tool does not provide enough control over the deformation of the geometry, you can use driven keys to achieve a much better deformation for the elbow and the elbow crease, just like in the previous flexor exercise. You can also use driven keys to bulge the bicep.

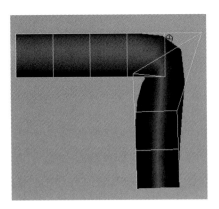

The edited rigid bind membership

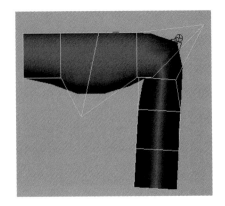

Driven lattice

Smooth binding

The most advanced type of skinning is called smooth binding. Smooth binding allows an object vertex or CV to be influenced by multiple bones, according to a certain percentage. For instance, a vertex's influence can follow a particular bone at 100%, or that influence can be spread across multiple bones in varying percentages, such as 50%-50% or 25%-75%. Doing so will move the vertex accordingly between all the influence bones.

1   **Set up the scene**

   • Using the scene from the previous exercise, set the *middle joint* rotation to zero.

   • Select **Edit** → **Delete All by Type** → **History** to remove the lattice object.

2   **Smooth bind**

   • Select the *first joint*, then **Shift-select** the *polygonal cylinder.*

   • Select **Skin** → **Bind Skin** → **Smooth Bind**.

3   **Test joint rotations**

   • Select the *middle bone* and rotate it to
     see the result of the smooth binding
     on the geometry.

4   **Edit smooth bind influence**

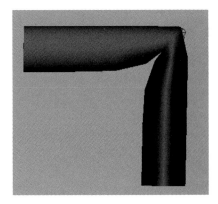

   Modifying the influences of each bone
   on each vertex can be a tedious task,
   but you can use the *Paint Skin Weights
   Tool* to paint the weights of the vertices
   directly on the geometry in the viewport.
   The *Paint Skin Weights Tool* will display an
   influence of 100% as white, an influence
   of 0% as black, and anything in between
   as grayscale. This makes it easier to
   visually edit the influence of bones on
   the geometry.

Default smooth binding

- Select *polyCylinder* and go to **Shading** → **Smooth Shade All**.

- Select **Skin** → **Edit Smooth Skin** → **Paint Skin Weights Tool** → ❑.

  The painting option window opens and the geometry gets displayed in grayscale.

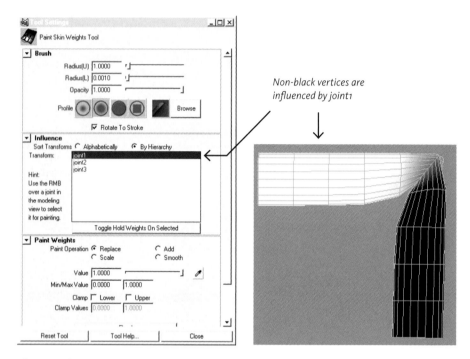

Non-black vertices are influenced by joint1

The Paint Skin Weights Tool and the weights on the geometry

Painting skin weights requires a solid understanding of bone influences. Since the tool is based on the Artisan Tool, you can edit the skin weighting on your own. Smooth binding, along with its various related tools, will be covered in greater detail in the intermediate Learning Maya 2010 | The Modeling & Animation Handbook.

Binding the character

Since the character is mostly composed of deformable skin objects, you will bind its geometry using smooth binding. You will also use binding for the eyes and claws. You could parent those objects directly to the skeleton, but it is an easier workflow to keep geometry in one hierarchy and the character skeleton in another.

1   **Open the scene from the previous lesson**

- **Open** the file *09-skeleton_01.ma*.

2 Set Preferred Angle

When binding geometry on a skeleton, you need to test the binding by rotating the bones. By doing so, you should be able to return the skeleton to its default position quickly. Maya has two easily accessible commands called *Set Preferred Angle* and *Assume Preferred Angle*. These commands allow you to first define the default skeleton pose, then return to that pose whenever you want.

Note: *The preferred angle also defines the bending angle for IK handles.*

- Select the *pelvis* joint.

- In the viewport, **RMB** over the *pelvis* joint to pop-up the contextual marking menu.

- Select **Set Preferred Angle**.

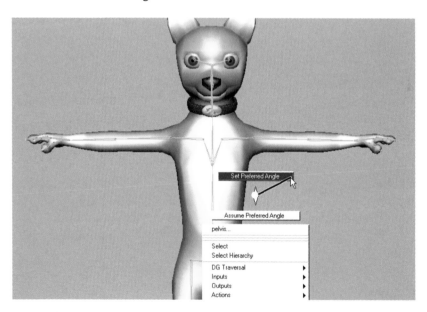

Joint marking menu

Note: *These commands are also available in the **Skeleton** menu.*

3   **Assume Preferred Angle**

- **Rotate** several joints to achieve a pose.

- Select the *pelvis* joint.

- In the viewport, **RMB** over the *pelvis* joint and select **Assume Preferred Angle**.
  The skeleton should return to its preferred angle (set in the previous step).

4   **Bind the body**

- Select **Skin** → **Bind Skin** → **Smooth Bind** → ❑.

- In the smooth bind options, change **Bind To** to **Selected Joints**.

Tip: *It is recommended that you select the joints to which you want to bind the geometry, in order to avoid having unwanted influence from other bones.*

- Select the following joints, which should play an important role in the binding of the character:

	lClavicle	*lHip*	*tail*
pelvis	*lShoulder*	*lKnee*	*tail1*
spine	*lElbow*	*lAnkle*	*tail2*
spine1	*lWrist*	*lToes*	*tail3*
neck			
neck1	*rClavicle*	*rHip*	*lEar*
head	*rShoulder*	*rKnee*	*lEar1*
jaw	*rElbow*	*rAnkle*	
	rWrist	*rToes*	*rEar*
			rEar1

- Also select all the finger and thumb joints, except the ending ones, which will not be used.

- **Shift-select** the *body* geometry.

- Click the **Bind Skin** button in the Smooth Bind option window.
  You will notice that the wireframe of the bound geometry is now purple, which is a visual cue to show the connection to the selected joint.

- **Rotate** the *pelvis* joint to see if the geometry follows correctly.

5   Smooth bind the eyeballs

- Select the *lEyeball* geometry, then **Shift-select** the *lEye* joint.

- Select **Skin** → **Bind Skin** → **Smooth Bind**.

- **Repeat** to bind the right eyeball.

- **Rotate** the *eye* joints to see if the geometry follows correctly.

6   Rigid bind the eyelids

- Select the *lEyelid* and *rEyelid* geometry, then **Shift-select** the *head* joint.

- Select **Skin** → **Bind Skin** → **Rigid Bind** → ❏.

- In the rigid bind options, change **Bind To** to **Selected Joints**.

- Click the **Bind Skin** button.

- **Rotate** the *head* joints to see if the geometry follows correctly.

7   Rigid bind the collar

- Select all the pieces of the collar, then **Shift-select** the *neck* joint.

- Select **Skin** → **Bind Skin** → **Rigid Bind.**

8   Ensure everything is bound

- To ensure all the geometry is bound, select the *pelvis* joint and **translate** it.
  You will easily notice if a piece is left behind.

- Pose the character to see the effect of the binding and note problematic areas.

Note: *Do not translate any bones except the root joint (pelvis). The preferred angle command only keeps rotation values.*

9   Reset the skeleton position

- **Undo** the last movement to bring the skeleton back to its original position.

  OR

- Select the *pelvis* joint, then select **Skeleton → Assume Preferred Angle**.
  Doing so will ensure all the skeleton rotations are set to their preferred values.

10   Save your work

- **Save** your scene as *10-skinning_01.ma*.

11   Paint Skin Weights Tool

Once the geometry is bound to the skeleton, you must refine the weighting so that every joint bends the geometry as expected. Perhaps the easiest way to edit a smooth skin is to use the Paint Skin Weights Tool. As mentioned earlier, this tool works just like the 3D Paint Tool, except that you paint bone influences in grayscale instead of colors, where white is fully influenced by a joint and black is not influenced at all by a joint.

Since painting skin weights is considered an advanced topic, this lesson will not cover the painting weights workflow. Consider experimenting on your own with this tool.

- To see the final skinned character scene file, open the scene *10-skinning_02.ma*.

The bound character with Smooth Preview enabled

Joint degrees of freedom and limits

A character is usually unable to achieve every possible pose. In this case, the character's articulation works in a similar way to the human body. Some joints cannot be rotated a certain way or exceed a certain rotation limit. Bending joints too much or in the wrong way might cause the geometry to interpenetrate or appear broken. Joints have many options to let you control how they are bent by the animator.

1   **Degrees of freedom**

By default, all three rotation axes on a joint are free to rotate. If you need to, you can limit the degrees of freedom on a joint. In the case of the character, the elbows and knees cannot bend in all three directions due to the nature of a biped skeleton. Therefore, you need to limit these joint rotations to a single axis.

- Select the *lElbow* joint.

- Notice on which axis the joint should be allowed to bend.

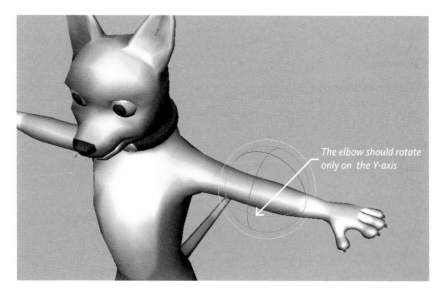

The elbow should rotate only on the Y-axis

The elbow rotation axes

Tip: *The* **Rotate Tool** *must be in* **Local** *mode.*

- Open the Attribute Editor and scroll to the **Joint** section.

- Turn **Off** the **X** and **Z** checkboxes for the **Degrees of Freedom** attribute.

  Notice that the **Rotate X** *and* **Rotate Z** *attributes in the Channel Box are now locked.*

2 Joint limits

A joint limit allows you to specify the minimum and maximum values allowed for a joint to rotate. In this case, the elbow joint needs to stop rotating when it gets fully bent or fully extended.

- Select the *lElbow* joint.

- **Rotate** the joint to bend it on the **Y-axis** and stop just before it interpenetrates with the upper arm.

- In the Attribute Editor, open the **Limit Information** section.

- In the **Rotate** section, turn **On** the **Rot Limit Y Min** attribute.

- Click the **<** button to put the **Current** value in the **Min** field.

- **Rotate** the *lElbow* joint on the **Y-axis** the other way, and stop when the arm is perfectly straight.

- Back in the Attribute Editor, turn **On** the **Rot Limit Y Max** attribute.

- Click the **>** button to put the **Current** value in the **Max** field.

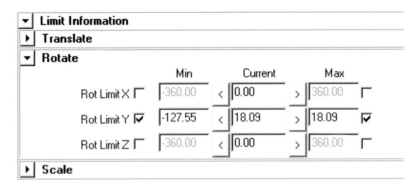

The lElbow rotation limits

3   **Remainder of skeleton limits**

You can now set the freedom and limitations on the character skeleton as you would like them to be.

4   **Save your work**

The completed version of the bound character can be found in the support files as *10-skinning_03.ma.*

Conclusion

You have now explored the various skinning types required to bind a character to its skeleton. You have also learned how to change a joint's degrees of freedom and set limit information.

In the next lesson, you will learn about the Blend Shape deformer, which will be used for facial animation.

Lesson 11
Blend Shapes

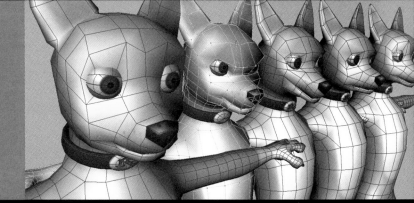

In this lesson, you will create a Blend Shape deformer, which is a type of deformer that blends between different geometry shapes. This will allow you to model facial expressions for the character to be used for animation.

In this lesson, you will learn the following:

- How to sculpt surfaces by painting with Artisan

- How to use different brush operations

- How to create Blend Shapes

- How to mix Blend Shapes

Sculpting a surface

You will now test the Artisan Sculpt Tool. You will use the tool on a sphere to get a feel for it. Once you are more familiar with the tool, you will apply brush strokes to the character geometry.

1   **Make a test sphere**

   • **Create** a polygonal primitive sphere.

   • Set its construction history for both **Subdivisions Axis** and **Subdivisions Height** to **60**.

   • To better see the effect of your painting in the viewport, assign a new *phong* material to the sphere by selecting **Lighting/Shading** → **Assign New Material** → **Phong** from the **Rendering** menu set.

   • Press the **5** key to turn on **Smooth Shade All**.

2   **Open the Sculpt Geometry Tool**

   • With the *pSphere* selected, select **Mesh** → **Sculpt Geometry Tool** → ❏ from the **Polygons** menu set.

   *This opens the **Tool Settings** window, which includes every Artisan sculpting option.*

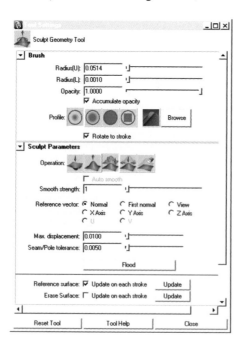

Tool Settings window

- Click the **Reset Tool** button to make sure that you are starting with Artisan's default settings.

- Set the following attributes:

  Under **Brush**:

  Radius (U) to **0.2**.

  Under **Sculpt Parameters:**

  Max Displacement to **0.1**.

- Place the Tool Settings window to the right of the *sphere* and keep it open.

3   **Paint on the surface**

- Move your cursor over the *pSphere* geometry.

  The cursor icon changes to show an arrow surrounded by a red circular outline. The arrow indicates how much the surface will be pushed or pulled, while the outline indicates the brush radius. Artisan's brush icon is context sensitive. It changes as you choose different tool settings.

- **Click+drag** the *sphere*.

  You are now painting on the surface, pushing it toward the inside.

Tip: *Artisan works more intuitively with a tablet and stylus, since the input device mimics the use of an actual paintbrush.*

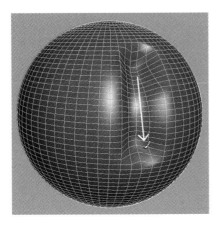

First brush stroke

4   **Change the Artisan display**

- Open the **Display** section in the Tool Settings window.

- Click **Show Wireframe** to turn this option **Off**.

  Now you can focus on the surface without displaying the wireframe lines.

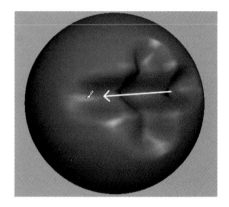

5   **Paint another stroke**

- **Paint** a second stroke across the mask surface.

  Now it is easier to see the results of your sculpting.

Second brush stroke

The sculpting tools

You will now explore some of the Artisan sculpting operations to see how they work. So far, you have been pushing on the surface. Now you will learn how to pull, smooth, and erase.

1   **Pull on the surface**

- In the Tool Settings window, scroll to the **Sculpt Parameters** section.

- Under **Operation**, click **Pull**.

- **Tumble** around to the other side of the sphere.

- **Paint** on the surface to create a few strokes that pull out.

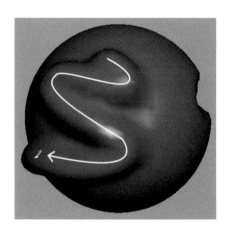

Pulling the surface with several brush strokes

2   Smooth out the results

- Under **Operation**, click **Smooth**.

- Under **Brush**, change the **Radius (U)** to **0.6**.

  This increases the size of your brush. You can see that the red outline has increased in size. This is the brush feedback icon.

> **Tip:**   *You can hold the* **b** *hotkey and* **click+drag** *in the viewport to interactively change the brush size.*

- **Paint** all of the strokes to smooth the details.

  If you stroke over an area more than once, the smoothing becomes more evident.

3   Erase some of the brush strokes

- Under **Operation**, click the **Erase** option.

- **Paint** along the surface to begin erasing the last sculpt edits.

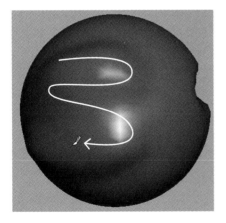

Smoothing the brush strokes

Erasing the brush strokes

4   Flood

- Under **Operation**, click the **Pull** option.

- In the **Sculpt Parameters** section, click the **Flood** button.

  This uses the current operation and applies it to the entire surface using the current opacity setting.

- Under **Operation**, click the **Erase** option.

- In the **Sculpt Parameters** section, click the **Flood** button.

  The sphere comes back to its original shape.

Fully erased surface

Updating the reference surface

When you paint in Artisan, you paint in relation to a *reference surface*. By default, the reference surface updates after every stroke so that you can build your strokes on top of one another. You can also keep the reference surface untouched until you decide to update it manually.

1   Change the brush attributes

- Under **Operation**, click **Pull**.

- Set the following attributes:

  Under **Brush**:

    Radius (U) to **0.2**.

  Under **Sculpt Parameters**:

    Max Displacement to **0.2**.

2   Pull the surface with two strokes

- **Paint** on the surface to create two crossing strokes that pull out.

  The second stroke is built on top of the first stroke. Therefore, the height of the pull is higher where the two strokes intersect.

3   Change the reference update

- In the Tool Settings window, scroll down in the **Sculpt Parameters** section and turn **Off** the **Reference Surface: Update On Each Stroke**.

4   Paint more overlapping strokes

- **Paint** on the surface to create a few strokes that pull out.

  *This time, the strokes do not overlap. The reference surface does not update, therefore, the strokes can only displace to the **Maximum Displacement** value. You cannot displace beyond that value until you update the reference surface.*

5   Update the reference layer

- Still in the **Sculpt Parameters** section, click the **Update** button next to **Reference Surface**.

6   Paint on the surface

- **Paint** another stroke over the last set of strokes.

  The overlapping strokes are again building on top of each other.

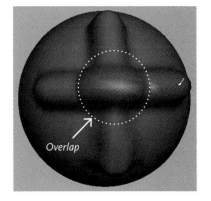

Painting with reference update

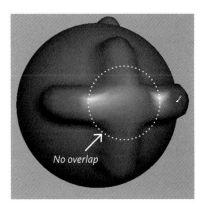

Painting with no reference update

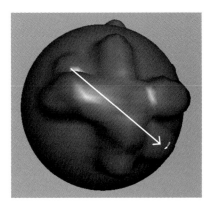

Painting on updated reference layer

7   Flood erase the surface

- Under **Operation**, click the **Erase** option.

- Click the **Flood** button.

Sculpting the character

You will now use the Artisan Sculpt Tool to create a few facial shapes for the Romeo character. You will first duplicate the body of the character in order to have multiple copies to use for the blend shape deformer.

1   Scene file

- Continue with your own scene file from the previous lesson.

    OR

- Continue with *10-skinning_03.ma*.

2   Skin envelope

Before you start making blend shapes, you must ensure that the geometry is in its original position. One way to get the skin back to its exact original position is to turn off the skin's influence.

- Select the character's *body*.

- In the Channel Box, highlight the *skinCluster1*node.

- Set **Envelope** to **0**.
  Doing so temporarily turns off the skinCluster, thus removing any influence of the skeleton and placing the geometry back to its exact original position.

3   Duplicate the character

The blend shape deformer requires that the original untouched character and character duplicates be deformed.

- **Hide** the joints in the viewport.

- Select all of the character's geometry.

- Press **Ctrl+d** to **Duplicate** it all.

- Highlight every locked attribute in the Channel Box, then **RMB** and select **Unlock Selected**.

Highlight and unlock the attributes

- Press **Ctrl+g** to group all the geometry together.

- **Move** the new group next to the original character.

- **Rename** the new *body* geometry *smile*.

- **Duplicate** the group you have just created and **rename** the *body* geometry for the following:

  sad;
  browUp;
  browDown.

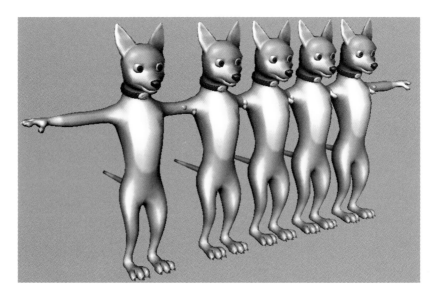

The duplicates

Tip: *It is good to duplicate the other objects such as the eyes, since you will be able to use them as a reference for when you model the Blend Shapes. Never modify an object other than the one intended for deformation.*

- Select the character's original *body*.

- In the Channel Box, highlight the *skinCluster* node.

- Set **Envelope** to **1**.

4   **Sculpt the smile shape**

You will use Artisan to paint and deform the smile geometry.

- With the *smile* geometry selected, select **Mesh → Sculpt Geometry Tool → ❑** from the **Polygons** menu set.

- Click the **Reset Tool** button to make sure that you are starting with Artisan's default settings.

- Set the following attributes:

  Under Brush*:*

      Radius (U) to **0.3**.

  Under Sculpt Parameters:

      Operation to **Pull**;

      Reference Vector to **Y-axis**;

      Max Displacement to **0.1**.

  Under Stroke:

      Reflection to **On**.

  This option allows you to sculpt only one side of the geometry to create the complete shape.

  Under Display:

      Show Wireframe to **Off**.

  This last option will turn off the wireframe display on the geometry. It is up to you whether to turn this on or off.

Note: *In the previous test sphere example, you were painting using the normals of the surface as the direction to be pushed and pulled. In this case, you will pull along the Y-axis, which will move the vertices up.*

- **Paint** directly on the model to get a shape similar to the following:

Smile shape

5 **Sculpt the other shapes**

- **Repeat** the previous steps to sculpt the three other shapes and any other shape you would want.

Sad shape   *Brow up shape*   *Brow down shape*

Blend shape deformer

In order to make character animation more realistic, you will need facial animation. This will be done using a deformer that will blend between the original character geometry and the geometry displaying emotion that you just created. That kind of deformer is called a Blend Shape *deformer*. Blend Shapes are very useful in 3D, especially to animate facial expressions on characters, but they can also be used for plenty of other things.

1   Creating the deformer

- Select, in order, the *smile*, *sad*, *browUp*, and *browDown* shapes, and then **Shift-select** the original *body* shape.

Note: *It is important to select the original object last.*

- From the **Animation** menu set, select **Create Deformers** → **Blend Shape** → ❑.

- In the Blend Shape option window, make sure to set **Origin** to **Local**.

- Select the **Advance** tab and make sure **Deformation Order** is set to **Front of chain**.

  The Front of chain option tells Maya that you need the Blend Shape deformer to be inserted before any other deformers, such as the skinCluster.

- Click the **Create** button.

2   Testing the deformer

- Select the original *body* geometry.

  In the Channel Box, you should see a blendShape1 node and its construction history.

- Highlight the *blendShape1* node.

  Notice that the attributes have the same names as the geometry you duplicated earlier. These attributes control the blending between the original shape and the sculpted ones.

The Blend Shape node

- Highlight the *smile* attribute's name.

- **MMB+drag** from left to right to access the virtual slider and see the effect of the deformer on the geometry.

- Experiment blending more than one shape at a time to see its effect.

Sad and browDown shapes mixed together

3   **Tweaking the Blend Shape**

Since construction history still links the Blend Shape with the deformed surface, you can still tweak the sculpted geometry as needed.

- Make modifications on any of the sculpted geometry with the Artisan Sculpting Tool.

Tip: *Your changes must be made on the sculpted blend shape geometry and not on the original geometry.*

4   **Delete targets**

- Select all the duplicated groups used to create the Blend Shapes.

- Press **Backspace** or **Delete** to dispose of them.

> **Note:** *When you delete Blend Shape targets, Autodesk® Maya® software keeps the blend values in the Blend Shape node instead of using the geometry in the scene. Because of this, it is important to not delete the history on the model unless you want to get rid of the Blend Shapes.*

5   Save your work

- **Save** your scene as *11-blendshapes_01.ma*.

Conclusion

You are now more familiar with the very useful Blend Shape deformer, as well as the Artisan Sculpting Tool. You now have the skills to create extremely powerful deforming animations, such as lip-synching, facial expressions, and reactive animations.

In the next lesson, you will refine your character setup by using IK handles, constraints, and custom attributes. You will also create a reverse foot setup that will help maintain the character's feet on the ground.

Lesson 12
Inverse Kinematics

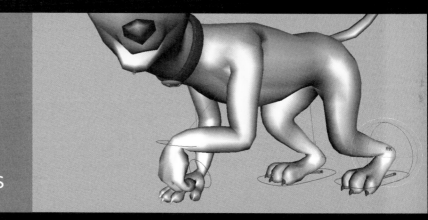

In this lesson, you will add inverse kinematics (IK) handles and constraints to the existing character skeleton in order to make the character easier to animate. You will also create a reverse foot setup, which simplifies floor contact when animating, and hand manipulators, which will help lock hands upon contact with the environment. Lastly, you will learn about pole vector constraints.

In this lesson, you will learn the following:

IK handles

There are several types of IK handles and you will experiment with two types in this lesson: the *single chain IK* and the *rotate plane IK*. The difference between these two is that the single chain IK handle's end effector tries to reach the position and orientation of its IK handle, whereas the rotate plane IK handle's end effector only tries to reach the position of its IK handle.

Single Chain IK

A single chain IK handle uses the single chain solver to calculate the rotations of all joints in the IK chain. Also, the overall orientation of the joint chain is calculated directly by the single chain solver.

1   **Open the previous character scene**

 • **Open** the file *11-blendshapes_01.ma*.

2   **Joint rotation limits**

For better results using IKs, it is not recommended to have rotation limits on joints that are part of an IK handle. Limiting joint rotations will prevent the IK solver from finding good joint rotations and may cause it to behave unexpectedly.

 • **Remove** rotation limits and enable all degrees of freedom for the arm and leg joints, if any.

Note: *Rotation limits and degrees of freedom are especially useful on joints intended to be animated manually.*

3   **Single Chain IK**

 • Select **Skeleton → IK Handle Tool → ❏**.
 The tool's option window will be displayed.

 • Change the **Current Solver** to **ikSCsolver**.

 • Click the **Close** button.

 • In the viewport, click the *lShoulder* bone.
 The joint will be highlighted. This is the start joint.

- Click the *lWrist* bone.

  The IK handle is created, starting at the shoulder and going down to the wrist of the character.

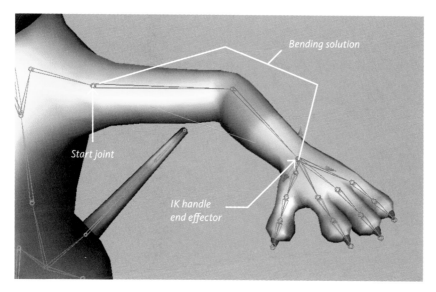

Single chain IK

In the Hypergraph, you can see the end effector connected to the hierarchy and the IK handle to the side. The end effector and the IK handle are connected, along with the appropriate joints at the dependency node level. When you control the handle, you control the whole IK chain.

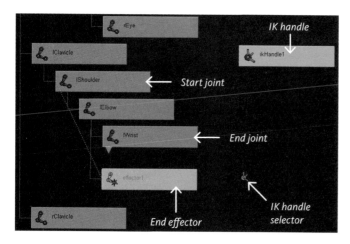

IK chain and nodes in Hypergraph

4   **Experiment with the IK handle**

- Press **w** to enter the **Translate Tool**.

- **Translate** the IK handle and notice the resulting bending of the arm.

Tip: *If the IK handle does not bend the arm or if it bends it the wrong way, it is because the angle in the arm joint chain was not appropriate. To remedy the situation, delete the IK handle, bend the arm appropriately, and then recreate the IK.*

- Press **e** to enter the **Rotate Tool**.

- **Rotate** the IK handle and notice the resulting bending of the arm.

  Rotating the IK handle will change the bending solution, but will not affect the wrist's rotation. You will create a hand setup in a later exercise.

- **Rename** the IK handle *lArmIk*.

5   **Preferred angle**

- With the IK selected, **RMB** in the viewport and select **Assume Preferred Angle**.

  The arm joints and the IK handle will move back to the preferred angle set in the previous lesson.

6   **Right arm IK**

- **Create** another single chain IK for the right arm and rename it *rArmIk*.

Tip: *IK handles have a higher selection priority than joints and geometry. To choose an IK handle, simply make a selection bounding box over it.*

Rotate Plane IK

A rotate plane IK handle uses the rotate plane solver to calculate the rotations of all joints in its IK chain, but not the joint chain's overall orientation. Instead, the IK rotate plane handle gives you direct control over the joint chain's orientation via the pole vector and twist disk, rather than having the orientation calculated by the IK solver.

> **Note:** *The twist disk is a visual representation showing the vector defining the chain's overall orientation. You will experiment with the twist disk in the following steps.*

1   **Rotate Plane IK**

- Select **Skeleton** → **IK Handle Tool** → ❑.

- Change the **Current Solver** for **ikRPsolver**.

- Turn **On** the **Sticky** option.
  This option snaps the IK to its effector at all times.

- Click the **Close** button.

- In the viewport, click the *lHip* bone.

- Click the *lAnkle* bone.
  The IK handle gets created, starting at the hip and going down to the ankle of the character.

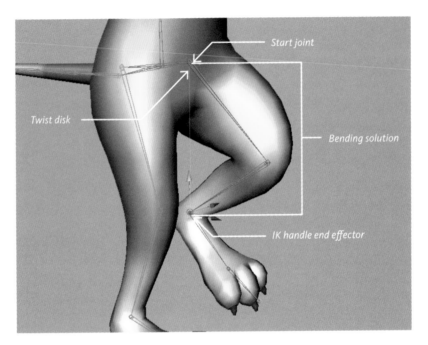

Start joint

Twist disk

Bending solution

IK handle end effector

Rotate plane IK

2 Experiment with the IK handle

One differentiating feature of this type of IK handle is the ability to control the twist of the solution using the *twist* and *pole vector* attributes.

- **Move** the IK handle up.

- Press **t** to show the IK handle manipulators.

- **Move** the pole vector manipulator located next to the twist disk.
  This manipulator affects the pointing direction of the IK chain.

- Highlight the **Twist** attribute in the Channel Box and **MMB+drag** in the viewport.
  This attribute also affects the pointing direction of the IK chain, but overrides the pole vector attributes.

- **Rename** the IK handle *lLegIk*.

3   **Reset the IK handle's position**

- With the IK selected, **RMB** in the viewport and select **Assume Preferred Angle**.

4   **Right leg IK**

- **Create** another rotate plane IK for the right leg.

- **Rename** the IK handle *rLegIk*.

5   **Save your work**

- **Save** the file as *12-IKs_01.ma*.

Reverse foot

When you animate a walking character, you need one of the character's feet to plant itself while the other foot is lifted into position. In the time it is planted, the foot needs to roll from heel to toe. A reverse foot skeleton is the ideal technique for creating these conditions.

1   **Draw the reverse foot skeleton**

- Change the viewport to a *four-view* layout.

- Dolly on the feet of the character in all views.

- Select **Skeleton → Joint Tool**.
  *The **Orientation** of the tool should be set to **XYZ**.*

- In the *side* view, create the first joint on the heel of the character's foot geometry.

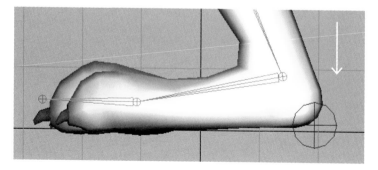

The heel joint

- In the *front* view, **MMB+drag** the new joint to align it with the rest of the foot joints.

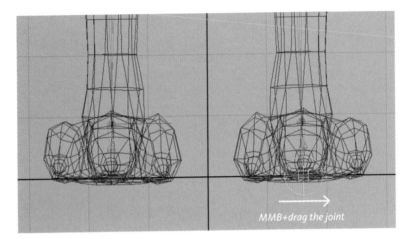

MMB+drag the joint

Move the heel joint

- In the *Perspective* view, turn **Off** the geometry display by selecting **Show** → **Polygons**.
- Hold down the **v** hotkey to enable **Snap to Point**.
- **Draw** three other bones, snapping them to the *toesEnd*, *toe*, and *ankle* joints respectively.

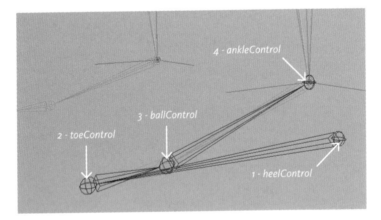

4 - ankleControl

3 - ballControl

2 - toeControl

1 - heelControl

The complete reverse foot

- Press **Enter** to exit the tool.
- **Rename** the joints as shown in the previous image.

Project 02

Set up the reverse foot

To control the foot and have a proper heel-to-toe rotation, you will now constrain the IK handle, ankle, and toe joints to the reverse foot chain. This will allow you to use the reverse foot chain to control the foot and leg.

1   **Point constrain the IK handle**

* Select the *ankleControl* joint on the reverse foot chain.

* **Shift-select** the IK handle.

> **Tip:**   *You may want to use the Hypergraph panel to help you select the joint.*

* Select **Constrain → Point**.

    The point constraint forces an object to follow the position of a source object. The IK handle is now positioned over the reverse foot's ankleControl joint.

2   **Test the reverse foot chain**

* Select the *heelControl* joint.

* **Move** the joint to test the foot setup so far.

    The ankle moves with the reverse foot chain, but the joints do not stay properly aligned.

* **Undo** your moves.

3   **Orient constrain the toes**

To align the rest of the foot, you will orient constrain the *toes'* joint to the reverse foot.

* Select the *toeControl* joint on the reverse foot chain.

* **Shift-select** the *toes'* joint from the leg chain.

* Select **Constrain → Orient → ❑.**

* In the orient constraint options, turn **On** the **Maintain Offset** option.

- Click the **Add** button.

  The orient constraint forces an object to follow the rotation of a source object. The Maintain Offset option forces the constrained object to keep its position.

- **Rotate** the *heelControl* joint to test the foot setup so far.

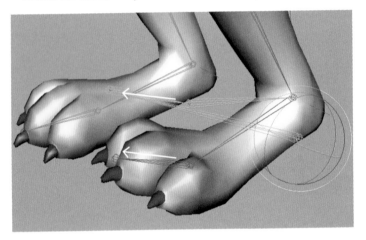

Orient constrained toes' joint

- **Undo** your moves.

4   **Orient Constrain the ankle joint**

You will now repeat these last few steps for the *ankle* joint.

- Select the *ballControl* joint on the reverse foot chain.

- **Shift-select** the *ankle* joint from the leg chain.

- Select **Constrain** → **Orient**.

  Now the foot joints and reverse foot joints are aligned.

5   **Test the movement of the reverse foot**

- **Rotate** the different joints of the foot setup to test them.

  Notice how you can easily achieve the motion of peeling the foot off the floor. You can also easily roll the toes or the heel on the floor, which would otherwise be very difficult to achieve.

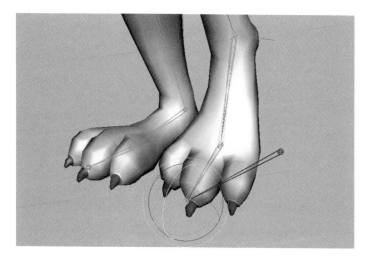

Orient constrained foot setup

- **Undo** your moves to bring the foot setup back to its original position.

Creating the heel-to-toe motion

You can now control the rotation of the foot by rotating the various control joints on the reverse foot. Instead of requiring the rotation of several joints to achieve a heel-to-toe motion, you will use Set Driven Key to control the roll using a single attribute on the *heelControl* joint.

1   **Create a foot manipulator**

- Make sure **Show → NURBS Curves** is turned on in the viewport.

- Select **Create → NURBS Primitives → Circle**.

- **Rename** the circle *lFootManip*.

- Press **w** to access the **Translate Tool**.

- Hold down the **v** hotkey and snap the *circle* to the *heelControl* joint.

- **Tweak** the shape of the circle to resemble the foot sole.

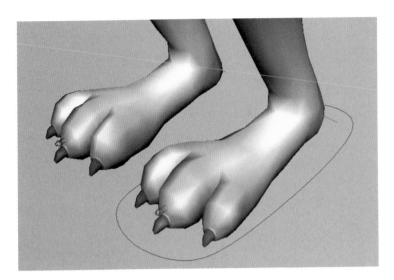

The foot manipulator

- Select **Modify** → **Freeze Transformations**.

- **Parent** the *heelControl* joint to the new *lFootManip*.

2   **Add a Roll attribute**

- Select the *lFootManip* joint.

- Select **Modify** → **Add Attribute...**

- Set the following values in the Add Attribute window:

    Long Name to **roll**;

    Data Type to **Float**;

    Minimum to **-5**;

    Maximum to **10**;

    Default to **0**.

- Click **OK** to add the attribute.

    You can now see this attribute in the Channel Box. The minimum and maximum values give reasonable boundary values for the roll.

The roll attribute in the Channel Box

3 **Prepare the Set Driven Key window**

- Select **Animate** → **Set Driven Key** → **Set...**

- Select the *lFootManip* and click **Load Driver**.

- In the **Driver** section, highlight the **roll** attribute.

- Select the *heelControl, ballControl,* and *toeControl* joints and click **Load Driven**.

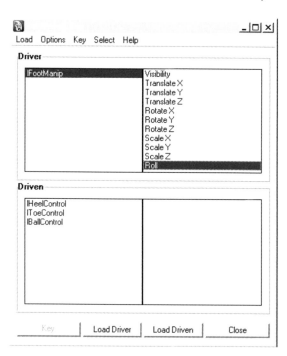

Set Driven Key window

4   Key the heel rotation

- In the **Driven** section, highlight **heelControl** and the **rotate Z** attribute.

- Click the **Key** button to set the starting rotation.

- In the Channel Box, set the **roll** value to **-5**.

- Set the **Rotate Z** to **20**.

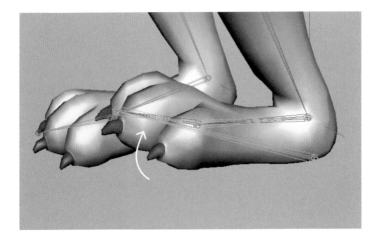

Foot rotated back on heel

- Again, click the **Key** button.

- You can now test the **roll** attribute by clicking on its name in the Channel Box and **MMB+dragging** in the viewport. You can see that the foot rolls from the heel to a flat position.

- Set the **Roll** attribute to **0**.

5   Key the ball rotation

- In the **Driven** section, click **ballControl** and then click **rotate Z**.

- Click the **Key** button to set the starting rotation.

- Click **lFootManip** in the **Driver** section and set the **roll** value to **5**.

- Click **ballControl** and set the **Rotate Z** to **30**.

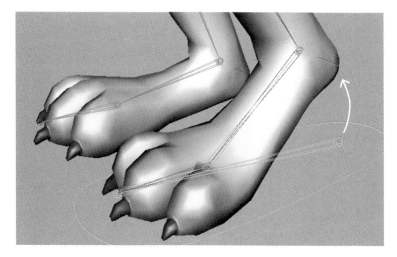

Foot rotated forward on ball

- Again, click the **Key** button in the Set Driven Key window.

> **Tip:** When working with Set Driven Key, always set the value of the driver before setting
> the driven. If you set the driver second, it will reset your driven value because of
> earlier keys.

6   Key the toe rotation

- In the **Driven** section, click **toeControl** and then click **rotate Z**.

- Click **lFootManip** and Make sure the **Roll** value is set to **5**.

  The toeControl rotation will kick in only after the ballControl joint has rotated to its maximum.

- Click the **Key** button to set the starting rotation.

- Set the **Roll** value to **10**.

- Click **toeControl** and set the **Rotate Z** to **30**.

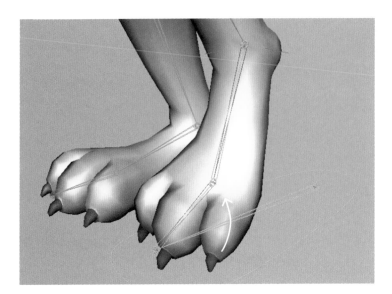

Foot rotated forward on toe

- Again, click the **Key** button.

7   **Test the foot roll**

- Select the *lFootManip*.

- Click the **roll** attribute name in the Channel Box and **MMB+drag** in the viewport to test the roll.

- Set the **roll** back to **0**.

- Click the **Close** button in the Set Driven Key window.

8   **Right foot joint setup**

You will now create another reverse foot setup for the right leg. In order to simplify the task, you will duplicate the left foot setup in separate steps.

- Select the *heelControl*.

- Select **Edit** → **Duplicate Special** → ❑.

- In the options, turn **On** the **Duplicate input graph** option.

- Click the **Duplicate Special** button.

  By duplicating the input graph, you will keep the driven keys you have just made.

- Press **Shift+p** to unparent the new reverse foot from its manipulator.

- Set the **TranslateX** attribute of the new *heelControl* joint to the same value, but **negative**.

- Snap the new reverse foot joints to their respective right foot joints.

- **Recreate** the different constraints for the right foot.

9 **Right foot manipulator**

- In the Outliner, select the new *lFootManip1* node.

  This node was created when you used Duplicated Special on the heelControl. This node is connected to the Set Driven Keys of the new reverse foot joints.

- **Snap** to point the *lFootManip1* to the new *heelControl* and **rename** it *rFootManip*.

- Select **Modify → Freeze Transformations**.

- **Parent** the new *heelControl* joint to the new *rFootManip*.

- **Rename** all the joints appropriately with their left and right prefixes.

10 **Test the setup**

- Select the *pelvis* joint.

- **Move** and **rotate** the *pelvis* to see the effect of the constrained IK handles.

- Try to pose the feet using the new reverse foot setups.

- **Undo** the last moves to bring the character back to its original position.

11 **Save your work**

- **Save** the scene as *12-IKs_02.ma*.

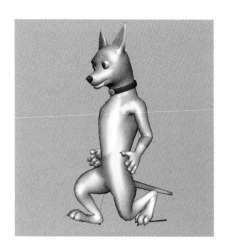

Moving the pelvis joint

Hand setup

It is good to be able to plant the feet of your character, but it would also be good to control the hand rotations. In this exercise, you will create a basic hand setup that will allow you to control the hand rotations.

1   **Change the arm IK type**

Single plane IKs are best used when you do not need to bother with the hands' rotation or with the bending solution. This means that they are not ideal for the type of control you are looking for in this case. You will need to delete the ones you have on the arms and create new rotate plane IKs.

- Select the two arm IK handles.

- Press **Delete** on your keyboard.

- Select **Skeleton → IK Handle Tool**.
  The IK type should already be set to ikRPsolver.

- **Create** IK handles for both arms.

- **Rename** the IK handles properly.

2   **Create a hand manipulator**

- Make sure **Show → NURBS Curves** is turned on in the viewport.

- Select **Create → NURBS Primitives → Circle**.

- **Rename** the circle *lHandManip*.

- Press **w** to access the **Translate Tool**.

- Hold down the **v** hotkey and snap the *circle* to the *lWrist* of the skeleton.

- **Rotate** and **scale** the circle to fit the wrist.

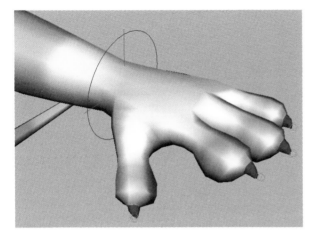

The hand manipulator

- Select **Modify** → **Freeze Transformations**.

3   Constrain the IK handle

- With the *lHandManip* still selected, **Shift-select** the *lArmIk* handle.

- Select **Constrain** → **Parent**.

  The parent constraint forces the constrained object to follow a source object, just as if it were parented to it.

4   Constrain the wrist

- Select the *lHandManip*, then **Shift-select** the *lWrist* joint.

- Select **Constrain** → **Orient**.

5   Test the wrist manipulator

- **Move** and **rotate** the *lHandManip* to see how it affects the arm and hand.

- **Move** and **rotate** the *pelvis* joint to see how it affects the arm and hand.

  Notice how the hand stays planted wherever it is. This is exactly the behavior you are looking for.

- **Undo** the last steps to return the *pelvis* and *lHandManip* to their original locations.

6   **Create a pole vector constraint**

- Select **Create** → **Locator**.

- Hold down **v** to enable **Snap to Point**, then snap the locator on the *lElbow* joint.

- **Move** the *locator* back on the **Z-axis** by about **5 units**.

- Select **Modify** → **Freeze Transformations**.

- With the *locator* selected, **Shift-select** the *lArmIk* handle.

- Select **Constrain** → **Pole Vector**.

  The pole vector constraint will connect the locator's position to the IK handle's **Pole Vector** *attribute. By doing this, you can now control the rotation of the arm using a visual indicator.*

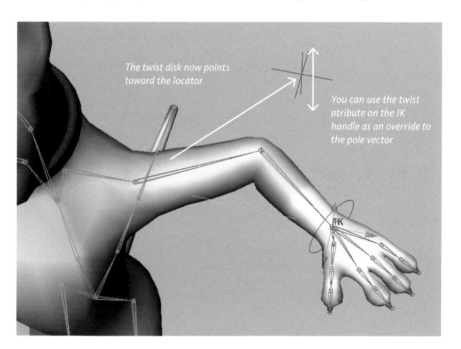

A pole vector locator

- **Rename** the locator *lArmPv*.

7   **Right hand manipulator**

- **Create** the same type of manipulator on the right hand.

The completed IK setup

8   **Save your work**

   • **Save** the scene as *12-IKs_03.ma*.

Conclusion

In this lesson, you learned the basics of how to use IK handles in a custom setup. You experimented with some of the most popular tricks, such as the reverse foot setup and manipulators. You also used the twist attribute and pole vector constraints, which are required for any good IK handle animation.

In the next lesson, you will refine the current character setup even more. Steps will include creating an eye setup, locking and hiding nonrequired attributes, adding and connecting custom attributes, and creating a character set. Doing so will make your character rig easier to use, limiting manipulation errors that could potentially break it. You will also generate a higher resolution version of the geometry.

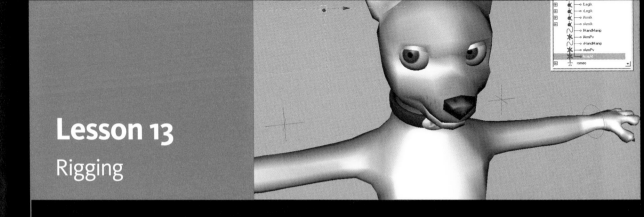

Lesson 13
Rigging

Character rigging requires a thorough knowledge of Autodesk® Maya® objects and lots of experimentation. The more you experiment with creating and animating character rigs, the better you will become at producing first-rate setups.

In this lesson, you will finalize the character rig by making it animator friendly. This means that you will make the various useful setups and attributes easy to find, as well as hide unnecessary ones. You will also create a high-resolution polygonal version of the character, in order to get better visualization once you are finished animating.

In this lesson, you will learn the following:

- How to organize the rig's hierarchy

- How to create selection sets

- How to create visibility layers

- How to strategically place attributes

- How to use aim constraints

- How to use the jiggle deformer

- How to lock and hide nodes and attributes

- How to create a Smooth node and hook it to the rig

- How to create a character set for keyframing

Rig hierarchy

When you look in the Outliner, your character's hierarchy should be clean, well-named, and simple to understand. For instance, all the Setup nodes should be parented together under a Master node. You can then use that Master node for the global placement of the character in a scene.

1   Open the previous scene

- **Open** the file *12-IKs_03.ma*.

2   Geometry group

- Select all the body and collar geometry and the eye groups.

Tip: *It might be simpler to select the geometry and groups from the Outliner.*

- Press **Ctrl+g** to group it all together.

- **Rename** the group *geo*.

3   Create a Master node

- Change the current view to the *top* view.

- Select **Create → EP Curve → ❑**.

- Change the **Curve Degree** for **1 Linear**.

- Click the **Close** button.

- Hold down **x** and draw a four-arrows shape as indicated:

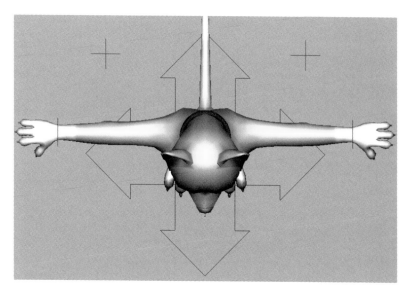

The master node curve

- Press **Enter** to complete the curve.

- **Rename** the curve *master*.

4   **Hierarchy**

- Select **Panels** → **Saved Layouts** → **Persp/Outliner**.

- In the Outliner, select all character Setup nodes and **Parent** them to the *master* node.

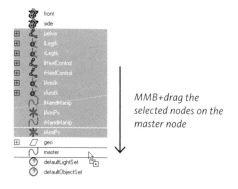

MMB+drag the selected nodes on the master node

Parent setup nodes to master

Note: *Do not parent bound geometry or the geometry group to the master node.*

There should now be only two main groups in the Outliner, which are geo and master.

5   **Node names**

- Make sure all nodes are named correctly.

Note: It is recommended to have unique names for all your objects.

6   **Visibility layers**

- In the Layer Editor, click the **Create a new layer** button.

- **Double-click** the new layer's name and **rename** it *setupLayer*.

- Click the **Save** button to confirm the new name.

- Select the *master* node in the *Perspective* view, then **RMB** on the *setupLayer* and select **Add Selected Objects**.
  All the character rig nodes can now be hidden by hiding the setupLayer.

- Click the **Create a new layer** button and **rename** the new layer *geoLayer*.

- Select the *geo* node in the *Perspective* view, then **RMB** on the *geoLayer* and select **Add Selected Objects**.

Selection sets

Selection sets are meant to simplify the selection process of multiple objects. In the character setup, it would be nice to select all the tail joints at once in order to be able to bend the character's tail easily.

1   **Select the tail joints**

- Select the *tail, tail1, tail2,* and *tail3* joints.

2   Create a set

- Select **Create** → **Sets** → **Quick Select Set**...

- In the Create Quick Select Set window, enter the name *tailSet*.

- Click the **OK** button.
  If you scroll down in the Outliner, there will be a set called tailSet.

The new set

3   Use the selection set

- Select *tailSet* in the Outliner.

- **RMB** to pop up a contextual menu and choose **Select Set Members**.
  All the objects in the set are selected.

- Press **e** to access the **Rotate Tool**.

- **Rotate** all the joints simultaneously.

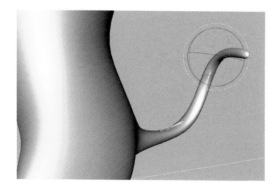

Rotate all joints simultaneously

Tip: *If you notice that some joint local rotation axes are not aligned correctly, you can go into Component mode and adjust them, even after a skin is bound.*

4   Edit a selection set

The last tail joint does not need to be selected at the same time as the other joints when you rotate the character's tail. The following will remove the last joint from the selection set.

- **Undo** the last rotation.

- Select **Window** → **Relationship Editors** → **Sets**.

- On the left side of the Relationship Editor, click the **+** sign next to the *tailSet* to expand it. *All the objects in that set are displayed.*

- Still in the left side of the Relationship Editor, highlight the *tail3* joint from the set *spineSet*.

- Select **Edit** → **Remove Highlighted from Set**.

Note: *When you highlight a set in the Relationship Editor, its members are highlighted on the right side of the panel. Toggle objects on the right side to add them to or remove them from the current set.*

- **Close** the Relationship Editor.

5   Save your work

- **Save** your scene as *13-rig_01.ma.*

Custom attributes

As you will notice by working in the current rig, some attributes are not easy to access. You should place useful attributes on strategic nodes for easy access.

Since you control the arm and leg IK handles using custom setups, it is a good idea to place useful IK attributes on the hand manipulator and the reverse foot bones.

1   Add new attributes

- Select the *lHandManip,* the *rHandManip,* the *lHeelManip,* and the *rHeelManip.*

- Select **Modify** → **Add Attribute...**

- Set the following:

  Long Name to **twist**;

  Data Type to **Float**;

  Default to **0**.

- Click the **OK** button.

  *This will add the **Twist** attribute to all selected nodes. The Add Attribute window will remain open for further attribute additions.*

2   Connect the new attributes

- Select **Window** → **General Editors** → **Connection Editor**.

- Select the *lHandManip*.

- In the Connection Editor, click the **Reload Left** button.

- Scroll down and highlight the **Twist** attribute.

- Select the *lArmIk*.

- In the Connection Editor, click the **Reload Right** button.

- Scroll down and highlight the **Twist** attribute.

  *You have just connected the **Twist** attribute of the hand manipulator to the left arm IK handle **Twist** attribute.*

3   Repeat

- **Repeat** the previous steps in order to connect the remaining *rHandManip, lHeelManip,* and *rHeelManip* attributes to their respective IK handles.

- Click the **Close** button to close the Connection Editor.

4   Hide the IK handles

Since you have connected the *Twist* and *IK Blend* attributes of the IK handles to their manipulators, the IK handles can now be hidden since they are no longer required to be visible or selected.

- Select the *lArmIk*, the *rArmIk*, the *lLegIk,* and the *rLegIk*.

- Set the **Visibility** attribute in the Channel Box to **Off** by typing in **o** in the Channel Box.

  All the IK handles are now hidden.

- Highlight the **Visibility** attribute's name.

- **RMB** in the Channel Box and select **Lock Selected**.

  *Doing so will prevent the IK handles from being displayed, even when using the **Display** → **Show** → **All** command.*

Selection handles

There are several nodes that you will need to select when animating the character. Unfortunately, these nodes can be hidden under geometry or difficult to choose in the viewport. This is where a selection handle becomes helpful. Selection handles have a very high selection priority and are visible on top of your geometry in the viewport.

1   **Show selection handles**

- Select the *lClavicle*, the *rClavicle*, and the *pelvis* joints.

- Select **Display** → **Transform Display** → **Selection Handles**.

2   **Move selection handles**

- Go into **Component** mode.

- Make sure only the selection handle mask is enabled.

The selection handle mask

- Choose the selection handles for the *lClavicle*, the *rClavicle*, and the *pelvis* joints.

- Press and hold **w** and then click in the viewport to bring up the Move Tool option menu, and select **World**.

  You are changing the Move Tool option to World because it is easier to move the selection handles all at once that way.

- **Translate** the selection handles toward the back of the **Z-axis** until they are outside the geometry.

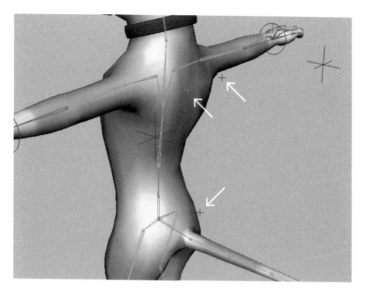

The selection handle outside the geometry

- Go back into **Object** mode.

- Press and hold **w** and then click in the viewport to bring up the Move Tool option menu, and select **Object**.

3   **Save your work**

- **Save** your scene as *13-rig_02.ma*.

Eye setup

The eyes of the character need to be able to look around freely. To do so, you will create an aim constraint, which forces an object to aim at another object. You will also need to define a new attribute for blinking.

1   **LookAt locator**

A locator will be used to specify a point in space where the eyes will be looking.

- Select **Create → Locator** and **rename** it *lookAt*.

- **Snap** the locator to the *head* joint.

- **Move** the locator in front of the character about **20 units** on the **Z-axis**.

The lookAt locator

- **Parent** the *lookAt* locator to the *master* node.

2   **Freeze transformations**

In order to be able to easily place the *lookAt* locator at its default position, you should freeze its transformations.

- Select the *lookAt* locator.

- Select **Modify → Freeze Transformations**.

3   Aim constraint

- Select *lookAt*, then from the Outliner, **Ctrl-select** the *lEye* joint.

Note: *You might have to expand the hierarchy in the Outliner using the + sign to reach the desired node.*

- Select **Constrain → Aim → ❏**.
- Turn **On** the **Maintain Offset** checkbox, then click the **Add** button.
- **Repeat** for the *rEye* joint.

4   Experiment with lookAt

- Select the *lookAt* locator and **move** it around to see how the *eyeball* reacts.

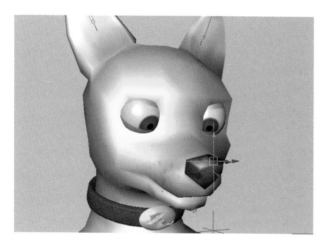

The eyes looking at the locator

5   Eye blink attribute

It would be good to have a *blink* attribute on the locator, to make it easy to blink the character's eyes.

- Select the *lookAt* locator and select **Modify → Add Attribute**...

- Set the following in the new attribute window:

    Long Name to *blink*;

    Data Type to **Float**;

    Minimum to **0**;

    Maximum to **2**;

    Default to **1**.

- Click the **OK** button to add the new attribute.

6   **Eye blink driven keys**

- Select the **Animate** → **Set Driven Key** → **Set...**

- Load the *lookAt* node and the *blink* attribute as the driver.

- Select both *eyelid* geometries, then highlight the *makeNurbsSphere* in the Channel Box.

> **Note:** *If the makeNurbsSphere node is not listed in the Channel Box, it means that you have deleted the history on the eyelid. To remedy the situation, rebuild the eyelid starting from a new primitive sphere.*

- Click the **Load Driven** button.

- Highlight the two *makeNurbsSphere* nodes and highlight their *startSweep* and *endSweep*.

- Click the **Key** button.

- Set the **blink** attribute to **0**, then set the **sweep** attributes to set the eye closed.

- Click the **Key** button.

- Set the **blink** attribute to **2**, then set the **sweep** attributes to set the eye wide open.

- Click the **Key** button.

7   **Test the eye blink**

- Test the **Blink** attribute using the virtual slider.

Jiggle deformer

The Jiggle deformer will make vertices jiggle as the geometry is moving. You will use a jiggle deformer on the ears of the character so they wobble as he is walking.

1   **Paint Selection Tool**

- Select the *body* geometry.

- In the toolbox, **double-click** the **Paint Selection Tool**.

- **Paint** on the *body* geometry to easily select the ear vertices.

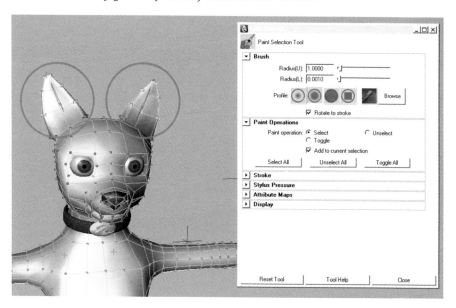

The vertices to be used with the jiggle deformer

Tip: *Use the Unselect paint operation to select unwanted vertices.*

2   **Create a jiggle deformer**

- With the wanted vertices still selected, select **Create Deformers → Jiggle Deformer → ❏**.

- In the option window, set the following:

  Stiffness to **0.2**;

  Damping to **0.05**;

  Weight to **0.8**;

  Ignore Transform to **On**.

- Click the **Create** button.

  The jiggle1 deformer will be added to the character's input history in the Channel Box.

3   Smooth the jiggle influence

With the default value, all the vertices selected are fully affected by the jiggle deformer. It is better to create a nice gradient effect by smoothing the jiggle's weight.

- Go into Object mode and select the *body* geometry.

- Select **Edit Deformers** → **Paint Jiggle Weights Tool** → ❑.

- Change the **Paint Operation** to **Smooth**.

- Click the **Flood** button to smooth out the jiggle weight to get the following:

The jiggle influence

- Close the tool window.

4   **Test the jiggle deformer**

In order to test the jiggle deformer, take some time to keyframe a very simple animation and then play back the scene. The attributes of the jiggle deformer to tweak can be found in the Channel Box, when the *body* geometry is selected. Once testing is over, remove the animation and make sure all the joints are at their preferred angle.

Tip: *Make sure to always set your Playback Speed to Play Every Frame and Max Playback Speed to Real-time when playing a scene with dynamics. Doing so will ensure an accurate representation of the final effect.*

5   **Save your work**

- **Save** your scene as *13-rig_03.ma*.

Lock and hide nodes and attributes

Many nodes and attributes in the character rig are not supposed to be animated or changed. It is recommended that you double-check each node and attribute to see if the animator requires them. If they are not required, you can lock and hide them.

The Channel Control window allows you to quickly set which attributes are displayed in the Channel Box and which ones are locked.

1   **Lock geometry groups**

Since all the geometry is bound to the skeleton, it must not be moved. All the geometry attributes should, therefore, be locked.

- Select **Window → Hypergraph: Hierarchy**.

- Make sure all nodes are visible in the Hypergraph by enabling **Options → Display → Hidden Nodes** to **On**.

- Select the *geo* group.

- Select **Edit → Select Hierarchy** from the main menu.

- In the Channel Box, highlight the **Translate**, **Rotate,** and **Scale** attribute names.

- **RMB** in the Channel Box and select **Lock and Hide Selected**.

  Doing so will leave only the **Visibility** *attribute in the Channel Box for all the geometry nodes.*

2 **Channel Control Editor**

- Select **Window** → **General Editors** → **Channel Control**.

  Under the **Keyable** *tab, all the keyable attributes shown in the Channel Box are displayed. If you highlight attributes and then click the* **Move >>** *button, the selected attributes will be moved in the* **Nonkeyable Hidden** *column. Notice that only the* **Visibility** *attribute is still visible in the Channel Box.*

  In the same manner, under the **Locked** *tab, you can move the wanted attributes from the* **Locked** *column to the* **Non-Locked** *column and vice versa.*

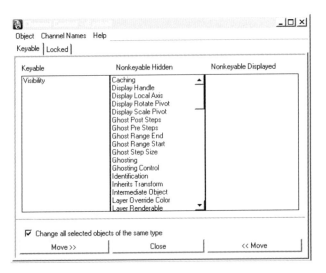

3 **Hide end joints**

End joints are usually not animated.

- Select all the end joints on your skeleton, except the eye joints.

- Set their **Visibility** attributes to **Off**.

- **Lock and hide** all the attributes of the end joints.

  An end joint is the last joint in a joint chain. They are usually created only for visual reference and often never used.

> **Tip:** *Try using* **Edit → Select All by Type → Joints,** *then press the* **down arrow** *repeatedly until all the end joints are selected. Do not forget the deselect the eye joints.*

4 **Lock joints**

Joints can usually rotate, but should not be translated or scaled. There are exceptions, such as *joint* roots, that usually need to be able to translate.

- **Lock and hide** the **Translate**, **Scale,** and **Visibility** attributes for all the joints in the scene, except for *pelvis*, *lHeelControl,* and *rHeelControl,* which require translation.

> **Tip:** *Try using* **Edit → Select All by Type → Joints**.

- **Lock and hide** the **Scale** and **Visibility** attributes for the *pelvis*.

5 **Rest of setup**

You should spend some time checking each node in your character rig hierarchy to lock and hide unwanted attributes or nodes. When you do not know what an attribute does, you should at least set it to non-keyable, so that it does not appear in the Channel Box. This will prevent it from being keyframed accidentally.

> **Note:** *As you learn more advanced character rigging techniques, you might not necessarily want to lock your rigs in the same way as shown here. The character rig from this book is simplified on purpose so you do not get lost with technicalities.*

Following are some general guidelines for this particular rig:

- The pole vector and *lookAt* locators should only translate.
- The reverse foot joints should be hidden and locked as they are not intended for manual animation.
- Any constraint attributes should be locked.
- All the scaling attributes should be locked unless you want to do cartoon-like animations.
- Any attributes controlled by a constraint or an IK handle should be hidden.
- IK handles that are controlled by a manipulator should be completely locked.
- Effectors should be completely locked.

6   Master scale

You should make sure to set the *master*'s scaling attributes to non-keyable, but you should not lock these attributes. By doing so, you can be sure no keyframes will be made on the global scaling of the character, but you will still be able to change the character's scaling to fit its environment.

7   Save your work

- **Save** your scene as *13-rig_04.ma*.

High resolution model

When animating a character, it is good to have the choice of displaying either the high-resolution or low-resolution model. In this case, the character geometry is already quite low resolution and it would be good to have a high-resolution version of the model to visualize the final result of your animation.

Here you will use a polygonal Smooth node and connect it to a new attribute on the character's master. Once that is done, you will be able to crank up the character's resolution easily.

1   Smooth polygons

- Select the *body* geometry.
- Select **Mesh** → **Smooth**.

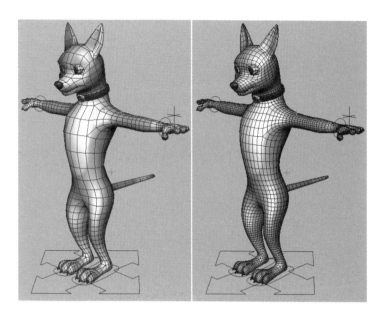

High-resolution geometry

2   **Smooth attribute**

- Select the *master* node.

- Select **Modify** → **Add Attribute**...

- Set the following in the new attribute window:

    Long Name to *smooth*;

    Data Type to **Integer**;

    Minimum to **0**;

    Maximum to **2**;

    Default to **0**.

- Click the **OK** button to add the new attribute.

- Using the Connection Editor, connect the new attribute to the *polySmoothFace1*'s **Divisions** attribute.

- **Test** the new attribute.

    You can now easily increase or decrease the resolution of the model.

Creating character sets

In the next lesson, you will use keyframing techniques to make the character walk. To organize all animation channels needed for keyframing, you can create character sets. These sets let you collect attributes into a single node that can then be efficiently keyed and edited as a group.

1   **Create a main character node**

- Select the *master* node.

- Select **Character** → **Create Character Set** → ❑ **from the Animation menu set.**

- Set the following:

    Name to *romeo*;

    Hierarchy below selected node to **On**;

    All keyable to **On**.

- Click **Create Character Set**.

    This character is now active and visible next to the Range Slider. It was created with all the keyframable attributes for the entire master hierarchy.

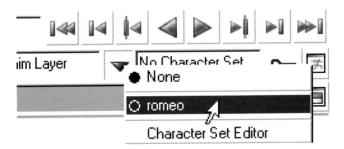

Character menu

2   **Remove unnecessary attributes from the character set**

- Select the *character* set from the Outliner.

romeo

The character node

> All the character's attributes are listed in the Channel Box.

> *If you scroll in the Channel Box, you will notice that some attributes are already connected (colored). They are being driven by constraints, therefore, they are not needed in the character.*

- Highlight the master's Smooth attribute in the Channel Box.

- Select **Character → Remove from Character Set**.

  The selected attribute is now removed from the character set.

- Also remove any colored attributes in the Channel Box from the *character* set since they are not intended for animation

3   **Reference geometry**

In order to simplify even more the selection of the character rig in the viewport, make sure to set the *geoLayer* display to **Reference**. Doing so will ignore the geometry when choosing the various rig nodes.

4   **Save your work**

- **Save** your scene as *13-rig_05.ma*.

Conclusion

You now have a biped character all hooked up and ready for a stroll. You made your character rig simpler for an animator to use and virtually unbreakable. You also created an attribute to set the resolution of the model, which will be very useful for visualizing animation.

In the next lesson, you will animate Romeo using the character rig and character set. It will put both your rigging and animation skills to the test.

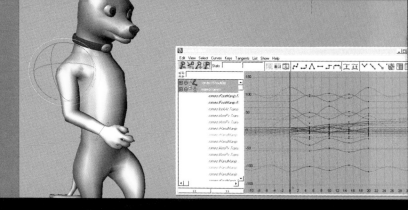

Lesson 14
Animation

The character you built is now ready to be animated. To create a walk cycle, you will build up the motion one part at a time. Starting with sliding the feet, you will then lift the feet, use the roll attribute and set the twist of the pelvis. When that is done, you will animate the upper body accordingly.

In this lesson, you will learn the following:

Reference

Instead of working directly with the file from the previous lesson, you will reference the *Romeo* scene file. A reference refers to another scene file that is set to read-only and loaded into the current scene. It allows you to animate the character, leaving the rig file untouched. That way, if you update the rig file the file referencing will also get updated.

1   **Create a reference**

- Select **File** → **New Scene**.

- Select **File** → **Create Reference** → ❑.
  Doing so will open the Create Reference options.

- Under **Name Clash Options**, set **Resolve all nodes with this string:** *romeo*.
  This will prefix all the Reference nodes with the string romeo.

Note: *For simplicity, the romeo prefix will not be cited.*

- Click the **Reference** button.

- In the browse dialog that appears, select the file *13-rig_05.ma*, then click **Reference**.
  The file will load into the current one.

  Notice the small diamond icon in the Outliner and the red names in the Hypergraph. This means that Romeo nodes are loaded from a reference file as read-only.

Note: *If you need to bring changes to the character setup from the previous lesson, you will need to open the rig file, make your changes, then save the file. Once that is done, you will need to open the animation file again so the new referenced rig gets reloaded. Be careful—if you remove or rename nodes or attributes in the rig file that are animated in the animation file, their animation will be lost.*

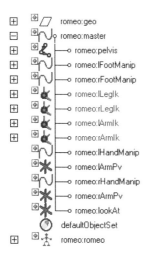
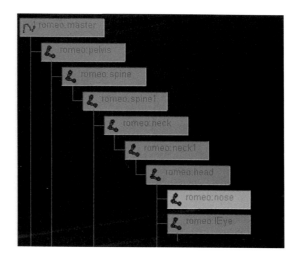

Hypergraph

2 Layers

- Turn the visibility **On** for the *geoLayer* and the *setupLayer*.

- Make sure the **smooth** attribute on the *master* node is set to **0**.
  You should now see only the low resolution model along with its rig.

3 Change the view panels

- Select **Panels** → **Layouts** → **Two Panes Stacked**.

- Change the top panel to a *side* view and the bottom panel to a *Perspective* view.

- For the *side* view, select **View** → **Predefined Bookmarks** → **Left Side**.

Tip: *You can also use the view cube to interactivly choose the proper camera view.*

- In the *side* view, turn **Off** both **Show** → **NURBS Surfaces** and **Show** → **Polygons**.

  This panel will be used to watch the movements of the rig.

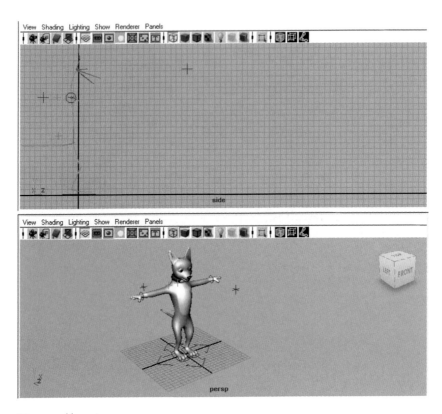

View panel layout

Animating a walk cycle

To create a walk, you will start with a single cycle. To create a cycle, you will need the start position and end position to be the same. There are several controls that need to be keyed, including the position of the feet, the roll of the feet, and the rotation of the pelvis.

Animate the feet sliding

You will now key the horizontal positions of the feet to establish their forward movement. This will result in a sliding motion of the feet.

> **Note:** *The animation values specified here depend on the scale of your character. To follow this lesson properly, either open the required support file or adjust the values to compensate.*

1   **Set your time range**

- Set the **Start Time** and **Playback Start Time** to **0**.

- Set the **End Time** and **Playback End Time** to **20**.

    This will give you a smaller time range to work with as you build the cycle. The cycle will be a full stride, using two steps of 10 frames each.

2   **Active character**

- In the **Current Character** menu next to the Range Slider, select *romeo*.

    Now any keys you set will be set on all the attributes of this Character node.

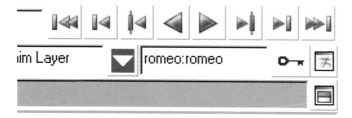

Active Character menu

3   **Position and key the lower body start pose**

You will key the starting position of the character in the position of a full stride.

- Go to frame **0**.

- Select the *lFootManip* selection handle and set the following:

  Translate Z to **9** units

  Roll to **-5**

- Select the *rFootManip selection handle* and set the following:

  Translate Z to **0** units

  Roll to **10**

 Tip: *Make sure the Translate Tool is set to be in World coordinates.*

- Set the *pelvis* **translate Z** to **5** units.

- **Move** the *pelvis* down until the knees bend.

 Note: *Leave the arms behind for now. Later, you will add secondary animation.*

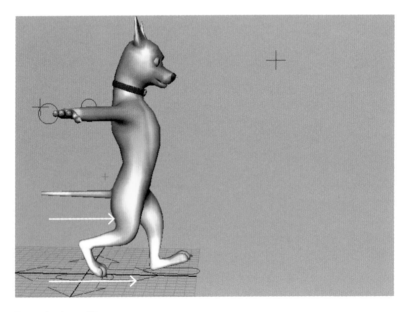

Lower body position

- Press **s** to set a key on all the channels of the *romeo* character.

  The entire character gets keyframed since the Romeo character is selected in the Current Character menu at the bottom right of the interface.

4   **Position and key the right foot**

- Go to frame **10**.

- Set the *rFootManip* **translate Z** to **18** units and **roll** to **-5**.

  This translation value is exactly double the value of the initial left foot key. This is important to ensure that the two feet cycle together later.

- Set the *lFootManip* **roll** to **10**.

- Set the *pelvis* **translate Z** to **14** units.

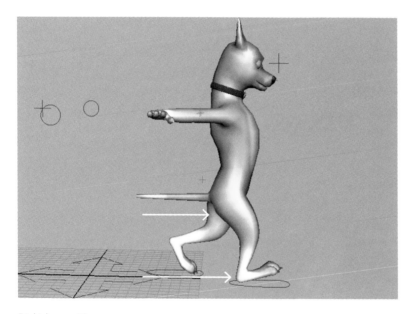

Right leg position

- Press **s** to set a key on all the channels of the *romeo* character.

5   Position and key the left foot

You will move the left foot into a position that is similar to the starting position.

- Go to frame **20**.

- Set the *lFootManip* **translate Z** to **27** units and **roll** to **-5**.
  Again, the value is set using units of 9. This will ensure a connection between cycles later.

- Set the *rFootManip* **roll** to **10**.

- Set the *pelvis* **translate Z** to **23** units.

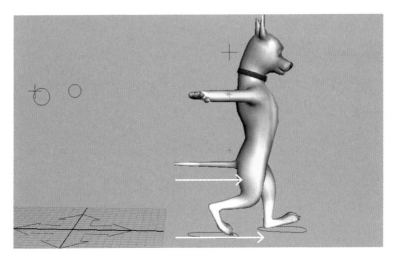

Left leg position

- Press **s** to set a key on all the channels of the *romeo* character.

Edit the animation curves

To refine the in-between motion of the feet, you can use the animation curves to view and change the tangent options for the feet.

1   View the curves in the Graph Editor

You will edit the animation curves produced by the keys in the Graph Editor.

- Clear the selection.

- Select **Window** → **Animation Editors** → **Graph Editor**.

- Press the **Ctrl** key (**Apple** key on Macintosh) to select *lFootManip.TranslateZ* and *rFootManip.TranslateZ* in the Outliner section of this window.

- Select **View** → **Frame Selection**.

  The pattern of the animation curves you have created should look as follows:

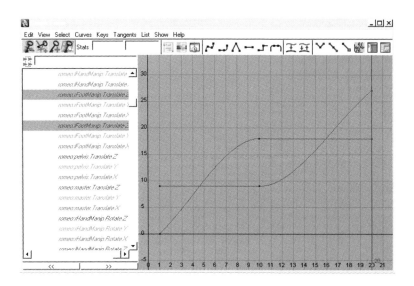

Animation curves in Graph Editor

- **Playback** the animation to see the motion.

Note: *If you open the Graph Editor when the feet are selected, you will see an animation channel with keys set in the negative direction. This is the animation curve connecting the Rotate Z of the foot to the Roll attribute.*

---

2   **Edit the curve tangents on the feet**

The curve tangent type should be changed so that the steps cycle smoothly. The default tangent type is *Clamped*.

- Select the two animation curves for *lFootManip.TranslateZ* and *rFootManip.TranslateZ*.

- Select **Tangents** → **Flat**.

   The visual difference between clamped and flat tangents in the Graph Editor is subtle. Look at the start and end keyframes on the curves. The flat tangents will create a smooth hookup for the cycle between the start frame and end frame.

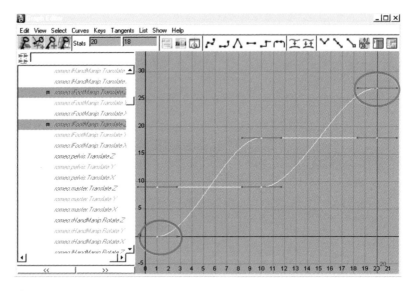

Flat tangents

Animate the feet up and down

You will now key the vertical raising and lowering of the feet to establish the stepping action.

1   Turn on Auto Key

   You will now use **Auto Key** to help with the raising of the feet. The Auto Key feature will automatically keyframe any attributes on the selected nodes that already have at least one keyframe, and for which the value is changing.

   - Click the **Auto Keyframe** button in the right side of the Time Slider to turn it **On**.

   - Open the **Animation Preferences** window, using the button just to the right of the **Auto Keyframe** button.

- In the **Timeline** category, make sure the **Playback speed** is set to **Play every frame** and that **Max Playback Speed** is set to **Real-time**.

- Click the **Animation** category under the **Settings** category and set the following under the **Tangents** section:

  Default in tangent to **Flat**

  Default out tangent to **Flat**

  This will set all future tangents to flat.

- Click the **Save** button.

2   Raise the right foot at midstep

Key the high point of the raised foot in the middle of a step.

- Go to frame **5**.

- Select the *rFootManip*.

- **Translate** the foot about **1** unit up along the **Y-axis**.
  This sets a new key for the Y-axis channel of the foot using Auto Key.

3   Raise the left foot at midstep

- Go to frame **15**.

- Select the *lFootManip*.

- **Move** the foot about **1** unit up along the **Y-axis**.
  Again, a key is automatically set.

- **Playback** the results.

4   Save your work

- **Save** your scene as *14-walk_01.ma*.

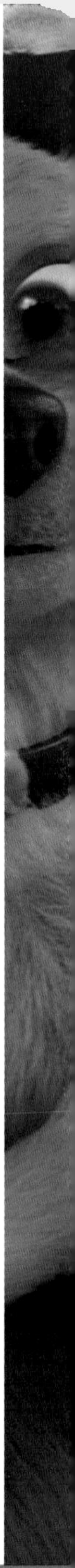

Animate the pelvic rotations

To create a more realistic action, the pelvis' position and rotation will be set to work with each step. You will again set keys for the translation and rotation of the pelvis using Auto Key.

1   **Set the pelvis Y rotation**

You will now animate the pelvis rotation to give the walk a little more motion.

- Go to frame **0**.

- Select the *pelvis* node using its selection handle.

- In the *top* view, **rotate** the *pelvis* using the red rotation manipulator handle in a clockwise direction by about **-10 degrees**.
  This points the left hip toward the left foot and the right hip toward the right foot.

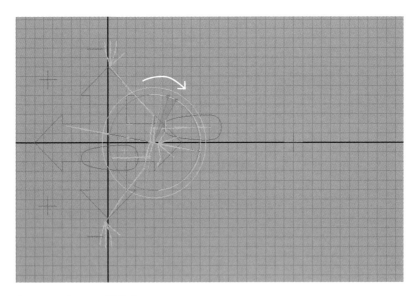

Rotate pelvis toward left foot

2   **Rotate in the opposite direction**

- Go to frame **10**.

- **Rotate** the pelvis in the opposite direction by about **10 degrees**.

3   **Copy the first Y rotation**

- Go to frame **0**.

- In the Time Slider, **MMB+drag** the current time to frame **20**.

  The display has not changed, but the time has changed.

- With the *pelvis* still selected, highlight the **Rotate** attribute in the Channel Box, then **RMB** and select **Key Selected**.

  *By doing so, you have manually set a keyframe on the rotation value of the pelvis from frame **0** to frame **20**.*

- **Refresh** the Time Slider by dragging anywhere in the time indicator.

  *Notice that the pelvis' **Rotate** attributes have the exact same value at frame **20** that they do at frame **0**.*

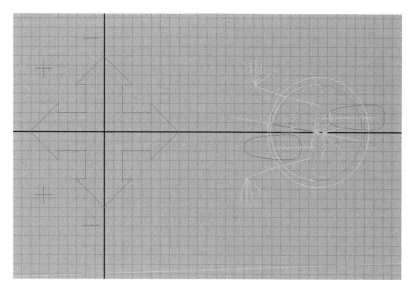

Copied rotation value at frame 20

4   **Pelvis in front view**

- Go to frame **5**.

- In the *front* view, **Translate** the *pelvis* on the **X-axis** by about **0.5** units so that the weight of Romeo is on the left leg.

- **Rotate** the *pelvis* on its **Y-axis** by about **-3** degrees so that the upper body arc to maintain its balance over the left leg.

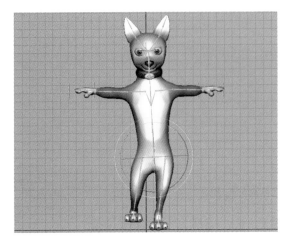

Offset pelvis with right foot raised

- Go to frame **15**.

- **Translate** the *pelvis* on the **X-axis** so that the weight of Romeo is on the right leg.

- **Rotate** the *pelvis* on the **Y-axis** in the opposite direction to arc the body to maintain its balance.

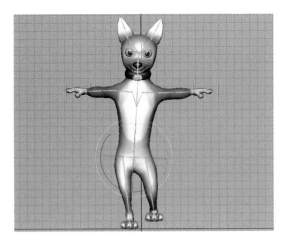

Offset pelvis with left foot raised

5   Edit the keys

To prepare the file for creating cycles later, you will need to ensure that the rotations match at the start and end of the cycle.

- Make sure the *pelvis* is selected.

- In the Graph Editor, press the **Ctrl** key and highlight the **Translate X**, **Rotate X,** and **Rotate Y** attributes.

- Select **View → Frame All**.

  Since you copied frame 0 of the pelvis' X rotation onto frame 20 in Step **3**, *the start and end values of the animation curve are a perfect match. If they were different, you could have fixed the curve in the Graph Editor so that the cycled motion is smooth.*

- Change the tangents so the curves look like the following:

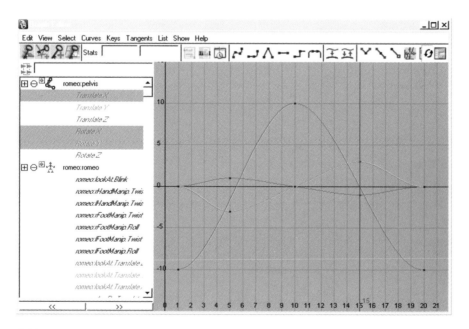

Pelvis curves

Add a bounce to the walk

To create a bouncing motion for the walk, you will add keyframes to the Y translation of the *pelvis* node.

1 Edit the pelvis height

- In the Graph Editor, highlight the *pelvis.TranslateY* channel.

2 Insert keys

- Select the **Insert Keys Tool** found in the Graph Editor.

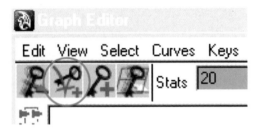

The Insert Key Tool

- Select the **translateY** curve, then with your **MMB** insert a key at frame **5** and frame **15**.

3 Edit the Y translation value of the keys

- Press **w** to select the **Move Key Tool**.

- Select the new keys at frame **5** and frame **15** by holding down **Shift,** and select the two keyframes.

- **Click+drag** with the **MMB** to move these keys to a value of about **9.0** to add some bounce to the walk.

- Drag the other keys to a value of about **8.5** to ensure the knees are not overextended.

Tip: *If the current time in the Time Slider is either on frame 5 or 15, you will see the effect of the change directly on the character. Make sure the value you are using does not overextend the legs.*

- Press **a** to frame the curve.

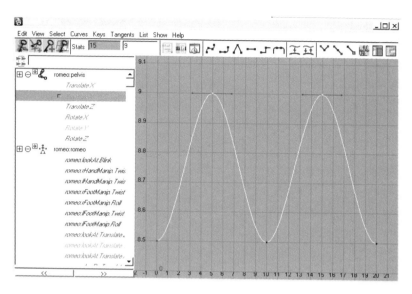

Pelvis Y Translate channel

Refine the feet rotation

When you created the reverse foot setup, you spent a great deal of time preparing the foot for the *heel-to-toe* motion that occurs when walking. So far, you have only rolled the feet so the legs would not snap. You are now going to refine the animation of the foot rotations.

1   **Set a key on the left foot's roll**

As you play back, you will notice that the feet do not pound on the ground after the heel contact.

- Select the *lFootManip* using its selection handle.

- Go to frame **2**.

- Set the *lFootManip*'s **Roll** attribute to **0**.

- Go to frame **5**.

- Set the *lFootManip*'s **Roll** attribute to **0**.

2   Set a key on the right foot's roll

- Select the *rFootManip* using its selection handle.

- Go to frame **12**.

- Set the *rFootManip*'s **Roll** attribute to **0**.

- Go to frame **15**

- Set the *rFootManip*'s **Roll** attribute to **0**.

3   Walking in a straight line

Take some time to animate the feet on their X-axes so Romeo appears to be walking in a straight line.

- Set the *lFootManip* **Translate X** to be **-0.5** at frame **0, 5, 10,** and **20** and **0.5** at frame **15**.

- Set the *rFootManip* **Translate X** to be **0.5** at frame **0, 10, 15,** and **20** and **-0.5** at frame **5**.

- Set the **Twist** attribute on the *lFootManip* to be **-10** for the whole animation.

- Set the **Twist** attribute on the *rFootManip* to be **10** for the whole animation.

4   Play back the results

You have now covered most of the leg animation. Play back the results and try to fix the lower body animation so it appears like a natural walk.

Do not try to add more keyframes at this time. Instead, try to tweak the existing animation until you have no choice but to add more keyframes.

> **Tip:**   *You should always try to keep the required amount of keyframes to a minimum and group them on the same frame if possible. Later in the animation process, the animation curves can become quite complex and having fewer keyframes makes them easier to modify.*

5   Save your work

- **Save** your scene as *14-walk_02.ma*.

Animate the arm swing

The character needs some motion in his arms. To do this, you will animate the translation of the arm manipulators to create an animation that can be cycled.

To add some secondary motion, you will also set keyframes on the rotation of the head.

1   **Set keys for the start position**

   • Go to frame **0**.

   • **Rotate** the clavicles down on their **Z-axes** by about **-10** degrees.

   • **Move** and **rotate** the *lHandManip* behind the body and low down.

Tip: *Make sure to not keyframe the arms while they are overextended. They should always be slightly bent.*

   • **Move** the *lArmPv* to bend the elbow to a good angle pointing slightly out.

   • **Move** and **rotate** the *rHandManip* in front of the body and up.

   • **Move** the *rArmPv* to bend the elbow to a good angle.

   Now the arms are opposite to how the feet are set up. This makes the swinging motion work with the feet.

   • **Rotate** the fingers to get a natural, relaxed hand pose.

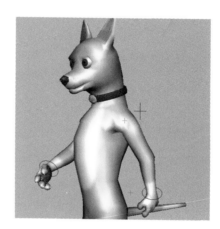

Arm positions

- Select the *head* joint and **rotate** it around the **Y-axis** by about **10 degrees**.

  This has the head and hips moving in opposite directions, where the head always aims straight forward.

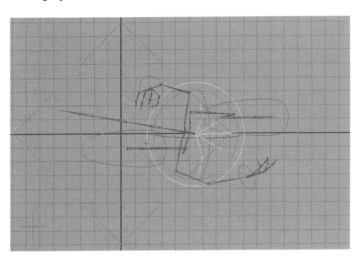

Top view of head rotation looking straight forward

2 Copy keys for the end position

In order to create a smooth transition for the arm cycle, you must have matching values at the start and end of the cycle.

- Select the *lClavicle, lArmPv, lHandManip, rClavicle, rArmPv,* and *rHandManip.*

- In the timeline, **MMB+drag** the Time Slider from frame **0** to frame **20**.

  *The character will not move when you scrub along the timeline when the **MMB** is pressed.*

- Highlight the **translation** and **rotation** attributes in the Channel Box.

- **RMB** and select **Key Selected** from the pop-up menu.

  This sets keyframes only on the attributes you have selected in the Channel Box.

Note: *Because you have multiple nodes selected, you can see three dots after the node's name in the Channel Box. This indicates that other nodes are active, and that they will also receive the keyframes.*

- **Refresh** the Time Slider at frame **20**.

You will see that you have set keyframes at the current position on the manipulators, but they are not following the character.

> **Note:** *You can also use the Dope Sheet to copy and paste selected keyframes, or you can cut and paste keyframe values from the Graph Editor.*

3   Add to attributes

You must now set the right offset to the values already in the Translate Z attributes of the arm manipulators and pole vectors. The Channel Box can allow you to enter a simple mathematical expression in the attribute value field.

- Go to frame **20**.

- With the *lArmPv, rArmPv, lHandManip,* and *rHandManip* nodes selected, type **+=18** in the **Translate Z** attribute in the Channel Box, then press **Enter**.

  Doing so adds 18 units to whatever value is in the attribute for each node.

4   Set keys for the head

Use the method outlined in Step 2 to set the last keyframe for the head rotation.

- Select the *head* joint.

- **MMB+drag** the Time Slider from frame **0** to frame **20**.

- **LMB** over the *head* **Rotate Y** attribute in the Channel Box to highlight it.

- **RMB** and select **Key Selected** from the pop-up menu.

5   Set keys for the middle position

- Go to frame **10**.

- **Move** the arm manipulators opposite to the legs.

- **Rotate** the *head* joint opposite to the hips.

6   **Fix the fingers**

- Select the *lWrist* and *rWrist* joints.

- Select **Edit → Select Hierarchy.**
  Doing so selects all the fingers for which you need to tweak the animation.

- Open the **Graph Editor** and select all the keyframes at frame **0.**

- In the Graph Editor, select **Edit → Copy.**

- **Go to frame 10.**

- In the Graph Editor, select **Edit → Paste → ❑.**

- In the option window, set the Paste method to Merge.

- Click the **Paste Keys** button.

- Go to frame **20.**

- In the Graph Editor, select **Edit → Paste.**
  The fingers should now have a proper position throughout the animation.

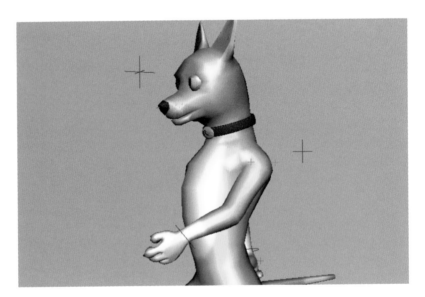

Arm positions at frame 10

7   **Add in-between keyframes**

   • Make sure to set a good position for the arms at frames **5** and **15**.

8   **The arm manipulator curves**

   • In the Graph Editor, select the arm manipulator's **Translate** and **Rotate** attributes.

   • Select all keyframes between frames **5** and **15**.

   • Select **Tangents** → **Spline**.

9   **The lookAt manipulator**

   • Go to frame **0**.

   • Set the *lookAt* **Translate Z** attribute to **5**.

   • Go to frame **10**.

   • Set the *lookAt* **Translate Z** attribute to **14**.

   • Go to frame **20**.

   • Set the *lookAt* **Translate Z** attribute to **23**.

10   **Refine the animation**

Take some time to refine the actual animation without adding any keyframes. Look at the character's walk and try to figure out what could be improved. For instance, Romeo's chest should counter-animate the pelvis Y rotation, so his back stays straight and facing right in front of the character.

When viewed from the front, a biped skeleton will compensate the hips' animation with the shoulders while the head tries to stay straight, as in the following image:

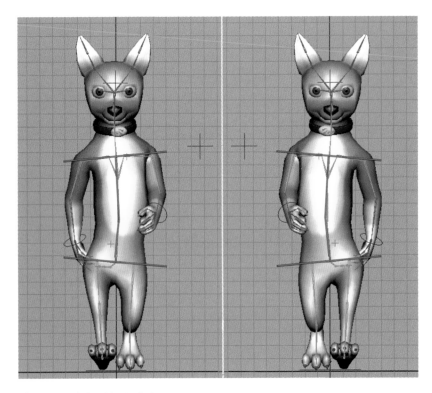

The hips' and shoulders' relation

Tip: *For a more cartoon-y look, exaggerate the hips and shoulder compensation. For a more feminine look, reduce the shoulder animation, but exaggerate the hips' motion.*

11   Secondary animation

You should now pose or animate the secondary body parts, such as the ears and tail.

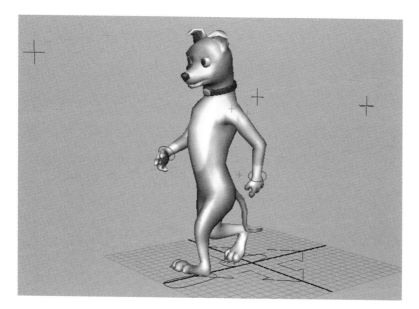

The keyframed secondary animation

12 Make sure the animation cycles

A quick trick to see if an animation cycles is to look at your character from the front view and toggle between frame 0 and 20. If nothing appears to be moving, your animation is probably a perfect cycle; if, however, the character is slightly changing position, then you need to copy the keyframes from frame 0 to frame 20 or vice versa.

13 Delete the static channels

If a curve is flat its whole length, the value of the attribute it represents does not change. This attribute is a static channel. Static channels slow Maya processing, so it is beneficial to remove them.

- Select **Edit → Delete All By Type → Static Channels**.

14 Turn off Auto Key

15 Save your work

- **Save** your scene as *14-walk_03.ma*.

Cycle the animation

So far, you have animated one full step for the walk cycle. Next, you will use the Graph Editor to complete the cycle.

1   Set your time range

- Set the **Start Time** and **Playback Start Time** to **0**.

- Set the **End Time** and **Playback End Time** to **300**.

2   View all curves in the Graph Editor

- Select **Window → Animation Editors → Graph Editor.**

- Select *romeo* from the Outliner portion of the window, then press the **a** hotkey to see all the animation curves for the character.

3   View the cycle

In order to check if the cycle works smoothly, you can display the curves' infinity and set it to cycle.

- In the Graph Editor, select **View → Infinity** and zoom out to see the dotted infinity curves.

- Select all the animation curves.

- Select **Curves → Pre Infinity → Cycle with Offset**.

- Select **Curves → Post Infinity → Cycle with Offset**.
  Cycle with Offset appends the value of the last key in the cycled curve to the value of the first key's original curve. You can now see what the curves are like when cycled.

- **Play** the animation for the entire **300** frames.

4   Adjust the curves

As the animation plays, make sure nothing moves increasingly away from the character. If an object gets out of control, you need to tweak the original animation between frame 0 and 20.

- Zoom on the curves and adjust the tangency of the keyframes on frames **0** and **20** so that the connection between the curves and cycle is smooth.

- If needed, adjust the in-between keyframe tangencies.

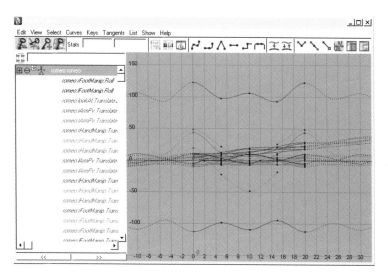

Animation cycle

- Go to frame **300**.

  At this frame, you should clearly see if there are any problems with the offset of your cycle where an object keeps moving farther and farther away.

- Fix any problems in your cycle by changing either frame **0** or **20**.

Tip: *You should not set a keyframe outside the cycle''s boundary, otherwise, you will break up the cycle.*

Bake the keyframes

Ultimately, you will use this animation inside the Trax Editor, so you will bake the keyframes of the post infinity onto the curves. The Trax Editor cannot use post infinity curves from the Graph Editor, so you will generate the actual keyframes by baking them.

1 **Select the character**

   - In the Graph Editor, select *romeo*.

2   **Bake the keyframes**

- In the Graph Editor, select **Curves** → **Bake Channel** → ❏.

- Set the following options:

  Time Range to **Start/End**;

  Start Time to **0**;

  End Time to **120**;

  Sample by **5**;

  Keep Unbaked Keys to **On**;

  Sparse Curve Bake to **On**.

- Click the **Bake** button.

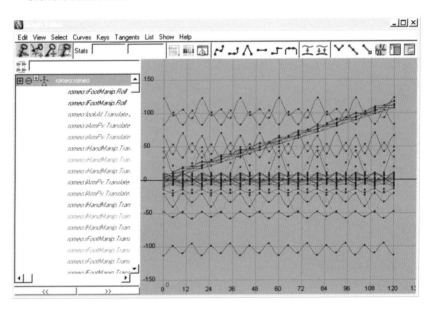

Baked curves

3   **Save your work**

- **Save** your scene as *14-walk_04.ma*.

Create a Trax clip file

The animation is finished, but since you will be working with the Trax Editor later in this book, you will now create a Trax clip file and export it for later use.

1   Open the Trax Editor window

- Select **Window** → **Animation Editors** → **Trax Editor**.

- Make sure the *romeo* character is set as current.

- In the Trax Editor, enable **List** → **Auto Load Selected Characters**.
  You should not see anything in the Trax Editor at this time.

2   Create a clip

- From the Trax Editor, select **Create** → **Animation Clip** → ❑.

- Set the following options:

   Name to *walk*;

   Leave Keys in Timeline to **Off**;

   Clip to **Put Clip in Trax Editor and Visor**;

   Time Range to **Animation Curve**;

   Include Subcharacters in Clip to **Off**;

   Create Time Warp Curve to **Off**;

   Include Hierarchy to **On**.

- Click the **Create Clip** button.

- Press **a** in the Trax Editor to frame all.
  A clip is created and placed in the Trax timeline. A corresponding clip source file called walkSource is also placed in the Visor.

  Until you export the clip, it can only be accessed through this scene file.

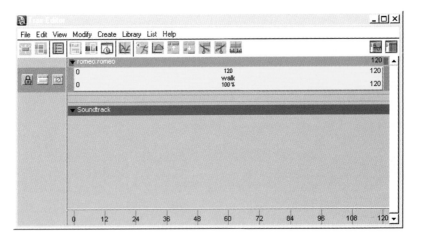

Walk clip in the Trax Editor

3   **Export the clip**

- Select **File → Visor...**

- Select the **Character Clips** tab to see the clip source.

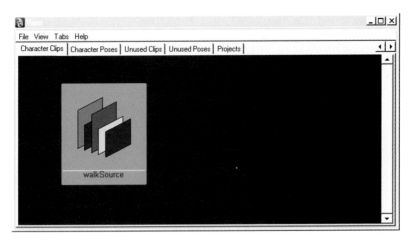

Walk source clip in Visor

- Select the *walkSource* clip.

- **RMB** on the clip and select **Export.**

  A pop-up menu will browse to the clips directory of your current project.

- **Export** the clip as *walkExport.*

  Now you can import this clip into another scene. You will do so later in this book.

- **Close** the Visor**.**

4   **Save your work**

- **Save** your scene as *14-walk_05.ma.*

Conclusion

Congratulations, you have completed a walk cycle! You learned how to reference a file, and then you animated Romeo using a character set. You produced a perfect cycle and exported a Trax clip.

In the next project you will build a scooter from NURBS, texture it, and rig it up so that Romeo can interact with it.

Image Gallery

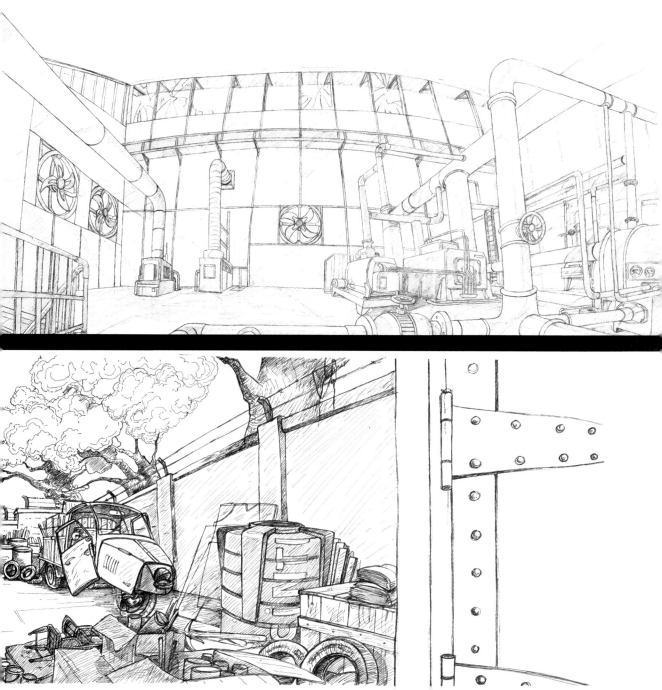

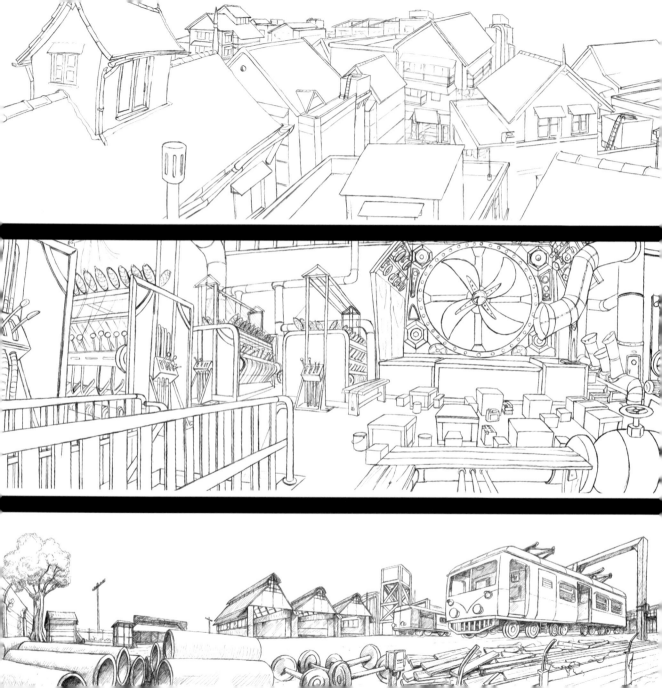

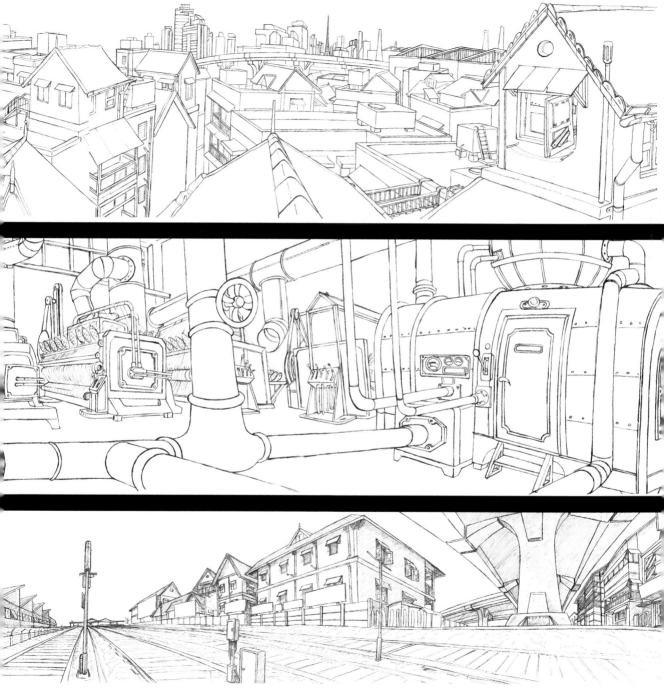

INT/COMPARTMENT DETAIL

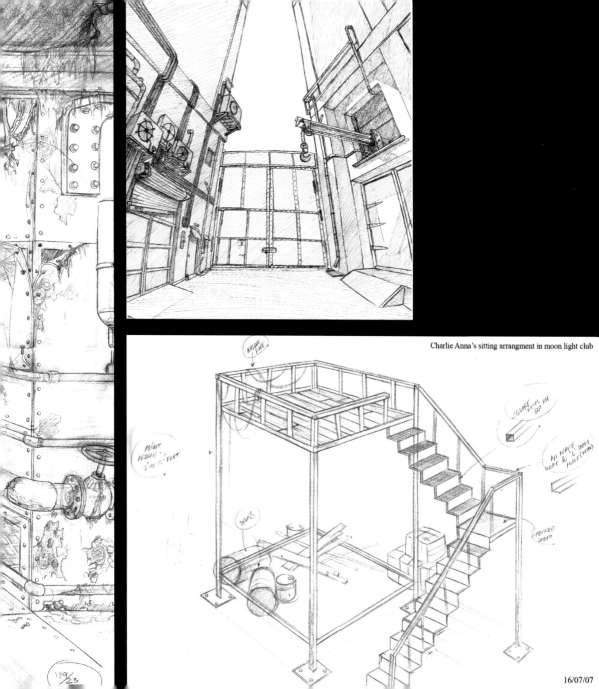

Charlie Anna's sitting arrangment in moon light club

16/07/07

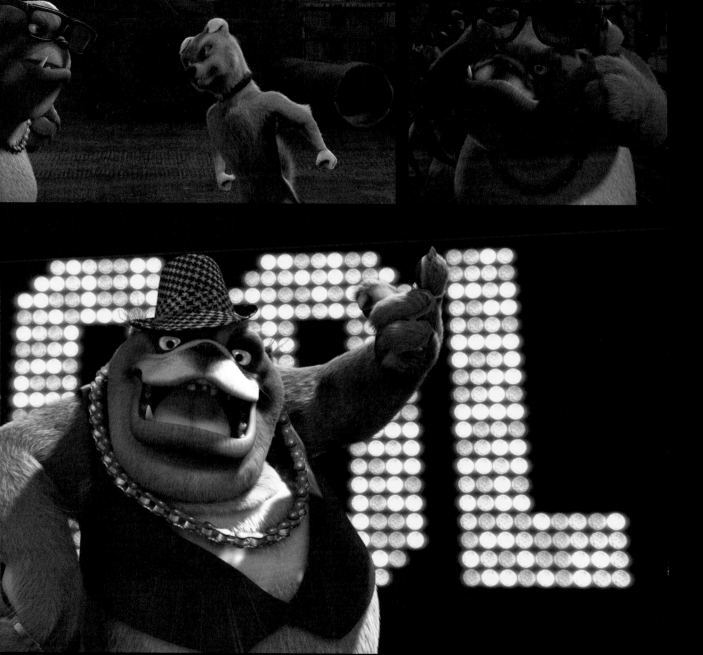

Project 03

In this project, you will model a scooter, which Romeo will interact with. You will begin by modeling, texturing, and rigging the NURBS scooter. Once that is done, you will test various deformers and use Paint Effects to add vegetation to the set built in the first project. Finally, you will add lights to your scene and experiment with the different renderers available in Autodesk® Maya® software.

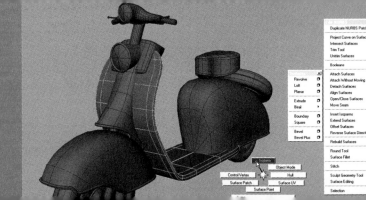

Lesson 15
NURBS Modeling

Set up your project

Since this is a new project, it is recommended to set a new current project directory.

1   **Set the project**

- If you copied the support files onto your drive, go to the **File** menu and select **Project** → **Se**
  A window opens, pointing you to the Maya projects directory.

- Click the folder named *project3* to select it.

- Click the **OK** button.

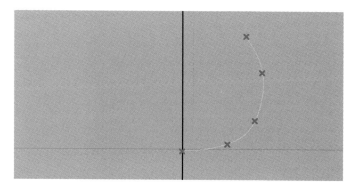

The tire profile curve

2   Duplicate and attach curves

In order to ensure that the profile curve is symmetrical, you will now duplicate the existing curve and attach the two curves together.

• With the curve selected, press **Ctrl+d** to duplicate it.

• Set the new duplicate's **Scale X** to **-1**.

• Select both curves.

• From the **Surfaces** menu set, select **Edit Curves** → **Attach Curves** → ❏.

• In the option window, set the following:

    Attach method to **Connect**;

    Multiple knots to **Remove**;

    Keep originals to **Off**.

• Click the **Attach** button to execute the tool.

You should now have a single curve, perfectly symmetrical, in the shape of a horseshoe.

Tip: *If for some reason the curves do not attach correctly, highlight the attachCurve node in the Channel Box and toggle the Reverse1 or Reverse2 attribute.*

• **Delete** the **history** for the curve.

3   Revolve

- With the profile curve selected, select **Surfaces** → **Revolve** → ❑.

- In the option window, se**t Axis preset** to **X**.

- Click the **Revolve** button to execute the tool.

- In the *Perspective* view, translate the profile curve on its **Z-axis** to set a proper diameter for the wheel.

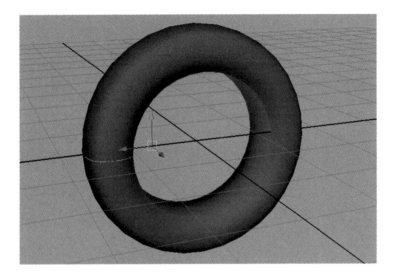

The revolved tire

- **Rename** the new surface *tire*.

4   Rim surface

You will now repeat the last steps to create a tire rim.

- Select **Create** → **EP Curve Tool** → ❑.

- In the option window, make sure **Curve** degree is set to **1 Linear**.

- Close the tool option window.

- From the *top* view, draw half a rim profile curve of your liking, making sure to snap to the **Z-axis** the last curve point.

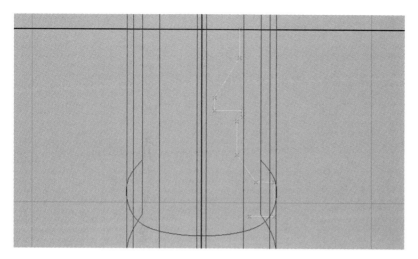

The base surface

Tip: *Hold down the **Shift** key while drawing new curve points to draw straight lines.*

- With the profile curve selected, select **Surfaces** → **Revolve**.

- In the *Perspective* view, tweak the profile curve to your liking.

- **Rename** the new surface *rim*.

- Duplicate the *rim* surface and set the **Scale X** attribute to **-1**.

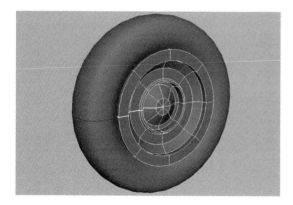

The completed tire

5   Rear wheel

- Select the tire and rim surfaces and select **Edit** → **Delete by Type** → **History.**

- Press **Ctrl+g** to group the surfaces together.

- **Rename** the new group *frontTireGrp.*

- **Duplicate** the *frontTireGrp* and **translate** it on its **Z-axis** by about **-10** units.

- **Rename** the new group *rearTireGrp.*

- From the Outliner, **delete** the profile curves.

6   Front wheel cover

You will now create the front wheel cover from a simple NURBS sphere.

- **Create** a primitive **NURBS sphere**.

- **Rotate** it on its **Z-axis** by **-90** degrees.

- Select the **Scale Tool**.

- Hold down the **Ctrl** key and **click+drag** the **Y-axis** to about **2.5** units. *Doing so will proportionally scale the X and Z axes.*

- **Tweak** the *sphere* shape to you liking.

7   Cover trim curve

- Select **Create** → **EP Curve Tool** → ❑.

- In the option window, make sure **Curve** degree is set to **3 Cubic**.

- Close the tool option window.

- From the *side* view, draw a line that will be used to trim the surface as follows:

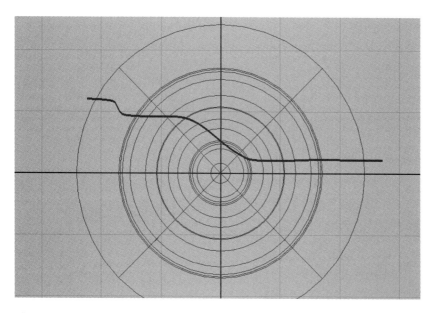

The trim curve

- Select both the *sphere* and the *curve*, then select **Edit NURBS → Project Curve on Surface.**

  A new curve is now drawn on the sphere surface.

Note: *Make sure to project the curve when the side view is active. The project curve tool uses the current view as the projection vector.*

8 **Trimming a surface**

- Select the *sphere* and select **Edit NURBS → Trim Tool.**

  The surface is now displayed in stippled wireframe, waiting for you to choose the section of the surface to keep visible.

- Click in the portion at the top of the *sphere*.

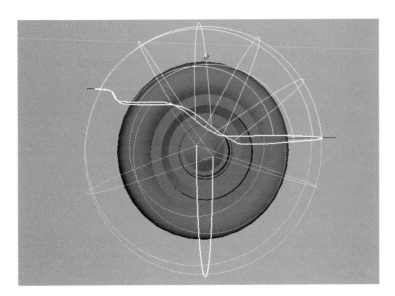

The surface section to keep

- Press **Enter** to complete the tool.

- **Rename** the trimmed surface *cover*.

- **Delete** the **history** on the *cover* and **delete** the *curve* used for the projection.

9   **About trimmed surfaces**

When trimming a surface, the NURBS surface is not actually cut; it rather has a portion of its surface hidden.

- With the *cover* selected, go in **Component** mode.
  Notice how the original surface CVs are still present.

- **Tweak** the cover to your liking.

10   **Save your work**

- **Save** your scene as *15-nurbsModeling_01*.

Front of scooter

Next, you will model the scooter's frame, steering mount, and headlight.

1   **Frame profile curves**

The scooter frame will be built by lofting a series of profile curves.

- Select **Create → NURBS Primitives → Circle.**

- In the **Channel Box**, highlight the *makeNurbCircle1* input node and set its **Sections attribute** to **12**.

- Tweak the circle to get the following floor profile shape:

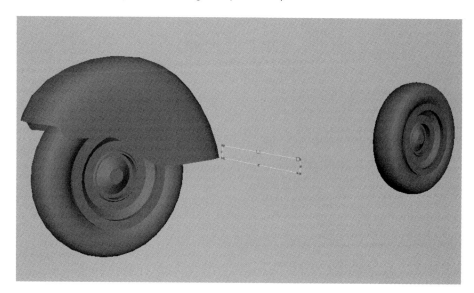

The floor profile curve

2   Establish the frame shape

•   **Duplicate**, **move**, and **rotate** the new curve several times to define the basic frame shape.

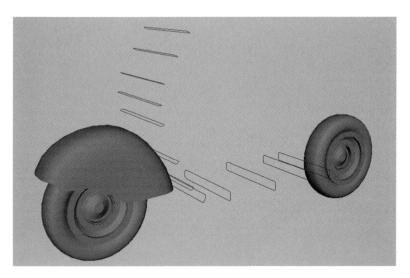

The duplicated profile curves

3   Loft

To create a surface from the profile curves, you must use the Loft Tool. This tool will generate a surface by linking the points of profile curves. It is thus very important that all the curves have the same number of CVs.

•   Select the profile curves in order from the top of the frame to the bottom rear of the frame.

Note: *It is very important to select the curves in order since this specifies how to create the lofted surface.*

•   Select **Surface** → **Loft.**
    The surface is automatically created.

- **Tweak** the curves or the resulting surface to your liking.

The basic scooter frame shape

- **Rename** the new loft surface *frame*.

- **Delete** the **history** on the *frame* and **delete** the profile curves.

4   **Steering mount**

Using a similar technique as in the previous step, you will now create the frame section that connects the steering to the front wheel.

- **Create** a **NURBS Circle**.

- Place it so it looks like the following:

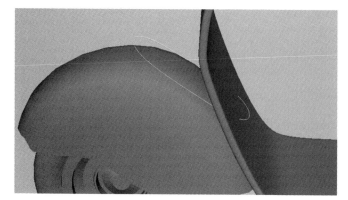

The base of the steering mount

- **Duplicate** and offset several copies of the curve up to the base of the steering.

The steering mount profile

- **Loft** the curves together.

- **Tweak** the resulting surface to your liking.

- **Rename** the new loft surface *mount*.

- **Delete** the **history** on the *mount* and **delete** the profile curves.

5   **Headlight**

You will now create the front headlight.

- **Create** a **NURBS Cylinder**, and place it so it becomes the frame of the headlight.

- **Rename** the cylinder *headLight*.

6   **Moving the seam**

Notice the NURBS seam on the headlight surface. The seam is shown as a thicker line on the wireframe while in shaded mode. When modeling with NURBS, it is important to carefully place the seam for two reasons. First, when attaching and detaching surfaces, it is better to have seams aligned on every surface. Second, when texturing, it is better to hide the seams as much as possible since this is where the opposite texture edges meet. For this piece of geometry, the seam will be placed underneath it so that it is never visible.

- In the *Perspective* view, look under the *headLight* surface.

- **RMB** on the *headLight* and select **Isoparm**.

  Isoparms are similar to edge loops on polygonal geometry. They define continuous lines going across the entire NURBS surface.

> **Note:** *When you click directly on an isoparm to select it, the isoparm gets highlighted with a continuous yellow line. If you **click+drag** an isoparm, a dotted yellow line shows you the isoparm at the cursor's position.*

- **Click** to highlight in yellow the isoparm located at the bottom of the *headLight* surface.

- Select **Edit NURBS → Move Seam.**

  The seam should now be located under the base surface.

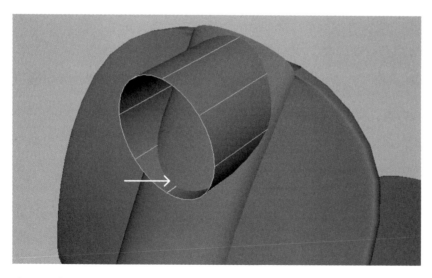

The moved seam

7   **Headlight glass**

To create the headlight glass, you will cut a NURBS sphere to fit within the headlight frame.

- **Create** a **NURBS Sphere**.

- **Rotate** it by **90** on the **Rotate X** attribute and by **-90** on the **Rotate Z** attribute.

  Doing so places the seam underneath the sphere.

- **Move** the *sphere* so it intersects with the *headLight* surface.

- **RMB** on the *sphere* and select **Isoparm**.

- **Click+drag** the vertical isoparm to define a new isoparm near intersection with the *headLight* cylinder.

- Select **Edit NURBS** → **Detach Surfaces.**

  Doing so will cut the sphere at the selected isoparm.

- **Delete** the unwanted sphere surface**.**

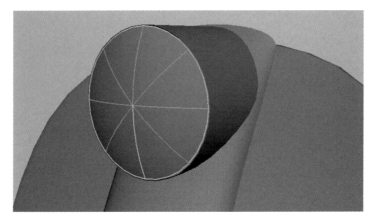

The cut sphere

- **Rename** the new surface *glass.*

8   **Decorative border**

To create a decorative border around the headlight glass, you will duplicate a surface curve and extrude it to create a tubular border.

- **RMB** on the *glass* surface and select **Isoparm.**

- **Click+drag** to select the outer circular isoparm.

- Select **Edit Curves** → **Duplicate Surface Curves.**

  Doing so will duplicate the isoparm and generate a NURBS curve out of it.

- With the new curve selected, select **Modify** → **Center Pivot.**

- Scale the border curve a little bigger.

- Create a **NURBS Circle** and scale it down to the border profile size you would like.

- Select the new profile circle, then **Shift**-select the duplicated border curve.

- **Select Surfaces** → **Extrude** → ❑**.**

- In the option window, set the following:

  Style to **Tube**
  Result Position to **At path**
  Pivot to **Component**
  Orientation to **Profile normal**

- Click the **Extrude** button.

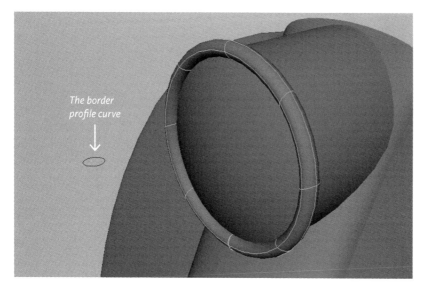

The decorative border

- **Rename** the new surface *border*.

9   **Clean up**

    • **Delete** all the construction history in the scene.

    • **Delete** all the construction curves.

10   **Save your work**

    • **Save** your scene as *15-nurbsModeling_02*.

Rear of scooter

Next, you will model the rear of the scooter, which includes the engine cover, the seat, and the spare tire.

1   **Engine cover**

    • **Create** a NURBS Sphere and change its attributes as follows:

        Rotate X to **-90**
        End Sweep to **180**
        Sections to **6**
        Spans to **6**

    • **Rename** the new surface *engineCover*.

    • **Tweak** the *engineCover* so it looks like the following:

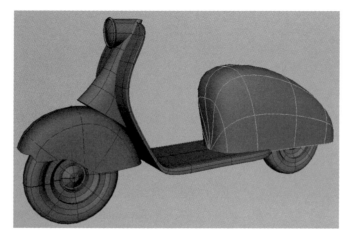

The engine cover

Seat profile curves

The seat will be created starting from lofted curves to create three surfaces. These surfaces will then be joined together and mirrored to create a full seat.

- From the *top* view, **draw** the following curve seat curve, making sure the first and last curve points are snapped to the central grid **Z-axis**.

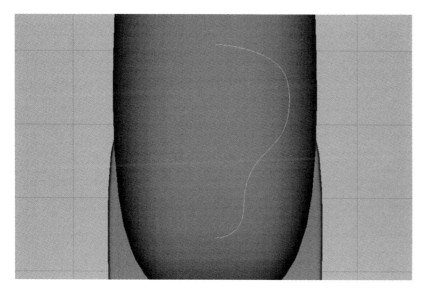

The seat curve

- Select **Modify → Center Pivot.**

- Press the **Insert** key to evoke the **Move Pivot Tool.**

- Hold down the **x** hotkey and snap the pivot to the central grid Z-axis.

- Press the **Insert** key again to exit the **Move Pivot Tool.**

- Place and tweak the seat curve to your liking.

- Duplicate the curve and translate it down to create the lower edge of the seat.

- Duplicate the bottom curve and scale it down to create the inner border of the seat.

- Duplicate the original seat curve and set its **Scale X attribute** to **0**.
  You should now have four profile curves defining half the seat.

- **Modify** the seat profile curves to your liking.

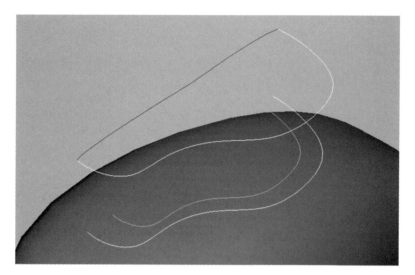

The seat profile curves

3   **Loft the seat**

- **Loft** the two side curves to create the side of the seat.

- **Loft** the two bottom curves to create the inner border of the seat.

- **Loft** the two top curves to create the top of the seat.

- Change the **Section Spans** attribute to **2** in the **Channel Box**.

  You should now have three independent seat surfaces. You will now attach them together.

- Roughly shape the seat to your liking.

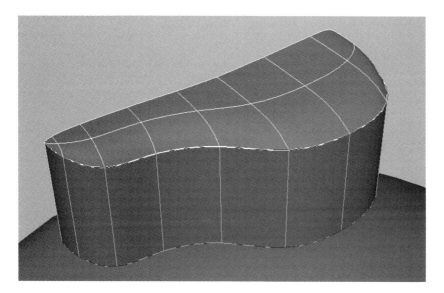

The separate seat pieces

4   **Attach surfaces**

You will now attach the three surfaces together so the entire seat is a single piece of geometry.

- Select the top and side surfaces.

- Select **Edit NURBS** → **Attach Surfaces** → ❑.

- In the option window, set the following:

    Attach method to **Blend**

    Blend bias to **0.5**

    Insert knot to **On**

    Insert parameter to **0.1**

    Keep originals to **Off**

- Click the **Attach** button.

    The two pieces should now have become a single surface.

- Select the new surface and the bottom border surface.

- Select **Edit NURBS → Attach Surfaces.**

  The entire seat is now a single surface.

- Finalize the shape of the seat to your liking.

  Because of construction history, you can still manipulate the original curves and the lofted surface will update properly.

- **Duplicate** the seat and set its **Scale X** attribute to **-1** to create a mirrored copy.

- Select **Edit NURBS → Attach Surfaces → ❑.**

- In the option window, set the **Insert knot** option to **Off**, then click the **Attach** button.

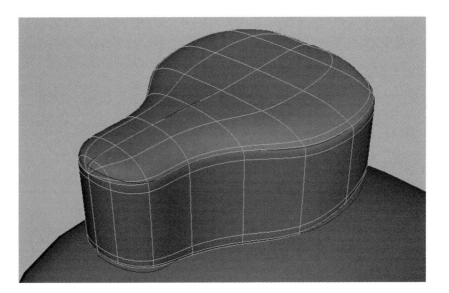

The completed seat surface

- **Rename** the surface *seat*.

- **Delete** the **history** on the *seat* and **delete** the profile curves.

5   **Save your work**

- **Save** your scene as *15-nurbsModeling_03*.

Finish the scooter

The remaining steps to create the scooter should be pretty straightforward. The following steps overview the rest of the objects to create, which will be much easier to model out of polygons.

1   **Rear of the scooter**

-   Build a seat stand out of a polygonal cube.

-   To refine the look of the seat stand, select the border edges, and then select **Edit Mesh** → **Bevel.**

-   Add a spring under the seat using **Create** → **Polygonal Primitives** → **Helix**.

-   Duplicate a tire group to have a spare tire at the back of the scooter.

-   Make the suspension frame and axel to attach the rear wheel to the scooter.

-   Create an engine cover decorative border as seen earlier in this lesson.

The final scooter rear

Front of the scooter

- From a polygonal cylinder, create the steering shaft.

- Create the front wheel suspension frame and axel.

- Create decorative border where needed.

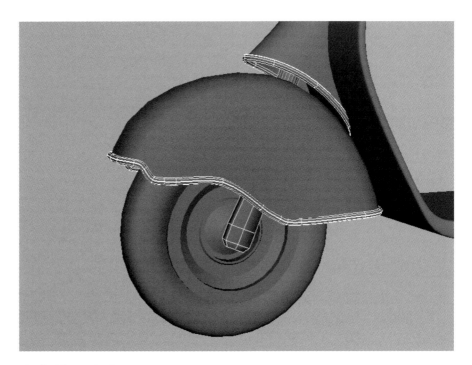

The final front wheel

Tip: *Always make sure to move the seam of any NURBS surfaces to where it is the least likely to be seen.*

3   **Create the steering**

- From a polygonal cube with Smooth Preview enabled, create the steering casing.

- Duplicate the headlight to make a second smaller headlight.

- Model a steering box.

- Create one set of handle and brake lever.

- Duplicate, group, and mirror the handle and brake lever.

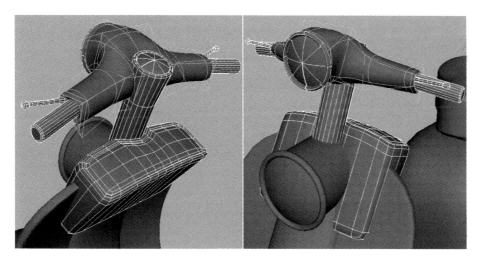

The final steering geometry

Tip: *You can model only half the surfaces, and then mirror them and attach them. Doing so will ensure that you model symmetrically.*

- Convert any Smooth Preview geometry using **Modify** → **Convert** → **Smooth Mesh Preview to Polygons.**

4 Clean up

- **Rename** each node correctly.

- Use **Modify** → **Freeze Transformations** on all nodes.

- Select **Edit** → **Delete All by Type** → **History**.
  Since you do not require any construction history, it is good to frequently clean up your scene.

- **Delete** any obsolete nodes from the Outliner.

The final scooter

Tip: *To speed up the display in the viewport, you can select NURBS surfaces and press 1 to set the NURBS display to coarse.*

5   **Save your work**

   • **Save** your scene as *15-nurbsModeling_04*.

Conclusion

In this lesson, you experimented with several NURBS curves and surface tools. NURBS modeling for simple objects can be straightforward, but modeling organic and complex shapes requires much more experience and planning.

In the next lesson, you will assign materials and textures to the scooter.

Lesson 16
NURBS Texturing

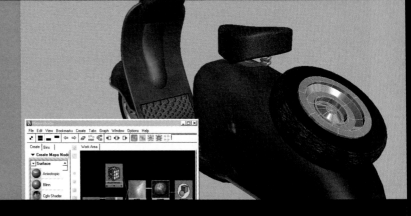

In this lesson, you will learn about NURBS texturing and other generic workflows. NURBS surfaces use a different UV system than polygons because they are always square and can automatically compute square UV mapping.

In this lesson, you will learn the following:

- About NURBS surface UVs

- How to texture using procedural textures

- How to break connections in the Attribute Editor

- How to project a file texture on a surface

- How to convert a shading network to a file texture

- How to place a texture using the Interactive Placement Tool

- About texture reference objects

- How to export and import a shading network

Texturing NURBS

Unlike polygonal geometry, UV mapping is not required on NURBS geometry since texture coordinates are determined by the U and V directions of the NURBS surface itself.

1   Scene file

- **Open** the scene from the previous lesson.

2   Checker texture

In order to view the default UV maps, you will create both a Lambert and checker texture, and then assign them to the scooter geometry.

- In the Hypershade, **create** a **Lambert** material.

- **Map** the **Color** of the new material with a **Checker** texture.

> **Tip:**   *Make sure the create option at the top of the Create Render Node window is set to* **Normal**.

- Press **6** on your keyboard to enable the **Hardware Texturing**.

- **Assign** the new material to the entire *scooter.*

- See how the texture is mapped on every object.

    On equally proportionate surfaces (as close to square as possible), the checker texture will not appear to be too stretched, but on long and thin surfaces, such as the borders, the texture will look stretched. Also, where a NURBS surface has a pole, the texture will look pinched.

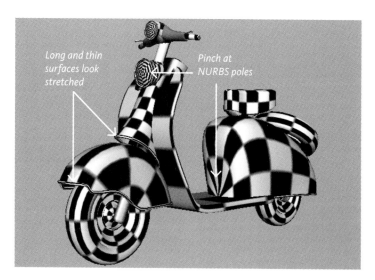

Long and thin
surfaces look
stretched

Pinch at
NURBS poles

NURBS texture mapping

Note: *Be aware that a NURBS pole is really multiple CVs at the exact same position. If you move a single CV from a pole, you will notice obvious stretching and creasing. Pole CVs should always be snapped all together.*

3   **Assign a file texture**

- Open the Attribute Editor for the Lambert material created in the previous step.

- At the top of the attribute list, set **Type** to **Blinn**.
  Doing so changes the type of the material without creating a new shader.

- Still in the Attribute Editor, **RMB** on the **Color** attribute's name and select **Break Connection**.
  This breaks the link between the shader and the checker.

- **Map** the **Color** of the material with a **File** texture.

- **Browse** to the *sourceimages* directory of the current project and choose *paint.tif* for the file texture.

The globally assigned texture

Notice how the texture is automatically mapped on the NURBS surfaces.

- **Rename** the material *paintM*.

- **Tweak** the *paintM*'s **Specular Shading** to your liking.

4   **Dirt ramp**

The scooter looks quite plain at this time, so you will improve the texturing of various pieces. You will be able to texture the scooter's engine cover quite well using procedural textures.

- In the Hypershade, select the *paintM* shader, and select **Edit** → **Duplicate** → **Shading Network**.

- Select **Graph** → **Rearrange Graph.**

- In the **Attribute Editor** for the *paintM1* shader, break the connection for the **Color** attribute.

- Map the **Color attribute** with a **Ramp** texture.

- Assign the new shade to the *engineCover* surface.

- Set the *ramp* Type to **U Ramp**.

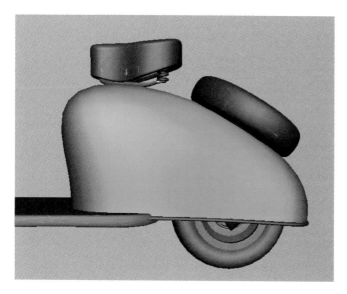

The assigned ramp texture

Note: *In this example, the red color is at the rear of the surface, but it is possible that on your surface, the NURBS UV mappings differ.*

- Select the color marker at the bottom of the ramp widget, which corresponds to the rear of the engine cover.

- Click in the color swatch of the **Selected Color** attribute.

- Set a **dark brown** color.

- Click the **Accept** button.

- Delete the color marker in the middle of the ramp widget.

- Highlight the color marker in the top of the ramp widget.

- With the Attribute Editor and the Hypergraph side by side, **MMB+drag** the *file2* paint texture onto the **Selected Color** attribute of the *ramp*.

  Doing so will map the texture in the ramp texture, allowing you to do gradients between the different ramp markers.

- Set the ramp **Noise** attribute to **0.1** and set the **Noise Freq** to **1.0**.

  These attributes change how evenly the gradient occurs along the ramp.

- **Tweak** the color markers for the ramp so the gradient between the paint texture and brown color properly defines a dirty engine cover.

The modified ramp texture

5   **Dirty metal**

Another technique for using a ramp texture to change the color of a texture is to map the texture in the Color Gain attribute rather than directly in the ramp's color markers.

- **Create** a new **Blinn** material.

- **Rename** the shader *metalM*.

- **Map** the **Color** attribute with a new **Ramp** texture.

- In the Attribute Editor for the ramp texture, scroll down to the **Color Balance** section.

- **Map** the **Color Gain** attribute with a **Noise** texture.

  Notice how the entire ramp texture is now affected by the noise texture. The colors mapped into the Color Gain of a texture act as multipliers to the existing colors.

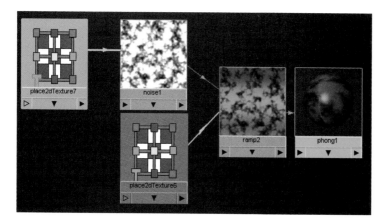

Noise texture assigned to the color gain

- **Assign** the *metalM* shader to the *rim* surfaces.

- Set the ramp texture's **Type** to **U Ramp**.

- **Tweak** the *ramp* texture so it looks as follows:

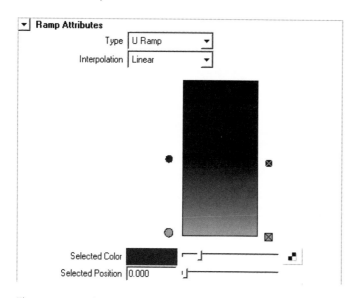

The new ramp colors

- **Tweak** the *noise* texture to your liking.

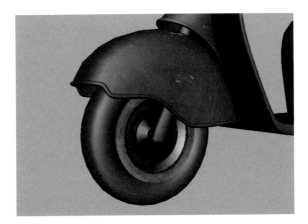

The new ramp color

6   **Tire material**

- **Create** a **Lambert** material.

- **Assign** the new shader to the *tires*.

- **Map** the **Color** attribute with a **File** texture, and set the **Image Name** to *thread.tif*.

The tire thread texture

7   **Save your work**

- **Save** your file as *16-nurbsTexturing_01.ma*.

Projections

You will now create a shading network to project a light glass texture onto the headlights of the scooter.

1   Normal texture mapping

You will first look at how a texture is applied onto a NURBS headlight surface by default.

- **Create** a new **Phong** material.

- **Assign** the new material to the main headlight surface.

- **Map** the **Color** attribute with a file texture.

- **Browse** to the texture file called *headlight.tif*.
  Notice how the texture is wrapped around the NURBS pole.

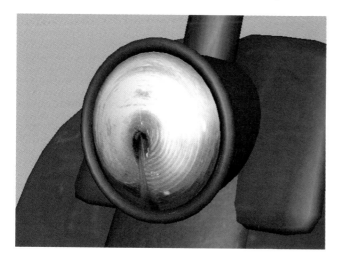

The normal texture mapping

2   Create a projection

You will now map the headlight surface. Since the texture must be applied in a special manner, you will use a projected texture.

- In the Hypershade, delete the previously created file texture.

- Click the **Map** button for the **Color** attribute of the *Phong* material from the previous step.

- At the top of the Create Render Node window, select the **As projection** option, then click the **File** texture button.

  Notice in the Hypershade that special projection nodes have been inserted between the shader and the file texture. The projection of the texture is determined by the 3D texture placement node located at the origin.

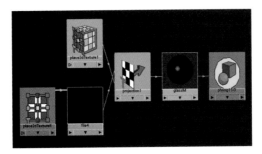

The projection and its 3D placement node

- **Browse** to the texture file called *headlight.tif*.

3 **Place the projection**

- Select the place3dTexture node in the Hypershade.

- In the *Perspective* view, **translate** and **scale** the projection node to the headlight surface.

- Alternatively, with the *place3dTexture* node selected, open the Attribute Editor and click the **Fit to Group BBox** button.

  Doing so will automatically fit the placement node to the bounding box of the assigned surface, in this case the headlight.

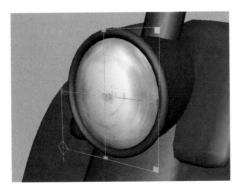

The 3D projection node and its manipulator

Convert to texture

It is wise to convert projected textures, which can be quite heavy to compute, and convert the shading network to a file texture. The following shows the basic workflow to do so.

1   Convert to shading network

You can convert a complex shading network into a single texture file through the Hypershade.

- Select the shader from the previous exercise and **Shift-select** its corresponding surface.

- From the Hypershade, select **Edit → Convert to File Texture (Maya Software) → ❑.**

- In the option window, set the following:

    UV Range to **Entire Range**;

    X Resolution to **512**;

    Y Resolution to **512**;

    Image Format to **Tiff (.tif)**.

- Click the **Convert and Close** button.

    The projected texture will be converted to a new file texture and automatically assign to the surface. The new texture is saved in the current project's sourceimages folder.

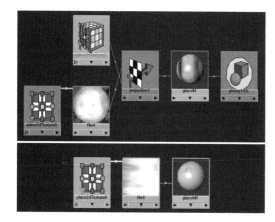

Before and after the conversion

Tip: *When converting textures assigned to polygonal objects, you must make sure that the UVs of the surface can accommodate a single texture to cover all of its geometry. If some UVs overlap, the texture might not reflect exactly what you were expecting.*

2   Delete unused Render nodes

Since the original shading network for the surface is no longer used, you can automatically delete unused Rendering nodes.

• In the Hypershade, select **Edit** → **Delete Unused Nodes.**

3   Edit the converted texture

If required, you can edit the converted texture found in the *sourceimages* folder of the current project to fix any problems with the projections and then reload your file texture to see your changes.

• **Assign** the new shader to the smaller headlight.

Interactive Placement Tool

The Interactive Placement Tool is designed to ease the placement of textures onto NURBS surfaces. This tool allows you to interactively set the different placement values of a 2D texture using an all-in-one manipulator.

1   Floor material

• Select the *frame* surface for which you will add a floor texture.

• In the Hypershade, select **Graph** → **Graph Materials on Selected Objects.**

• Select the shader and select **Edit** → **Duplicate** → **Shading Network.**

• Assign the new shader to the *frame*.
  You are duplicating the shading network on the surface because other surfaces with the same shader will also be affected by the upcoming steps.

2   Move seam

This particular example requires you to move the seam of the object to another location since the interactive placement tool will not work when trying to overlap a seam.

• **RMB** on the *frame* surface and select **Isoparm**.

• Select the isoparm underneath the surface.

• Select **Edit NURBS** → **Move Seam.**

3   **Interactive Placement Tool**

- **Break** the connection to the *paint* file texture.

- **Create** a new **File** texture with the **Normal** creation option rather than projection.

- **Browse** to the file texture called *floor.tif.*

- Select the *place2dTexture* node of the floor file texture.

- In the Attribute Editor, with the file texture's *place2dTexture* tab selected, click the **Interactive Placement** button.

  Doing so will access the **NURBS Texture Placement Tool**. *This tool displays a red manipulator on the NURBS geometry, which allows you to interactively place the texture in the viewport.*

Note: *You can also access the* **NURBS Texture Placement Tool** *via the* **Texturing** *menu when a NURBS surface is selected.*

- **MMB+drag** the manipulator's red dots to change the placement of the texture.

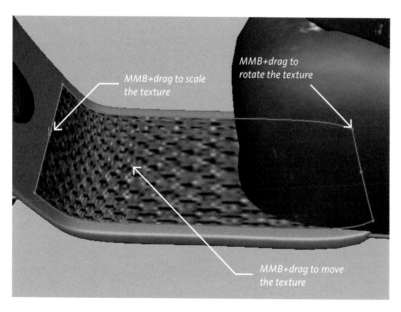

The interactive placement manipulator

Note: *Notice the value of the place2dTexture node updates as you drag the manipulator. You can also set the place2dTexture values manually.*

Tip: *This technique is perfect for placing a logo or image at a specific location on a NURBS surface.*

4 **Tweak the texture**

- To better see the texture in the viewport, select the shader, and set **Texture resolution** to **Highest** under the **Hardware Texturing** section.

- To change the default gray color of the region outside the texture, select the texture, and **map** the **Default Color** under the **Color Balance** section to the original *paint* texture.

Paint texture mapped in the default color

Texture reference objects

If while texturing you used projected textures or 3D textures, the results might be good on static geometry, but there can be unintended results when the surface is moving or deforming. This is because the object is moving without the 3D Placement node, which causes a texture sliding problem. To correct this, you can set up a nondeformed reference object to lock the texture on the geometry.

1   **Seat texture**

   • **Create** a B*linn* material and **assign** it to the *seat*.

   • **Map** the **Color** attribute with a **Leather** texture from the **3D Textures** section.

> **Note:** *You will need to render the scene in order to see the exact effect of procedural textures on the surfaces. Displayed in the viewport is only an approximation of the actual rendered effect.*

   • **Tweak** the 3D texture to your liking so it looks like black leather.

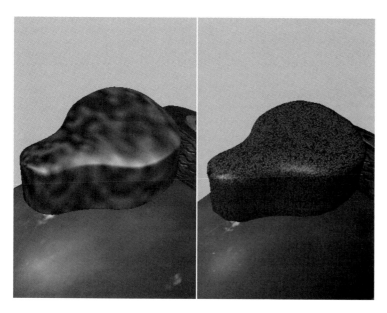

Viewport vs. rendered procedural texture

2 Texture reference object

Using texture reference objects is best when an object is deforming. Otherwise, it is easier to simply parent the projection node to the model itself, or convert the 3D texture to a file texture.

- Select the *seat*, which has projected texture assigned to it.

- Under the **Rendering** menu set, select **Texturing** → **Create Texture Reference Object**.
  An unselectable and unrenderable object duplicate will appear as wireframe in the viewport. This object is only selectable through the Outliner or the Hypergraph.

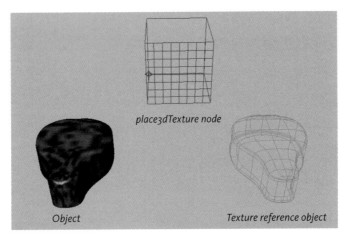

place3dTexture node

Object   *Texture reference object*

The object, its texture reference object, and place3dTexture

- **Group** the *place3dTexture* and *seat_reference* objects from the Outliner.

- **Rename** the group *txtRefGrp* and **hide** it.

Note: *By converting a shading network to a texture, you do not require a texture reference object.*

Finish texturing the scooter

You can now spend some time shading and creating textures for the remaining pieces of the scooter's geometry. Once you are satisfied with the results, you will make sure your scene is cleared of obsolete shading nodes.

1 **Texture the rest of the scooter**

The final scooter

2 **Optimize scene size**

- **Delete** all the **history** in the scene.

- Select **File → Optimize Scene Size**.

  Doing so will remove any unused nodes in your scene.

3 **Save your work**

- **Save** your file as *16-nurbsTexturing_02.ma*.

Import export of a shading network

When you need to texture lots of objects, it might be a good idea to build a library of shaders for generic materials such as metals, woods, rocks, and so forth. The following shows you how to export a material and import it when required without needing to re-create it from scratch.

1   **Exporting shading networks**

If you want to export one or more of your shading networks, do the following:

- Open the Hypershade and select the shader of your shading network. If you select more than one shader, they will all get exported at the same time in the same file.

- Still in the Hypershade, select **File** → **Export Selected Network.**

- Choose a file name that reflects the selected shaders and click the **Export** button.
  The shaders are exported by themselves in an Autodesk® Maya® software file located in the renderData/shaders of the current project.

2   **Import shading networks**

If you want to import a shader, do the following:

- From the Hypershade, select **File** → **Import...**

- In the browse window, select the file named *chrome.ma* from the folder *renderData\shaders* from the current project's *support_files*.

- Click the **Import** button.
  The shaders from this scene file are now in your scene.

3   **Assign the shaders**

- Under the **Materials** tab in the Hypershade, **MMB+drag** the *chromeM* shader onto a surface in your scene.
  Doing so assigns the shader to the object.

Conclusion

You now have experience texturing NURBS surfaces and have learned how to use procedural textures. You should now be comfortable creating textures from scratch using Maya nodes and converting networks to file textures.

In the next lesson, you will set up the scooter for animation.

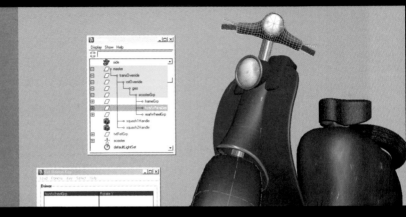

Lesson 17
Rigging

In this lesson, you will rig the scooter for animation. This rig will be slightly different than the Romeo character since the geometry is mechanical and, hence, you can have some automation built into it. You will first organize the scooter's hierarchy. Once that is done, you will set up driven keys that will automate some movements, such as the wheels turning automatically when moving it forward.

In this lesson, you will learn the following:

- How to rename multiple objects all at once

- How to add animation overrides in hierarchies

- How to set up reactive driven keys

- How to use the Distance Tool

- How to change the local rotation axis of objects

- How to add nonlinear deformers

Hierarchy

The first thing to do before rigging a model is to make sure that all of its nodes are in a good hierarchy where everything is easy to find and well named.

1   **Scene file**

- **Open** your scene from the last lesson.

    OR

- **Open** the scene file named *16-nurbsTexturing_02.ma* from the support files.

2   **Rename multiple objects**

When you create content, you should be renaming nodes fairly frequently. Since you usually need to rename all the nodes one by one, you will learn a way to rename several nodes simultaneously.

- Select all the objects that should have similar names, such as the tires.

- In the top-right corner of the interface, set the **Rename** option in the input field as follows:

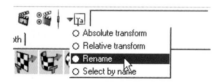

Rename option

- Enter *tire* in the input field and press **Enter**.

    Each and every selected object will be assigned a unique name starting with the defined string, followed by a unique number.

  Note: *The order of selection defines the order of the numbers appended to each name.*

- Take some time to appropriately **rename** every node in the scene.

3   **Hierarchy**

- **Group** basic, related objects together, such as *tireGrp*, *frontWheelGrp*, *rearWheelGrp*, *frameGrp,* and *scooterGrp*, leaving the *txtRefGrp* on its own.

  The idea is to define a hierarchy in which you could animate each group of objects individually, without modifying the hierarchy.

- **Group** everything together into a new group called *geo* as follows:

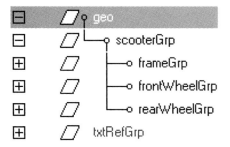

The grouped hierarchy

Tip: *Leave the txtRefGrp on its own since it is not intended to be part of the animation rig.*

- **Move** the *geo* group up on its Y-axis to place the scooter above the grid plane.

- **Move** the *geo* group forward on its Z-axis to place the scooter's center of mass above the origin.

4   **Pivots**

- Make sure every group's pivot is properly placed.

  To do this, make sure you look at every group and determine how it could be moving when animated. Once you know where a group should be moving from, place its pivot to that location. Doing so will allow you to animate any part of the scooter easily.

Note: *Unlike skinned characters, mechanical geometry and groups can be directly animated without a skeleton structure controlling them.*

5   Overrides

When animating any object as a whole, such as the scooter, it is important to have animation overrides on the top group. These overrides can then be used individually to isolate certain animation. For instance, the top group node will later be animated from path animation. Since this node will be controlled by its connection, you can then use lower overrides to add some custom animation such as rotations or translations.

- Select the *geo* group.

- Press **Ctrl+g** to group the hierarchy **three times**.

- **Rename** the top group *master*.

- **Rename** the group below it *transOverride*.

- **Rename** the group below *transOverride rotOverride*.

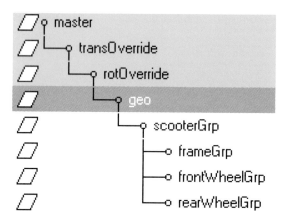

The overrides

6   Save your work

- **Save** your scene as *17-rig_01.ma*.

Automation

Sometimes, when creating rigs, you need to add some automation to ease the work of the animator. In this exercise, you will automate the wheel rotations using Set Driven Keys.

Automation is usually considered a good thing from the point of view of the setup artist, but can also introduce limitations for the animator. For instance, if a wheel movement is automated, the animator does not have the ability to spin the wheel or break it manually. Adding animation overrides, however, will allow the animator to gain control over the automation.

Note: *For simplicity reasons, this setup will only work when the scooter is rotated between 0 and 90 degrees on its Y-axis and translated forward. Having the wheels work in all possible directions would require a more complex exercise.*

1   **Wheel overrides**

- Select one of the *tireGrp*.

- Select **Edit → Group → ❑**.

- In the options, set **Group pivot** to **Center**.

- **Press the Group button.**
  The wheel is now grouped and the new group's pivot is centered with the wheel geometry.

- Make sure the group's pivot is centered on the wheel axel.

- **Rename** the new group appropriately with the *auto* prefix to clearly identify this group as being an automated node.

- **Repeat** for the other tire.

Tip: *Using animation overrides, such as groups, is an inexpensive way to give more control to the artist. Consider adding animation overrides even where it is not required; you will succeed in giving even more control over the rig.*

2   **Set Driven Keys**

You will now animate the wheels to rotate when the scooter moves forward.

- Select **Animate** → **Set Driven Key** → **Set...**

- Select the *master* node, and then click the **Load Driver** button.

- Highlight the *master* node and its **translateZ** attribute.

- Select the two tire *auto* groups, and then click the **Load Driven** button.

- Highlight all four wheel nodes and their **rotateX** attributes.

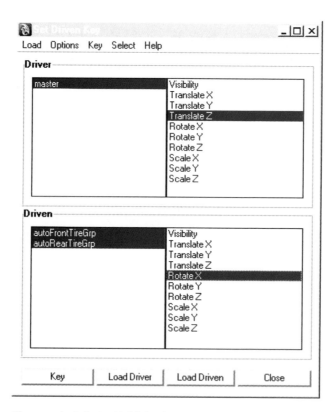

The correct attributes highlighted

- Click the **Key** button in the Set Driven Key window.
  This sets the initial keyframe in the default position.

3   **Mathematics**

Trial and error is helpful for determining the proper rotation on the wheels, but you can also use a simple formula to get the proper values.

The following is the formula for finding the distance when rotating a wheel by 360 degrees:

`pi * diameter = distance`

You will now use the Distance Tool to get the diameter of a wheel.

- Select **Create** → **Measure Tools** → **Distance Tool**.

  The Distance Tool shows in the viewport the distance between two points. Those two points are defined by locators.

- From the *side* view, click the center of a wheel and then click its perimeter to create the Distance nodes.

  You now have the radius of the wheel. You need to double that value to get the diameter of the wheel.

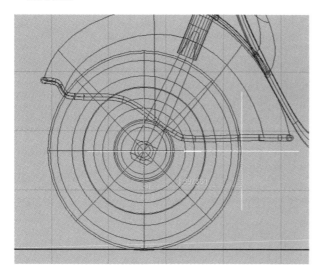

The Distance Tool

- If you solve the above formula with the returned value, you get:

  `3.14 * (1.69 * 2) = 10.61`

- **Note** down this value.

- **Delete** the *Distance* node along with its two locators from the Outliner.

4   **Set keys**

- In the Set Driven Key window, select the *master* node.

- **Move** the *master* on its **Z-axis** by **10.61** units.

- From the Set Driven Key window, select the two tire groups.

- **Rotate** them on their **X-axes** by **360 degrees**.

- Click the **Key** button.

5   **Animation tangent**

Since you have set the default tangent type to be flat in the animation preferences, the animation curves need to be changed.

- Select the two tire groups.

- Open the Graph Editor.

- Select all the animation curves that are visible.

- Select **Tangents → Spline.**

- **Translate** the *master* on its **Z-axis** to test the setup.
  The wheel should rotate correctly within the translation keys set above.

6   **Infinity**

The current driven animation curves are finite, and that is why when you translate the scooter, at some point, the wheels stop turning. To correct this, you need to change the infinity of the animation curve.

- Select all four wheel groups.

- Select all the animation curves that are visible in the Graph Editor.

- Select **Curves → Pre Infinity → Linear.**

- Select **Curves → Post Infinity → Linear.**

- To make sure the curves are set correctly, select **View → Infinity.**

- **Translate** the *master* on its **Z-axis** to test the setup.
  The wheels should no longer stop when you move the master far away from the origin.

7   **More driven keys**

The tires are now rotating correctly when you move the master on its Z-axis, but odds are that the scooter will not only move in a straight line. For instance, if you rotate the master on its Y-axis and translate it, the wheels will now slide or not rotate at all. The following will correct this behavior.

- Make sure to place the *master* back at the origin.

- Set its **rotateY** to **90 degrees**.

  Now if you translate the scooter forward, the wheels will not turn at all. As a result, you need to set new driven keys for the **translateX** *attribute.*

- Still in the Set Driven Key window, highlight **translateX** as the driving attribute.

- Click the **Key** button to set the initial keyframe.

- **Move** the *master* on its **X-axis** by **10.61** units.

- Select all four wheel groups.

- **Rotate** them on their **X-axes** by **360 degrees**.

- Click the **Key** button.

- Set the tangents of the new animation curves to **Spline**.

- Set the **infinity** of the new animation curves to **linear**.

- Close the Set Driven Key window.

8   **Test the driven keys**

The automation you have done so far now allows you to translate the scooter forward in any direction with its wheels moving correctly.

- **Double-click** the **Move Tool** in the toolbox.

- Set **Move** to **Object**.

- **Rotate** the scooter *master* and test the wheels by **translating** the scooter on the manipulator **Z-axis**.

- Place the *master* back at the origin.

9 Steering movements

All that is left to get a fully functional scooter rig is to be able to properly move the front wheel steering group. To do so, you will have to offset the rotation pivot so it is in the same angle as the steering axel.

- Select the *frontWheelGrp* and the press **e** to evoke the Rotate Tool.

- Try to **rotate** the group on its **Y-axis**.
  The local rotation axis of the steering group should be slightly offset on its X-axis in order to provide the proper animation.

- Go in **Component** mode and enable the **Local Rotation Axes** mask.

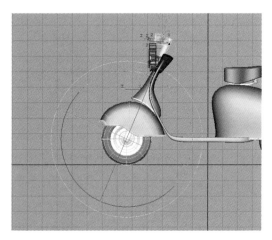

The steering group's local rotation axis

- Go back to **Object** mode and open the Attribute Editor for the steering group.

- Set the **Rotate Order** to start with the same axis you set to point in the direction of the steering axel. If you made the **Y-axis** point in the direction of the steering axel, select either **YXZ** or **YZX**.
  Doing so ensures that only the appropriate rotation axis changes when you rotate the steering group.

- **Test** the rotation of the *frontTireGrp* to see if the tire behaves as expected.

10 Save your work

- **Save** your work as *17-rig_02.ma*.

Non-linear deformers

The tires of the scooter will require some deformation when the scooter has some weight on it. This is a perfect opportunity to use a non-linear deformer. Non-linear deformers will deform objects according to a mathematical formula, such as bend, sine, wave, squash, and so on.

In this exercise, you will use a squash deformer.

1   **Assign a squash deformer**

- Select the front *tire*.

- Select **Create Deformers** → **Nonlinear** → **Squash**.
   The squash deformer is created and displayed as a vertical straight line.

- In the Channel Box, highlight the *squash1* node.

- Set **High Bound** to **0**.
   Doing so tells the deformer to only deform the lower part of the affected surface.

- **Scale** the *squash1Handle* so it fits only the lower part of the tire surface.

- In the Channel Box, set **Factor** to **-5** and **Expand** to **0.25**.
   The deformer does not deform as intended just yet.

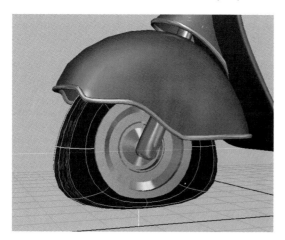

The effect of the squash deformer

- Set **Factor** to **0** to reset the deformation.

2   **Rear tire deformer**

- **Repeat** the last step to create the same squash deformer, but for the rear tire surface.

3   **Automation**

You really need this deformation to happen when moving the scooter down because of the weight of its passenger. In order to automate this, you will set driven keys on the *transOverride* group node.

- **Parent** the two *squashHandles* to the *transOverride* group node.

- Select **Animate → Set Driven Key → Set…**

- Select the *transOverride group* node, and then click the **Load Driver** button.

- Highlight the *transOverride* node and its **translateY** attribute.

- Select the two *squashHandle* nodes, and then highlight the *squash* input node in the Channel Box.

- Click the **Load Driven** button.

- Highlight the two squash nodes and their **Factor** attributes.

- Click the **Key** button.

- **Translate** down the *transOverride* group node on its **Y-axis** until the rims almost touch the grid plane.

- Set the **Factor** attribute of the *squash* nodes to **-5**.

- Click the **Key** button.

- In the Graph Editor with the squash nodes selected, change the tangent of the **-5** keyframes to be **linear**.

  Since the squash factor of the deformers works exponentially, you need the animation curve to start slowly and gradually speed up as the transOverride node moves down.

Note: *You can also set a driven key so the squash deformers stretch the tire when the transOverride node moves above the ground. Doing so will give a nice cartoon-y animation.*

- Close the Set Driven Key and Graph Editor windows.

4   **Lock and hide attributes**

- Make sure to **lock and hide** attributes that are not required to be changed by the animator.

Note: *Deleting the history on the scooter or its pieces would delete the squash deformer effect. Make sure to keep the history on the affected surfaces.*

5   **Visibility layer**

- **Create** a **new layer** and **rename** it *setupLayer*.

- Select the *master* node and add it to the *setupLayer*.

6   **Character set**

- Select the *master* node and select **Character** → **Create Character Set** → ❏.

- Select the **Name** to *scooter*.

- Click the **Create Character Set** button.

7   **Save your work**

- **Save** your scene as *17-rig_03.ma*.

Conclusion

The scooter is now ready to be animated. You have created some automation, but you also made sure that the animator could override that animation by placing the automation on groups. As well, you used a nonlinear deformer, which in this case was much easier to use than any other setup.

In the next lesson, you will learn how to fill your environment with one of the most powerful Autodesk® Maya® tools—Paint Effects.

Lesson 18
Paint Effects

For this next stage, you will generate lots of content for Romeo's environment. The Paint Effects Tool gives you access to preset brushes ranging from grasses to grass clumps and buildings to lightning bolts, which can be customized for your own scenarios.

In this lesson, you will use several Paint Effects brushes and how to test render your scene.

In this lesson, you will learn the following:

- How to paint on canvas

- How to paint on geometry

- How to optimize the way Paint Effects are displayed in the viewport

- How to share, blend, and customize brushes

- How to save brush presets

- How to auto-paint a surface

Paint on canvas

In order to experiment with various Paint Effects brushes, you will create a nature scene with grass clumps, flowers, and grass. First, you will test the tool on a canvas.

1   Open a new scene

2   Paint in the Paint Effects window

- Press **8** on your keyboard to display the Maya Paint Effects Canvas window.

- Select **Paint** → **Paint Canvas**.
  This will set the canvas to a 2D paint mode.

- In the Paint Effects window, select **Brush** → **Get Brush...**
  The Visor will open, letting you browse through the various template Paint Effects brushes.

- Open any brush folder, select a brush and paint on the canvas.
  You can now experiment with different brushes.

- Select **Canvas** → **Clear**.

3   Change the background color

- Select **Canvas** → **Clear** → ❏.

- Set the **Clear Color** to **dark blue**, then press the **Clear** button.

 Note: *You can also import an image as a starting point by selecting* **Canvas** → **Open Image**.

4   Paint your image

- In the Visor window, open the *clouds* folder.

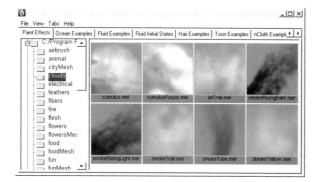

The Visor

- Select the *cumulus.mel* brush and paint some clouds onto your image.

Note: *Hold down* **b** *and* **LMB+drag** *to change the size of the current brush.*

- Continue painting elements onto your image using the different preset brushes.

- If you make a mistake, you can **undo** the last brush stroke by selecting **Canvas** → **Canvas Undo**.

Test image

5   **Save the image**

- When you are finished with your image, you can save it by selecting **Canvas** → **Save As** → ❑.

- In the Option window, you can decide whether or not you want to use the **Save Alpha** option.

- Click **Save Image** and name your image.

    If you want, you can then use this image as an image plane or as a texture.

> **Note:** *To set a saved image as an image plane, simply select the camera for which you would like to add a background image, then from the camera panel select **View** → **Image Plane** → **Import Image**.*

- Return to a single *Perspective* layout by clicking its icon in the toolbox.

Paint Effects strokes

You will now learn how to paint strokes on geometry and how strokes can share the same brush. As well, you will learn how to scale Paint Effects.

The following scenery will take place in the alley built in the first project.

1   **Scene file**

- **Open** the scene *04-animation_02.ma* from the first project's *scenes* directory.

2   **Delete the animation**

- Go to frame **1**, then select **Edit** → **Delete All by Type** → **Channels**.
    Doing so will delete the animation in the entire scene.

3   **Prepare the set**

- Select the *environmentGroup* and make sure its pivot is located at the origin.

- Set the *environmentGroup* **scale** to **5** on all axes.
    Doing so will give you room to eventually bring in Romeo and the scooter.

- In the Perspective view, select **View** → **Camera Attribute Editor**.

- Set the **Near Clip Plane** to **1.0** and the **Far Clip Plane** to **2000**.

  The clipping planes define the depth range for which the scene is visible. The near clipping plane defines how close an object can get to the camera, and the far clipping plane defines how far an object can be before getting clipped by the view.

- Set the display layers in the scene to be not referenced.

4   **Paint flowers**

- Press **F6** to select the **Rendering** menu set.

- With the *ground* selected, select **Paint Effects** → **Make Paintable**.

  Doing so will allow you to paint directly on the surface.

- Select **Paint Effects** → **Get Brush**...

- In the Visor, select the **Grasses** directory, then click the **grassClump.mel** brush preset.

  Clicking on a brush preset in the Visor automatically accesses the Paint Effects Tool.

- Hold down **b** and **click+drag** to resize the brush.

- **Paint** a single stroke on the *ground* to create a grass clump.

A Paint Effects stroke in the viewport

5   Optimized display

When working with Paint Effects, you can clutter your scene and computer with a lot of objects in no time. The following will change the display of a stroke in the viewport.

- Select the stroke from the Outliner.

- In the **Shapes** section of the Channel Box, set **Draw As Mesh** to **Off**.

  Rather than displaying meshes when painting the Paint Effects, only reference lines will be used. This drastically reduces the display refresh of the viewport, but does not affect the scene rendering.

- Select **Paint Effects → Paint Effects Tool → ❑**.

- In the option window, turn **Off** the **Draw as Mesh** option.

- **Paint** some more grass clumps around the alley.

More grass clumps

Tip: *To reduce the viewport refresh rate even more, you can also set the stroke's Display Percent to a lower value. This attribute specifies how many of the Paint Effects you want to see interactively in the viewport.*

6   Share one brush

At the moment, every stroke that you have drawn uses a different brush, letting you customize each one individually. To modify all the grass clumps simultaneously, you can set up the strokes so they share the same brush.

- Open the Outliner.

   You should see all the different strokes you have drawn on the ground.

- Select all the *strokeGrassClump* strokes.

- Select **Paint Effects → Share One Brush**.

   Now all the strokes use the same brush. Modifying this brush will change all the grass clumps at the same time.

7   Scale the grass clumps

- Press **Ctrl+a** to open the Attribute Editor for any of the selected strokes.

- Select the *grassClump* tab.

   This is the brush shared among all the strokes.

- Set the **Global Scale** attribute to your liking.

8   Test render the scene

- Select **Render → Render Current Frame**.

The rendered Paint Effects

Tip: *You might have to add some lights into your scene in order to properly see the alley and paint effects.*

9   Save your work

- **Save** your scene as *18-paintEffects_01.ma*.

Customize brushes

In this exercise, you will blend brushes together and customize your own brushes. You will also save your custom brush presets on your shelf for later use.

1   Flower bucket

- Build a simple polygonal flower bucket to place under a window in the alley.

- **Rename** the object to *flowerBucket*.

- Select **Paint Effects → Make Paintable.**

- **Parent** the *flowerBucket* to its respective *buildingGroup*.

2   Blending brushes

- Select **Paint Effects → Get Brush...**

- In the Visor, select the **flowers** directory, then click on the **lillyRed.mel** brush preset.

- Still in the Visor, **RMB** on the **violet.mel** brush preset.
  This will display a menu letting you blend the current brush with the new one.

- Select **Blend Brush 50%**.
  This will blend the second brush with the first brush, giving the stroke a little bit of profile from both brushes.

- **RMB** again on the **violet.mel** brush preset and select **Blend Shading 5%**.
  This will blend the shading of the two brushes together.

3   **Paint the new brush**

- Hold down **b** and **click+drag** to resize the brush.

- **Paint** one stroke of the new brush to fill the flower bucket.

- In the Channel **Box**, set the **Display Percent** attribute of the Paint Effects stroke to **50**.

- Set the **Global Scale** of the Paint Effects brush as desired.

The painted flowers

4   **Customizing brushes**

- In the Attribute Editor, select the *violet1* tab.

  Doing so will display all the Paint Effects attributes for the current brush and the current stroke.

- Try changing some of the values to see their affect on the current stroke. The following are some examples:

  Brush Profile → Brush Width

  Tubes → Creation → Tubes Per Step

  Tubes → Creation → Segments

  Tubes → Creation → Length Min

  Tubes → Creation → Length Max

  Tubes → Growth → Flowers → Petals In Flower

  Tubes → Growth → Flowers → Petals Color

  Behavior → Forces → Gravity

 Tip: *You may have to render the stroke in order to see changes.*

5   **Get brush settings from stroke**

In order to draw more customized flowers, you need to update the current template brush with the settings of the stroke you just modified.

- With the stroke selected, select **Paint Effects → Get Settings from Selected Stroke**.
  This will set the customized flower brush as the current template brush.

6   **Save custom brushes**

You can save the current template brush for later use. The brush can be saved either to your shelf or the Visor.

- Select **Paint Effects → Save Brush Preset**...

- To save to current shelf, set the following in the Save Brush Preset window:

  Label to *Custom Flower*;

  Overlay Label to *flower*;

  Save Preset to **To Shelf**.

OR

- To save to a Visor directory, set the following in the Save Brush Preset window:

   Label to *Custom Flower*;

   Overlay Label to *flower*;

   Save Preset to **To Visor**;

   Visor Directory to *brushes* from your *prefs* directory.

- Click the **Save Brush Preset** button.

7   **Automatically paint a surface**

If you do not need to paint strokes by hand, you can use the **Paint Effects → Auto Paint** command. This will automatically paint onto a surface according to the options set. For instance, you could cover a rock with lichen or flowers in a single click.

8   **Paint some more strokes**

Add to your scene some vegetation, or even some painted objects such as the *umbrellaBench. mel* found under the **objectsMesh** category.

An example render

Note: *Several Paint Effects brushes are preanimated so when you play your scene, some Paint Effect strokes might be animated.*

9   **Scene setup**

- Open the Outliner.

- **Group** the strokes together and **rename** the group to *pfxGroup*.

- **Lock** and **hide** all the attributes of the *pfxGroup*.

  Since the Paint Effect strokes rely on the position of the ground plane, the pfxGroup should never be moved as it would cause the strokes to double transform and offset themselves from the ground plane.

- **Create** a new layer called *pfxLayer* and add *pfxGroup* to it.

Tip: *To speed up the rest of the project, you can hide the pfxLayer.*

- **Delete** any lights you might have created during this lesson.

10   **Save your work**

- **Save** your scene as *18-paintEffects_02.ma*.

Conclusion

You have now experienced one of Autodesk® Maya® software's greatest tools, but you have only scratched the surface of the power available in Paint Effects. Learning how to use the Paint Effects Canvas, how to paint on objects, and how to customize your brushes will serve you well as you become more and more familiar with the tool. There are so many ways to use Paint Effects to generate scene content that there should be no reason for your future scenes to look dull and empty.

In the next lesson, you will learn how to convert Paint Effects and how to use deformers.

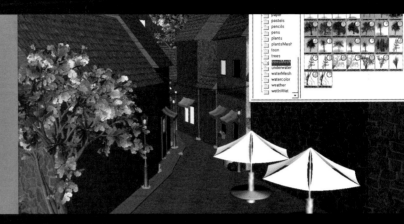

Lesson 19
Deformers

Deformers can be used for numerous reasons: for character set up and animation, for facial expressions, for modeling, and for creating dynamic surfaces. In this lesson, you will be introduced to various deformers to experiment with using a Paint Effects tree converted to polygons. These deformers will change the tree's shape while still keeping an organic feel to the geometry.

In this lesson, you will learn the following:

- How to convert Paint Effects to polygons

- How to use wire deformers

- How to use point on curve deformers

- How to use clusters

- How to use the Soft Modification Tool

- How to use nonlinear deformers

- How to change the deformation order

Convert Paint Effects

To begin, you will need geometry to deform. In this lesson, you will be using a polygonal tree originally from Paint Effects. Most Paint Effects' strokes can be converted to geometry and even animated dynamically.

For the sake of this lesson, you will only be using the output geometry of the conversion as a surface to deform.

1   **Open a new scene**

2   **Paint a tree**

   • From the Rendering menu set, select **Paint Effects → Get Brush**.

   • Under the **TreesMesh** directory, click the **birchSpringMedium.mel** brush preset.

   • **Paint** a single tree at the origin.

3   **Convert to polygons**

   • With the stroke selected, select **Modify → Convert → Paint Effects to Polygons → ❑.**

   • In the options, turn **On** the **Quad** output option.

   • Click the **Convert** button.

Paint Effects tree

4 Combine the model

If your model is composed of multiple meshes, for instance, the leaves, branches, and trunk, it will be simpler to combine them all together.

- Select all the meshes.

- Select **Mesh** → **Combine.**

5 Delete history

Some Paint Effects' brushes are animated by default, and when you convert the Paint Effects to polygons, the construction history keeps the ability to animate the mesh automatically. In this lesson, you will not require construction history.

Note: *Try to play your scene to see the Paint Effects' animation. If the playback is too slow, try to display the stroke as wireframe or playblast the scene.*

- Select **Edit** → **Delete All by Type** → **History**.
  The mesh has now lost its connection to the Paint Effects' stroke and is now a static model.

- **Delete** the stroke and curve from the Outliner.

6 Center the tree

- Select the mesh and **move** it so it grows straight up from the origin.

- **Freeze** its transformations.

- **Rename** it *tree.*

7 Save your work

- **Save** the scene as *19-deformers_01.ma.*

Wire deformer

You will now modify the tree using a wire deformer. A wire deformer is used to deform a surface based on a NURBS curve. You will use that type of deformer on the tree trunk.

1   Draw a curve

- Select **Create** → **EP Curve Tool**.

- From a *side* view, **draw** a curve along the trunk, then press **Enter**.

- **Tweak** the curve to follow the trunk in other views.

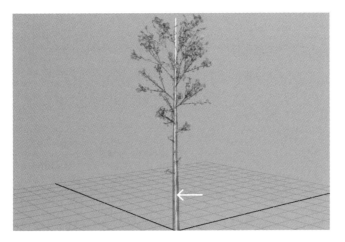

The curve to be used as a deformer

2   Create the wire deformer

- From the Animation menu set, select **Create Deformers** → **Wire Tool**.

  The Wire Tool requires two steps. First, you must select the deformable surfaces, then you must select the NURBS curve to be the deformer.

> **Note:** *You can read the tool's directives in the Help Line at the bottom of the main interface. The tool automatically sets the proper picking masks so you do not actually pick unwanted object types.*

- Select the *tree* geometry and press **Enter**.

- Select the NURBS curve and press **Enter**.

  The wire deformer is created.

3 **Edit the shape of the curve**

- With the *curve* selected, press **F8** to go into Component mode.

- Select some CVs and **move** them to see their effect on the geometry.

The default wire deformer effect

4 **Edit the deformer attribute**

As with any other deformers, the attributes of the wire deformer can be changed through the Channel Box.

- In the Channel Box, select the *wire1* history node.

- Highlight the **Dropoff Distance** attribute in the Channel Box.

- Hold down **Ctrl**, then **MMB+drag** in the viewport to see its effect.

  The effect of the wire deformer changes across the geometry.

Note: *Holding down the **Ctrl** key makes the virtual slider change with smaller increments.*

5   Edit the deformer membership

The **dropoff** has a nice effect, but the deformer might be affecting some undesired components. You can correct that by defining the membership of the geometry to the deformer.

- Select **Edit Deformers** → **Edit Membership Tool**.

- Select the *curve* to highlight the vertices affected by it.

  All the vertices of the tree geometry will be highlighted yellow.

- Hold the **Ctrl** key and **deselect** the branch vertices.

  Vertices that are no longer deformed will move back to their original positions.

The deformer's membership

Tip: *You can also use* **Edit Deformers** → **Paint Set Membership Tool** *to easily define the membership of the vertices.*

6   Experiment

Now that the deformer no longer affects the branches, you can set its **dropoff** to a higher value.

• Go back to **Object** mode.

• Press **q** to exit the **Edit Membership Tool** and enable the **Pick Tool**.

• Select the *curve* and try to change other deformer attributes from the Channel Box.

• Experiment with moving the *curve*'s CVs to see the effect of the deformer.

Point on curve and cluster deformer

The wire deformer is working well to deform the tree, but it is not practical to deform the curve for animation. Several other types of deformers can be used to deform the curve itself. Here you will experiment with the *point on curve* deformer and the *cluster* deformer.

1   Point on curve deformer

The point on curve deformer will create a locator linked to a curve edit point.

• **RMB** on the *NURBS curve* and select **Edit Point**.
Unlike CVs, edit points are located directly on the curve.

• Select the edit point located at the base of the trunk.

• Select **Create Deformers → Point on Curve**.
A locator is created at the edit point's position.

• Select **Modify → Center Pivot** to center the pivot of the *locator*.

• **Move** the locator to see its effect on the curve.

The point on curve deformer

Note: *Rotating a point on curve deformer has no effect on the curve.*

2   **Cluster deformer**

The point on curve works well, but has its limitations. For instance, it can only control one edit point at a time, and it cannot be used for rotation. The cluster deformer will create a handle that controls one or more vertices. When a cluster has multiple vertices in it, it can also be rotated.

- **RMB** on the *NURBS curve* and select **Control Vertex**.

- Select the two CVs in the middle of the trunk.

Tip: *It might be easier to locate the CVs by also displaying hulls. If you select only one CV, rotating the CV would have no effect.*

- Select **Create Deformers** → **Cluster**.
  *A cluster handle is displayed with a **C** in the viewport.*

The cluster handle

Note: Both the point on curve locator and cluster handle can be animated like any ot her node.

- **Move** and **rotate** the *cluster handle* to see its effect on the curve and the tree.

  By creating a cluster with more than one CV, you can rotate the cluster and you will see an effect on the geometry, but the geometry will not actually rotate. A CV has no rotation information, but a group of CVs can rotate their position in relation to each other.

Soft Modification Tool

The *Soft Modification Tool* lets you push and pull geometry as a sculptor would push and pull a piece of clay. By default, the amount of deformation is greatest at the center of the deformer, and gradually falls off moving outward. However, you can control the falloff of the deformation to create various types of effects.

1 **Scene file**

- **Open** the scene *19-deformers_01.ma* without saving your previous changes.

2   **Create the deformer**

- **RMB** on the *tree* surface and select **Vertex**.

- Select the tree's lower half vertices.

- Click the **Soft Modification Tool** in the toolbox, or select **Create Deformers** →
  Soft Modification.

  *An **S** handle similar to the cluster handle will be created. The tool's manipulator will also be
  displayed, and the influence of the deformer is shown. Yellow indicates areas that are fully
  deformed, while black areas are not deformed at all.*

The influence of the deformer

3   **Edit the deformer**

- **Move**, **rotate,** and **scale** the deformer to see its effect on the geometry.

- Press **Ctrl+a** to open the Attribute Editor for the deformer.
  The various deformer options can be edited here.

- Set the **Falloff Radius** to **2.0**.

- Click the button next to the **Falloff Curve** graph.

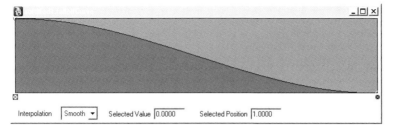

| Interpolation | Smooth ▼ | Selected Value | 0.0000 | Selected Position | 1.0000 |

Falloff curve

- See the effect of the deformer on the geometry.

The modified influence

Note: *The Soft Modification effect works best on high resolution models.*

4   Modeling with Soft Modification Tool

When modeling a high-resolution model, such as a character's face, you can create multiple Soft Modification deformers to achieve a final shape. The deformers can even overlap.

5   Delete Soft Modification deformers

If you want to delete the deformer, simply select its **S** handle and **delete** it. If you want to keep the shape of the geometry but remove the deformers, you must delete the model's history.

Nonlinear deformers

Maya has several *nonlinear deformers*. Non-linear deformers can affect one surface, multiple surfaces, or parts of a surface, and are very simple to use. In this exercise, you will experiment with all the nonlinear deformers.

1   Scene file

- **Open** the scene *19-deformers_01.ma* without saving your previous changes.

2   Bend deformer

- Select the *tree* geometry, then select **Create Deformers** → **Nonlinear** → **Bend**.
  The Bend handle is created and selected.

- In the Attribute Editor, highlight the *bend1* input.
  All the attributes for this deformer type are listed.

- Experiment and combine the different attributes to see their effect on the geometry.

> **Tip:**   *Most of the attributes have visual feedback on the deformer's handle in the viewport. You can also use the **Show Manipulator Tool** to interact with the deformer in the viewport.*

- **Moving**, **rotating**, and **scaling** the handle will also affect the location of the deformation.

Bend deformer

This deformer can have several uses, including simplifying modeling tasks, which would be otherwise difficult to achieve. In this case, it could be used to simulate wind animation.

- When you finish experimenting, select the deformer and **delete** it.

3   Flare deformer

- Select the *tree* geometry, then select **Create Deformers** → **Nonlinear** → **Flare**.
  The Flare handle is created and selected.

- In the Attribute Editor, highlight the *flare1* input.

- Experiment by moving, rotating, scaling, and combining the different attributes to see their effect on the geometry.

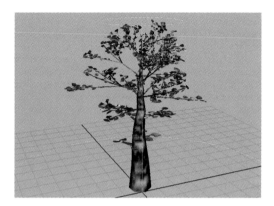

Flare deformer

This deformer is also versatile and can be used to simplify modeling tasks.

- When you finish experimenting, select the deformer and **delete** it.

4   **Sine deformer**

- Select the *tree* geometry, then select **Create Deformers** → **Nonlinear** → **Sine**.
  The Sine handle is created and selected.

- In the Attribute Editor, highlight the *sine1* input.

- Experiment by moving, rotating, scaling, and combining the different attributes to see their effect on the geometry.

Sine deformer

This deformer can help achieve refined randomization and could be used to simulate a flag animation or waves on a shore.

- When you finish experimenting, select the deformer and **delete** it.

5   **Squash deformer**

- Select the *tree* geometry, then select **Create Deformers** → **Nonlinear** → **Squash**.
  The Squash handle is created and selected.

- In the Attribute Editor, highlight the *squash1* input.

- Experiment by moving, rotating, scaling, and combining the different attributes to see their effect on the geometry.

Squash deformer

This deformer is useful for adding stretch and squash to an animated object.

- When you finish experimenting, select the deformer and **delete** it.

6 Twist deformer

- Select the *tree* geometry, then select **Create Deformers** → **Nonlinear** → **Twist**.
  The Twist handle is created and selected.

- In the Attribute Editor, highlight the *twist1* input.

- Experiment by moving, rotating, scaling, and combining the different attributes to see their effect on the geometry.

Twist deformer

  This deformer can add twisting animation to an object, among other uses.

- When you finish experimenting, select the deformer and **delete** it.

7 Wave deformer

- Select the *tree* geometry, then select **Create Deformers** → **Nonlinear** → **Wave**.
  The Wave handle is created and selected.

- In the Attribute Editor, highlight the *wave1* input.

- Experiment by moving, rotating, scaling, and combining the different attributes to see their effect on the geometry.

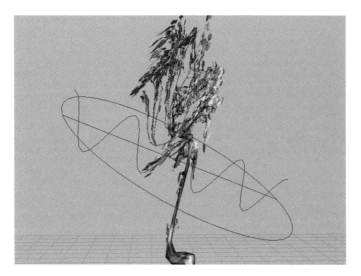

Wave deformer

As you can see, this deformer can have several uses, such as creating a rippling effect for water.

- When you finish experimenting, select the deformer and **delete** it.

8   **Experiment**

Spend some time deforming the tree as you wish. Keep in mind that you can add multiple deformers to the same object.

If you want to animate the tree later, consider keeping the deformers in the scene and making an animation setup.

Deformation order

The deformation order of a surface is very important to take into consideration. For instance, if you apply a *sine* deformer and then a *bend* deformer, the results are very different than if you apply a *bend* deformer and then a *sine* deformer.

The deformation order does not only apply to nonlinear deformers. For instance, a rigid binding and a polygonal smooth will have a very different effect than a polygonal smooth and a rigid bind.

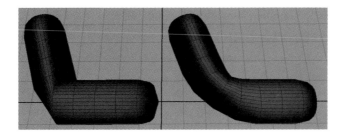

Smooth/Rigid bind vs. Rigid bind/Smooth

Note: In the previous statement, a rigid bind followed by a smooth would evaluate much faster and give better results than a smooth followed by a rigid bind, since the rigid binding would have to skin a higher resolution model.

1   **New Scene**

  • Select **File** → **New**.

2   **Create a cylinder**

  • Select **Create** → **Polygon Primitives** → **Cylinder**.

  • Edit the *cylinder* as follows:

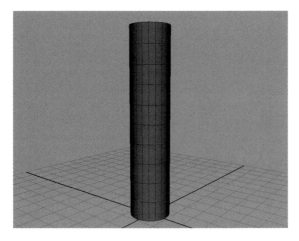

Example cylinder

3   **Apply deformers**

- Select the *cylinder*, then select **Create Deformers** → **Nonlinear** → **Bend**.

- Select the *cylinder*, then select **Create Deformers** → **Nonlinear** → **Sine**.

4   **Edit the bend deformer**

- Select the *cylinder*.

- In the Channel Box, highlight the *bend1* deformer.

- Set the **Curvature** attribute to **2**.

Bend deformer effect

5   **Edit the sine deformer**

- Select the *cylinder*.

- In the Channel Box, highlight the *sine1* deformer.

- Set the **Amplitude** attribute to **0.1**.

- Set the **Wavelength** attribute to **0.35**.

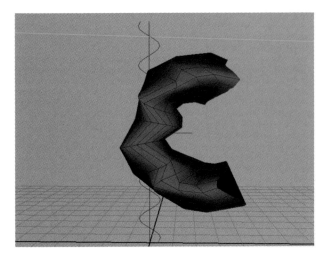

Sine and bend deformer effect

6   List input for the cylinder

- **RMB** on the *cylinder*.

- Select **Inputs → All Inputs**...
  Doing so will display a window with all the History nodes affecting the cylinder.

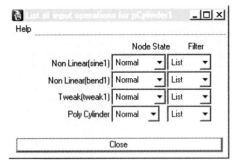

List of input for cylinder

7   Change the order of deformation

- In the Input window, **MMB+drag** the *Non Linear(sine1)* item over the *Non Linear(bend1)* item to change their order.

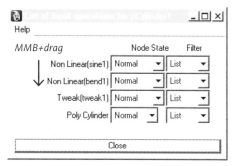

List of input for cylinder

8   **Result of the new order of deformation**

New deformation order effect

Conclusion

You should now be comfortable using basic deformers. Being aware of the results created by the deformation order will allow you to reorder them if needed.

In the next lesson, you will learn about lighting and effects, which can greatly improve the quality of your rendered scene.

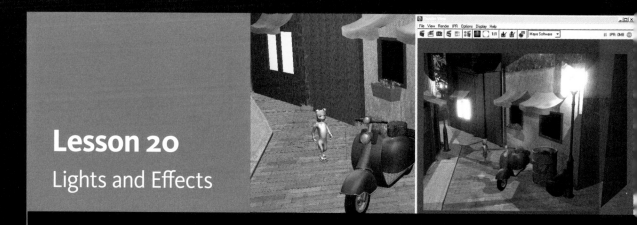

Lesson 20
Lights and Effects

In the real world, it is light that allows us to see the surfaces and objects around us. In computer graphics, digital lights play the same role. They help define the space within a scene and, in many cases, help to set the mood or atmosphere. As well, several other effects besides lighting can be added to the final image in order to have it look more realistic. This lesson explores and explains some of the basic Autodesk® Maya® software effects.

In this lesson, you will learn the following:

- How to add lighting to your scene

- How to enable shadows

- How to set up shader glow

- How to add light glow and lens flare

- How to set up motion blur

- How to batch render an animation

- How to use fcheck

References

When you first animated Romeo, you saw how to create a reference. You will now open that same animation file, but this time you will also reference the environment.

1   **Scene file**

- **Open** the scene file *14-walk_05.ma* from the second project's *scenes* directory.

2   **Create references**

- Select **File** → **Reference Editor** from the main interface menu.

- Select **File** → **Create Reference** → ❑ from the main interface menu or from the Reference Editor.

- Set **Resolve all nodes with this string:** *set*.

  This will prefix all the Reference nodes with the string set.

- Click the **Apply** button.

- In the browse window, select the file *18-paintEffects_02.ma*, and then click **Reference**.

  The file will load into the current one.

- Set **Resolve all nodes with this string:** *scooter*.

- Click the **Reference** button.

- In the browse dialog that appears, select the file *17-rig_03.ma*, and then click **Reference**.

> **Note:**   *You may have to re-link textures that are not automatically found. To do so, simply open the Hypershade, select the Texture tab, and change the path of the texture through the Attribute Editor.*

3   **Scene setup**

Looking at the three elements in your scene, you can clearly see that there is a scaling issue between the files.

> **Note:** *Scaling issues should be tackled when first creating a scene file, but it was not a required step in the scope of this book.*

- Select the *scooter:master.*

- Set its **Scale X**, **Y,** and **Z-axes** to **2.0,** or any other appropriate value.

> **Note:** *For simplicity reasons, you will overlook the fact that scaling the scooter will break the wheel automation created earlier since it was based on the wheel diameter. Now that you have doubled the global scaling, the wheels will slide slightly when the scooter is moved.*

- Select the Romeo *master.*

- Set its **Scale X**, **Y,** and **Z-axes** to **0.5,** or any other appropriate value.

- Select the *set:environmentGroup.*

- Set its **Rotate Y** to **90** so Romeo walks down the alley road.

The entire scene

Note: *If the top node's scale attributes are nonkeyable and unlocked, they will not show in the Channel Box, but the Scale Tool will still work. Alternatively, you can access the scale attributes in the Attribute Editor. If the scale attributes of the node are locked, you need to unlock them in the referenced file and reopen this file again.*

4   **Placing the characters**

- Place the Romeo *master* at the back of the alley and set a **keyframe** by pressing **Shift+w** to set a keyframe in translation and **Shift+e** to set a keyframe in rotation

  Since the character is controlled by a Trax clip, setting a keyframe will prevent it from snapping back at the origin.

- **Move** the scooter *master* next to the garbage drum.

5   **Save your work**

- **Save** this scene to *20-lightEffects_01.ma.*

Placing a point light

To create the primary light source in the scene, such as the lamp post, you will use a point light. This light type works exactly like a lightbulb, with attributes such as color and intensity.

1   **Create a point light**

- Select **Create → Lights → Point Light**.

  This places a point light at the origin.

- With the light still selected, **translate** the point light within any lamp post *bulb* geometry.

Tip: *Use snap to point to speed up the light placement.*

The light placement

2   **Turn on hardware lighting (if possible)**

One step beyond hardware texturing is *hardware lighting*. This lets you see how the light is affecting the surface that it is shining on.

* Press the **6** hotkey to display textures in the viewport.

* Select **Lighting → Use All Lights** or press the **7** hotkey.
  You will see the scene being lit by the point light.

The hardware lighting enabled

3   **Test render the scene**

- From the **Rendering** menu set, select **Render** → **Render Current Frame**.

  Notice the rendered image is dark and not very realistic.

The rendered scene

- Change the light **Color** to be slightly **yellow**.

4   **Shadows**

- In the Attribute Editor, expand the **Shadows** section for the point light.

- **Enable** shadow casting by checking the **Use Depth Map Shadows** attribute.

- **Render** the scene.

  Notice that you do not see the effect of the light anymore. This is because the point light is within the light bulb geometry, so the bulb geometry places the entire set in shadow. To correct this, you can disable shadow casting on the light bulb surface.

- Select the *lightBulb* surface and open its Attribute Editor.

- Under the **Render Stats** section, set the following:

  Casts Shadows to **Off**;

  Receive Shadows to **Off**.

- **Render** the scene again.

  You should now see shadows.

Shadows in the rendered image

5   **Refine the shadows**

Right now, the shadow resolution is coarse. The following shows how to increase the depth map shadow resolution:

- Open the Attribute Editor for the *pointLight1*.

- In the **Depth Map Shadow Attributes** section, set the following:

  Resolution to **1024** rather than **512**;

  Filter Size to **2**.

  Doing so will first increase the resolution of the shadow maps, and will then apply a blur filter smoothing out the shadow edges.

- **Render** the scene again to see how this makes the shadow smoother.

6   **Shader glow**

The light bulb geometry itself should look like its glowing, and right now, it seems a bit dull, not at all like if it was emitting light. To solve this, you will use the glow attribute of the light bulb shader.

- Select the *lightBulb* surface.

- In the Attribute Editor, select the *lightM* tab.

- Under the **Special Effect** section, set **Glow Intensity** to **0.5**.

- Test render you scene.

The shader glow effect

7   **Duplicate the lights**

- **Duplicate** the *pointLight* and place a copy in each *lightBulb*.

- Under the **Render Stats** section for each *lightBulb*, set **Casts Shadows** and **Receive Shadows** to **Off**.

Tip: *To speed up rendering time, you do not need to enable shadows on distant light source.*

8   **Light decay**

The light decay can be understood as how much the light looses its power over distance. It the current scene, each light post should not light up the entire city, but rather just a limited area around itself. You will now enable the light decay.

- Open the Attribute Editor.

- For each *pointLight* in the scene, set **Decay Rate** to **Linear** and increase the light **Intensity** to **25**.

  Since the light decay appends over distance, you need to increase the light intensity so the light reaches the other side of the alley.

9   Save your work

- **Save** your scene as *20-lightEffects_02.ma*.

Placing a directional light

So far, you used a point light to create a light bulb. Next you will use a directional light, which is a light type that mimics a light source so far away that rays are parallel. This light type is perfect for sunlight or moonlight.

1   Create a directional light

- Select **Create → Lights → Directional Light**.

  This places a directional light at the origin.

2   Edit the directional light's position

The Show Manipulator Tool provides a manipulator for the light's *look at point* and *eye point*. You can edit these using the same method as you would with a typical transform manipulator.

- Press the **t** key to access the **Show Manipulator Tool**.

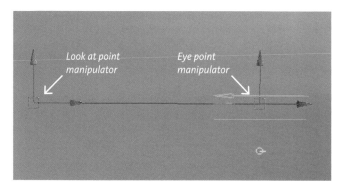

Show Manipulator Tool

- **Click+drag** the manipulator handles to reposition the light in the direction in which the sunlight should hit the set.

New light position

- In the Channel Box, set the **Intensity** attribute to **0.8**.

- Change the light **Color** to be slightly **blue**.

3   **Moon incandescence**

When you have created the moon shader, you did not make it incandescent. The following will show you how to map a texture file in the incandescence channel.

- Select the *moon* surface.

- In the Hypershade, click the **Graph materials on selected objects** button.

- **MMB+drag** the moon file texture onto the *moonM* shader node.

- Select **incandescence** from the pop-up menu.
  Doing so will map the color of the moon to its incandescence channel.

- Under the **Special Effect** section of the *moonM* shader, set **Glow Intensity** to **0.5**.

Note: *Even if the texture itself has a glowing effect around the moon, a shader glow will spill over other geometry in your scene, resulting in a better looking glow effect.*

- Test render the moon to see how it glows in the dark

4   **Adding ambient lighting**

In the real world, light rays bounce off surfaces, particles, and atmosphere, making the global lighting level of a set brighter. In order to mimic this, you could add several directional lights pointing from the back and from below, but instead you will use an ambient light, which can accomplish this effect.

- Select **Create** → **Lights** → **Ambient Light**.

- In the Channel Box, set the **Intensity** attribute to **0.2**.

- Change the light **Color** to be slightly **blue**.

- Place the light at the opposite side of the scene.

- Render the scene.

   Notice how the geometry that was previously entirely in shadow is now more visible. Also notice how the global light level raised like if your pupil would have adjusted to the light level in the scene.

The ambient light effect

Light effects

When the rendered camera is looking directly at bright light, a light glow and lens flare would add realism to your renders. You will now add light effects to one of the point lights.

1   **Light FX**

- Open the Attribute Editor for the *pointLightShape1*.

- Scroll down to the **Light Effects** section.

- Click the **map** button next to the **Light Glow** attribute.

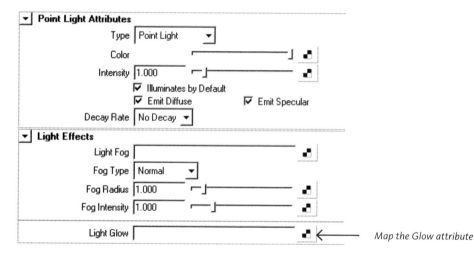

Light Glow attribute

Maya will automatically create, select, and display an opticalFX node in the Attribute Editor.

- Set the *opticalFX1* attributes as follows:

   Lens flare to **Enabled**;

   Glow Type to **Linear**;

   Halo Type to **Lens Flare**.

   Under **Lens Flare Attributes,** set **Flare Intensity** to **2**.

- **Place** the camera to look directly at the light bulb.

- **Render** your scene to see the lens flare.

The lens flare optical effect

2   Save your work

- **Save** your scene as *20-lightEffects_03.ma.*

Rendering animation

Now that you have defined the lighting in your scene and you are happy with your test rendering, it is time to render an animation. This is accomplished using the Maya *batch renderer.* In preparation, you will add motion blur to your scene, in order to simulate the blur generated in live action film and video work.

1   Render Settings

Render Settings are a group of attributes that you can set to define how your scene will render. To define the quality of the rendering, you need to set the Render Settings.

- In the Render View window, click with your **RMB** and choose **Options →
  Render Settings...**

  OR

- Click the **Render Settings** button located at the top right of the main interface.

- Select the **Maya Software** tab.

- Open the **Anti-aliasing Quality** section if it is not already opened.

- Set the **Quality** preset to **Intermediate quality**.

  Anti-aliasing is a visual smoothing of edge lines in the final rendered image. Because bitmaps are made up of square pixels, a diagonal line would appear jagged unless it was anti-aliased.

2   Set the image output

To render an animation, you must set up the scene's file extensions to indicate a rendered sequence. You must also set up the start and end frames.

- Select the **Common** tab in the Render Settings window.

- From the **File Output** section, set the following:

  File name prefix to *alley*.

  This sets the name of the animated sequence.

  Frame/Animation ext to name.#.ext.

  This sets up Maya to render a numbered sequence of images.

  Start frame to 1;

  End frame to 50;

  By frame to 1.

  This tells Maya to render every frame from 1 to 50.

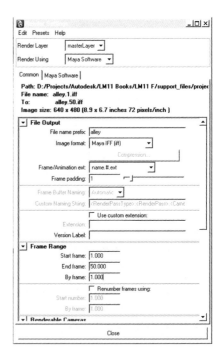

Render Settings

3   Turn on motion blur

- Select the **Maya Software** tab.

- Under the **Motion Blur** section, click the **Motion blur** button to turn it **On**.

- Set the **Motion blur type** to be **2D**.
  This type of motion blur renders the fastest.

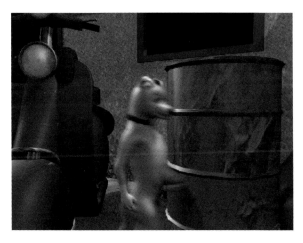

Motion blur on Romeo

Tip: *If you want to see more or less motion blur in your renders, you can set the Blur length in the Motion Blur section of the Render Settings.*

4   Place your camera

- In the Perspective view panel, select **View** → **Camera Settings** → **Resolution Gate**.

- **Place** the camera so you can see your animation from frames **1** to **50**.

5   Save your work

- **Save** your scene as *20-lightEffects_04.ma*.

6   **Batch render the scene**

- Press **F6** to change to the **Rendering** menu set.

- Select **Render** → **Batch Render**.

- If for any reason you want to cancel the current batch render, select **Render** → **Cancel Batch Render**.

7   **Watch the render progress**

- The sequence will be rendered as a series of frames. You can look in the Command Feedback line or through the **Window** → **General Editor** → **Script Editor** to see the status of the current rendering process.

Tip: *Once a batch render is launched, you can safely close the Maya software without interrupting the batch render.*

8   **View the resulting animation**

After the rendering is complete, you can preview the results using the *fcheck* utility.

- To open the *fcheck* utility, go into your programs, and then go to **Autodesk** → **Autodesk Maya 2010** → **FCheck.**

- In FCheck, select **File** → **Open Sequence**.

- Navigate to the *project3\images* folder.

- Select the file *alley.1.iff* and click **Open**.

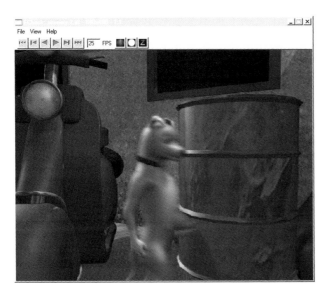

Animation previewed with fcheck utility

> The animation will load one frame at a time, and once in memory,
> it will play it back in real time.

Tip: *To learn more about the capabilities of fcheck for previewing your animations, enter* `fcheck-h` *in a command shell or select the Help menu.*

Conclusion

You are now familiar with the basic concepts of lighting and rendering a scene. You began by enabling various light options such as shadows, shader glow, light glow, and lens flare. Then you added 2D motion blur just before launching your first animation batch render. Once your render was complete, you viewed it in the fcheck utility.

In the next lesson, you will learn about rendering tasks and experiment with different renderers.

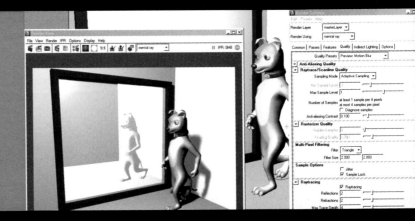

Lesson 21
Rendering

This lesson will make extensive use of the Maya Interactive Photorealistic Renderer (IPR). This tool allows you to create a rendering of the scene that can then be used to interactively update changes to the scene's lighting and texturing. You will see how fast and intuitive it is to texture your scene with the IPR.

So far, you have been using only the Autodesk® Maya® software renderer to render your scenes. In this lesson, you will also learn about three additional rendering types: Maya Hardware, Maya Vector, and mental ray® for Maya. Each has its own strengths and you should determine which rendering engine to use on a per project basis, depending on the final application.

In this lesson, you will learn the following:

- How to render a region and display snapshots

- How to open and save images

- How to display an image's alpha channel

- How to start the IPR

- How to make connections in the Hypershade

- How to enable high quality rendering in a viewport

- How to render with mental ray

- How to render with Maya Vector

- How to render with Maya Hardware

Rendering features

You are now ready to refine the rendering of your scene. In this section, you will experiment with the Render view features, such as snapshots, image storage, and region rendering.

1   Scene file

- Continue with the scene file you were using in the previous lesson.

    OR

- **Open** the scene *20-lightEffects_04.ma*.

2   Render setup

- In the *Perspective* view, select **Panels** → **Saved Layouts** → **Hypershade/Render/Persp**.

- Frame Romeo's *eyes* in the *Perspective* view.

- **Hide** the *pfxLayer* to speed up the rendering process.

- Temporarily turn **Off** the **Motion blur** in the render settings and the **Shadows** for the point lights.

- **RMB** click in the *Render* view and select **Render** → **Render** → **Persp**.

Note: *You can change the size of the panels by* **click+dragging** *their separators.*

3   Keep and remove image

When test rendering a scene, it is good to be able to keep previously rendered images for comparison with the changes you implement.

- To keep the current render for reference, select **File** → **Keep Image in Render View** or click the **Keep Image** button.
    Notice a slider bar appears at the bottom of the Render view.

- In the *Perspective* view, select the *eyeball* geometry.

- In the Hypershade, click the **Graph material on selected objects** button.

- In the **Create Maya Node** section, scroll down to the **2D Textures** section and click the **File** node.

- **Double-click** the *file1* node to open the Attribute Editor.

- Click the **Browse** button and select the *eyeball.tif* texture from the *sourceimage* folder. *This eyeball texture has much more detail than a simple ramp texture.*

- In the Hypershade work area, **MMB+drag** the *file1* node onto the *eyeM* material.

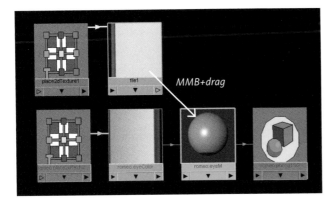

Dragging to create a connection

- Choose **Color** from the context menu to map the file in the color of the material.

- Make sure the *place2dTexture* node places the iris correctly on the eyeball by rotating the texture by **180** degrees.

- In the *Render* view, **render** the model again.

- Click the **Keep Image** button.

- Open the Attribute Editor for the *eyeM* node.

- Change the **Specular Color** to **white** and set the **Cosine Power** to **100**.

- In the *Render* view, **render** the model again.

- Click the **Keep Image** button.

- Open the Attribute Editor for the *file1* node.

- Under the **Color Balance** section, change the **Color Offset** to change the eye color.

- **Render** the model again.

- Once the rendering is done, scroll the image bar at the bottom of the *Render* view to compare the previous render results.

- Scroll the image bar to the right (the older image), and select **File** → **Remove Image from Render View** or click the **Remove Image** button.
  This will remove the currently displayed image stored earlier.

The eye render

Note: *You can keep as many images as you want in the Render view. The images will be kept even if you close and reopen the Render view window, but they will not be kept if you close Maya.*

4   **Region rendering**

You might think it is a waste of time to render the entire image again just for the small portion of the image that changed. With the Render view, you can render only a region of the current image.

- Select a region of the current image by **click+dragging** a square directly on the previously rendered image.

Select a region of the rendered image

- Click the **Render Region** button to render the selected region.

- To automatically render a selected region, **RMB** and enable the **Options** →
  Auto Render Region.

  *With this option, every time you select a region on the rendered image, it will automatically
  be rendered.*

Note: *You can still keep an image that has a region render in it.*

5   **Snapshots**

If your scene is long, you might not want to wait for a complete render before selecting a
region to render. The Render view allows you to take a wireframe snapshot of the image to
render so that you can easily select the region you want.

- **RMB** in the Render view and select **Render** → **Snapshot** → **Persp**.

  A wireframe image is placed in the Render view for reference.

- Select the region you would like to render.

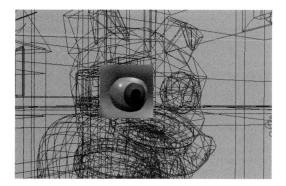

A snapshot in the Render view

6   **Open and save images**

You can open renders or reference images directly in the Render view.

- To open a reference image, select **File** → **Open Image**.

- **Browse** to the reference image *eyeReference.tif* located in the *images* folder of the current project.

The eye reference

You can also save your renders to disk from the Render view.

- To save your current Render view image, select **File → Save Image**.

7 Display the alpha channel

When rendering, you often want to display the image's alpha channel to see if it will composite well onto another image.

- Select the Romeo geometry group.

- Select **Display → Hide → Hide Unselected Objects**.

- Select **Display → Show → Lights**.

- Frame the character and render your scene.

The character's alpha channel

- Once the render is finished, click the **Display Alpha Channel** button located at the top of the Render view.

- To go back to the colored images, click the **Display RGB channels** in the Render view.

IPR

To give you access to interactive updating capabilities, you will set up an IPR rendering. An IPR rendering creates a special image file that stores not only the pixel information about an image, but also data about the surface normals, materials, and objects associated with each of these pixels. This information is then updated as you make changes to your scene's shading.

1   **IPR setup**

- From the *Render* view panel, click the **Render Settings** button.

- Click the **Maya Software** tab.

- From the **Anti-aliasing Quality** section, set **Quality** to **Production quality**.

  For IPR, you can use better settings if desired. Your initial IPR rendering will be slower, but the interactive updates will still be fast.

- Close the Render Settings window.

2   **IPR render**

- From your *Render* view panel, select **IPR** → **IPR Render** → **persp**.

  Now what seems to be a regular rendering of the scene appears. Notice the message at the bottom of the Render view saying: Select a region to begin tuning.

- **Click+drag** to select an area of the IPR rendering that will cover the entire character.

  This is the area that will be updated as you make changes.

Initial IPR rendering

3 **Tweak your materials**

- In the rendered IPR image, **click** directly on the character's *body*.

  Doing so will automatically select the body shading group.

- In the Hypershade, click the **Input and output connections** button to graph the shading network.

- **Drag** the *Romeo file1* onto the *bodyM* material and **drop** it in the **specularColor** attribute.

  Notice how the IPR updates every time you bring a change to the shading network.

- **Map** a **fractal** texture in the **bump map** attribute of *bodyM*.

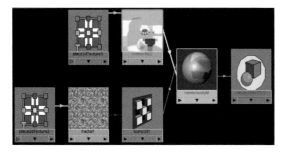

The updated shading network

- Select the *bump2D* node and change the **Bump Depth** to **0.01**.

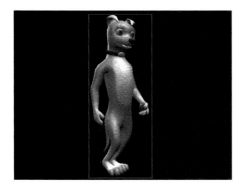

IPR update

4   Stop the IPR

- **Stop** the IPR by clicking the button located at the top right of the Render view.

IPR functions

5   Drag and drop feature

- Select the *eyeball* geometry and **graph** its shading network.

- In the Hypershade, select the *eyeM* material.

- Select **Edit** → **Duplicate** → **Shading Network** in the Hypershade.
  Doing so duplicates the entire selected shading network(s).

- Click the **Rearrange graph** button to order the work area.

- Frame the eyes in the *Perspective* view and **launch** another IPR.

- Select the render region surrounding the eyes.

- **MMB+drag** the duplicated *eyeM* and drop it on one of the *eyeballs* in the Render view.
  Each eye now has a separate material assigned.

Note: *Dropping a material directly in the IPR has the same effect as dropping it on a model in a viewport.*

6   IPR and the Attribute Editor

- Open the Attribute Editor.

- Single click any object in the IPR image and see the Attribute Editor update to show the related material node.

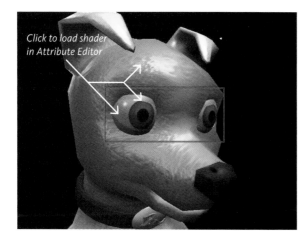

Click to load shader
in Attribute Editor

The IPR updates the Attribute Editor

7   Refresh the IPR image

When you have models outside the IPR region, you can refresh the entire image without losing your selected region.

- To refresh the entire image, click the **Refresh the IPR Image** button.

  The entire image gets redrawn and your original region is maintained.

8   IPR lighting

You can also use the IPR window to explore different lighting scenarios. Changing the light direction or properties will cause the IPR to redraw accordingly.

Note: *When you do not have any lights in your scene, the IPR creates a directional light for you by default. The defaultLight node gets deleted when you stop an IPR rendering.*

- Select any light from the Outliner.

- Change the light intensity or color to see the IPR update with the new lighting.

New light color and intensity in IPR

9   **IPR shadows**

The IPR might not update certain shadow tweaks. To correct this, do the following:

• Select **IPR → Update Shadow Maps**.

The IPR updates and the shadows are re-rendered.

• **Stop** the IPR.

High quality rendering

When high quality rendering is turned on, the scene views are drawn in high quality by the hardware renderer. This lets you see a very good representation of the final render's look without having to software render the scene.

1   **Enabling high quality rendering**

• In the Perspective view, press **5, 6,** or **7**.

Note: *High quality rendering is not available while in wireframe, and not compatible with all graphic cards.*

- Select **Edit → Select All by Type → NURBS Surfaces**, and then press the **3** hotkey to display the NURBS surfaces to there highest quality.

- Enable **Renderer → High Quality Rendering**.

- Enable **Lighting → Shadows**.

High quality rendering

mental ray

Perhaps the most complex and powerful rendering type available in Maya software is mental ray. It offers many solutions for the creation of photorealistic renders, such as Global Illumination, caustic reflections and refractions, support for High Dynamic Range Imaging (HDRI), custom shaders, and motion blurred reflections and shadows.

In this exercise, you will open an existing scene that includes the Romeo with animation, reflection, and lighting. Using mental ray, the shadows will have motion blur, and the motion blur on Romeo will be reflected in a mirror.

1   **Scene file**

- Select **File** → **Open** and choose *21-rendering_01.ma* without saving changes to the previous scene.

2   **Set up the depth map shadows**

- Select *pointLight1* and open the Attribute Editor.

- Under the *spotLightShape1* tab, expand the **Shadows** section.

- Set **Use Depth Map Shadows** to **On**.

- Change the **Shadow Color** to a **dark gray**.

3   **Open the Render Settings**

- Select **Window** → **Rendering Editors** → **Render Settings**...

- In the **Render Settings** window, select **Render Using** → **mental ray**.
  Doing so changes the renderer to mental ray instead of Maya software.

Tip: *If mental ray is not available, you must load the Mayatomr.mll plug-in in the* **Window** → **Settings/Preferences** → **Plug-ins Manager**.

4   **Set the rendering options**

To render the animation, you must set up the scene's file extensions to indicate a rendered sequence. You must also set up the start and end frames.

- Click the **Common** tab.

- From the **Image File Output** section, set the following:

    File Name Prefix to *mentalRay*

    This sets the name of the animated sequence.

    Frame/Animation Ext *to:*

    name.#.ext

    This sets up mental ray to render a numbered sequence of images.

    Start Frame to **1**;

    End Frame to **10**;

    By Frame to **1**.

5   **Set up the mental ray Render Settings for motion blur**

- Under the **Quality** tab, select **Quality Presets → Production: Motion Blur**.

    This image quality preset automatically turns on high quality motion blur. It also sets up raytracing, as well as high quality anti-alias and texture sampling values for mental ray.

6   **Perform a test render**

- Go to frame **5**.

- Make the *Perspective* view active.

- Select **Render → Render Current Frame**...

mental ray rendering

Note: *Notice that the reflection and shadows in the scene have motion blur.*

7   **Batch render**

*   Select **Render** → **Batch Render**.

Tip: *If you have a computer with multiple processors, it is recommended that you set* **Use all Available Processors** *to* **On** *in the batch render options, since the render can be time-consuming.*

*   When the render is complete, select **Render** → **Show Batch Render...** This will activate the fcheck utility to playback the animated sequence.

    OR

*   From the browser, select one of the frames of the animation, then click **Open**.

Maya Vector

The Maya Vector renderer can output files in 2D vector format. It can also be used to create stylized flat renderings seen in illustrations and 2D animation.

Using the previous scene, you will set up a Maya Vector render.

1   Open the Maya Vector Render Settings

- Select **Window** → **Rendering Editors** → **Render Settings** …

- In the **Render Settings** window, select **Render Using** → **Maya Vector**.

> **Tip:**   *If Maya Vector is not available, you must load the VectorRender.mll plug-in in the* **Window** → **Settings/Preferences** → **Plug-ins Manager**.

2   Set up the Maya Vector options

- Select the **Maya Vector** tab.

- In the **Fill Options** section, set the following:

    Fill objects to **On**;

    Fill style to **Single color**;

    Show back faces to **On**;

    Shadows to **On**;

    Highlights to **On**;

    Reflections to **On**.

- In the **Edge Options** section, select the following:

  Include edges to **On**;

  Edge weight preset to **3.0 pt**;

  Edge style to **Outlines**.

3 **Perform a test render**

   - Make the Perspective view active.

   - Select **Render** → **Render Current Frame**...

Maya Vector rendering

4 **Batch render**

   - **Repeat** step **7** from the previous exercise to render the sequence.

Note: *You might experience compatibility issues with the Maya Vector renderer on Intel®-based Macs ®.*

Maya Hardware

Not to be confused with the Hardware Render Buffer, which will be introduced in the next project, the Maya hardware renderer allows you to create broadcast resolution images faster than with the software renderer.

In many cases, the quality of the output will be high enough to go directly to broadcast, but some advanced shadows, reflections, and post-process effects cannot be produced with the hardware renderer. The final image quality of the Maya hardware renderer is significantly higher than that of the viewport and Hardware Render Buffer.

1   **Set up the depth map shadows**

  • Make sure the **Use Depth Map Shadows** attribute for the *pointLight1* is still **On** from the previous exercise.

2   **Open the Maya Hardware Render Settings**

  • Select **Window** → **Rendering Editors** → **Render Settings...**

  • In the **Render Settings** window, select **Render Using** → **Maya Hardware**.

Note: *It is possible that your graphic card does not support hardware rendering. If so, you will get a warning message in the Command Feedback line.*

  • Select the **Maya Hardware** tab.

  • Under the **Quality** section, set **Presets** to **Production Quality.**

  • Under the **Render Options** section, set **Motion Blur** to **On**.

3   Perform a test render

- Make the *Perspective* view active.

- Select **Render → Render Current Frame**...

  You cannot see a reflection in the mirror since the raytracing feature is unavailable with the hardware renderer. However, the renderer is otherwise capable of fast, high quality rendering, including texture mapped reflections, depth map shadows, and motion blur.

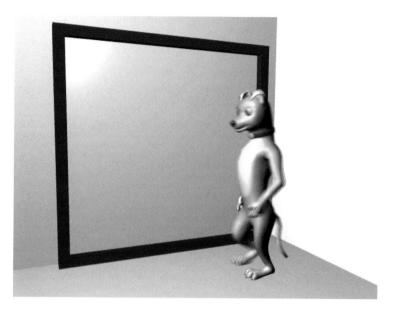

Maya hardware render

Note: *You might need to reverse some surfaces in order to render them correctly.*

4   Batch render

- **Repeat** step **7** from the mental ray exercise to render the sequence.

Conclusion

You have now completed this short introduction to the rendering engines available in the Maya software. The Maya IPR helps speed up the creative process and allows you to explore fast shading, lighting, and texturing possibilities. For more mental ray, Maya Vector, Maya hardware, and Maya software rendering tutorials, see the Maya online documentation.

In the next project, you will experiment with more animation techniques, rigid bodies, and particles.

Project 04

In this project, you will try more animation techniques using animation layers, Trax, motion paths, particles, and dynamics. You will also learn about MEL scripting to enable you to automate some tasks and simplify your everyday work.

Lesson 22

More Animation

Set up your project

Since this is a new project, it is recommended to set a new current project directory.

1 **Set the project**

- If you copied the support files onto your drive, go to the **File** menu and select **Project → Set...**

  A window opens, pointing you to the Maya projects directory.

- Click the folder named *project4* to select it.

2 **Set the time range**

- Set the **Start Time** and **Playback Start Time** to **1**.

- Set the **End Time** and **Playback End Time** to **30**.

3 **Current time**

- Move the current time indicator to frame **1**.

4 **Clear the Trax Editor**

As you may notice, Romeo is already animated in this scene. This is because the Trax Editor still contains the Trax walk cycle clip you created earlier. You will now clear the Trax Editor and start a new animation.

- Open the Trax Editor by selecting **Window** → **Animation Editors** → **Trax Editor**.

- If the walk clip is not visible, make sure to turn on the **List** → **Auto Load Selected Characters** options.

- Press **a** to frame all in the Trax Editor.

- Click the *walk* clip to highlight it.

- Press **Delete** to remove it.

  The animation has now been removed, but the character has kept its initial step position, which will be used as the starting pose of the new animation.

- Close the Trax Editor.

5 **Start pose**

- Press the **s** hotkey to keyframe the entire *character*.

- Enable the **Auto Key** button.

- **Translate** and **rotate** the character *master* so Romeo is next to the scooter.

The start pose

Tip: *Change display layers to be Reference layers to avoid accidentally picking unwanted objects.*

6   **Anticipation pose**

- Go to frame **5**.

- Hold down the **w** hotkey, click in the view, and choose **Object** from the marking menu.
  This changes the Move Tool's option to be oriented with the object rather than with the world.

- Bring the *rFootManip* next to the *lFootManip* to prepare for the jumping motion.

- Place the character as follows:

The anticipation pose

> **Tip:** *Anticipation usually goes in the opposite direction of the actual motion.*

- Press the **s** key to set a key on the character at this new position.

7   **Pushing pose**

- Go to frame **10**.

- Place the character as follows:

The pushing pose

8 **Jump pose**

• Go to frame **15**.

• Place the character in midair:

The jump pose

• Press the **s** key to set a key on the character at this new position.

9   Fix jump pose tangents

- **RMB** in the Time Slider at frame **15** and select **Tangents** → **Spline.**

10   Landing anticipation pose

- Go to frame **20**.

- Place the character as follows:

The landing anticipation pose

- Press the **s** key to set a key on the character at this new position.

- **RMB** in the Time Slider at frame **15** and select **Tangents** → **Spline.**

11   Landing pose

- Go to frame **25**.

- Place the character as follows:

The landing pose

- Press the **s** key to set a key on the character at this new position.

12   **End pose**

- Go to frame **30**.

- Place the character comfortably seated on the scooter.

The turning pose

- Press the **s** key to set a key on the character at this new position.

Tip: *It is a difficult task to rotate an entire character through space and you might experience some problems when doing so. For instance, you might inadvertently rotate a limb by more than 360 degrees, causing the limb to spin between keyframes. If you do so, you can try to delete the rotation keyframes using the Graph Editor and try to set the rotation again.*

13   Tune the jiggle

- Select the body geometry from the Outliner.

- In the **Inputs** section of the Channel Box, highlight the *jiggle1* deformer**.**

- Change the **Jiggle Weight** attribute to your liking.

14   Save your work

- **Save** this scene to *22-moreAnimation_01.ma*.

15   Playblast your animation

A playblast is a movie reflecting your scene animation. When making a playblast, Maya software generates the animation by grabbing the image directly from the active viewport, so make sure to display only what you want to see in your playblast.

- Frame the scene in the *Perspective* view to see it in its entirety.

- **Hide** the Romeo *setupLayer*.

Tip: *Creating setup display layers allows you to quickly hide the character rig before playblasting your scene.*

- From the **Show** menu in the *Perspective* panel, hide object types that you do not want in your playblast such as **Grids**, **NURBS curves**, **Lights**, **Locators,** and **Handles**.

- Press **6** if you want the textures to appear in your playblast and **7** if you want hardware lighting.

- Select **Window** → **Playblast**.

Maya will render every frame, recording it into the playblast. Once the scene has been entirely played through, the playblast is displayed in your default movie player.

Note: *For more options on the playblast, select* **Window** → **Playblast** → ❏.

16 Animation refinement

Once you have seen the playblast and animation at its real speed, you can concentrate on correcting the motion and timing.

- Note areas that appear to be too fast or too slow in the playblast.

- To move a pose to a different frame, hold down **Shift** and click a keyframe in the Time Slider.

- **Click+drag** the keyframe to the left to make the pose faster, and to the right to make the pose more slowly.

- Tweak the poses and tangents to make the motion between them more fluid.

Make sure you bring everything along when moving the character animation, such as the lookAt node and the pole vectors.

- Add secondary animation to enhance your animation, such as the scooter shaking when the character lands on it, the tail, the ears, and the fingers.

Note: *You might have to redo your playblast and perform some trial and error before finding the perfect animation speed.*

Tip: *Beginner animators tend to make everything slow motion when animating. Do not be afraid to have only two or three frames between your poses. An entire picking-up motion should take about one or two seconds, which is only 24 to 48 frames.*

17   **Save your work**

- **Save** this scene to *22-moreAnimation_02.ma*.

- In the *images* directory, you can view the playblasts recorded at blocking and refined stages of the animation.

Create a Trax clip file

The animation is finished, so you will now create another Trax clip file.

1   **Open the Trax Editor window**

- Make sure that *Romeo* is the current character set.

- Select **Window** → **Animation Editor** → **Trax Editor**.

2   **Create a clip**

- From the Trax Editor, select **Create** → **Animation Clip** → ❑.

- In the **Create Clip Options** window, select **Edit** → **Reset.**

- Set the following options:

    Name to *jump;*

    Leave Keys in Timeline to **Off**;

    Clip to **Put Clip in Trax Editor and Visor**;

    Time Range to **Time Slider**;

    Include Subcharacters in Clip to **Off**;

    Create Time Warp Curve to **Off**;

    Include Hierarchy to **On**.

- Click the **Create Clip** button.

- Press **a** in the Trax Editor to frame all.

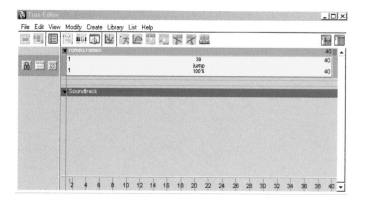

Clip in Trax Editor

3   Export the clip

• Select **File** → **Visor...**

• Select the **Character Clips** tab to see the clip source.

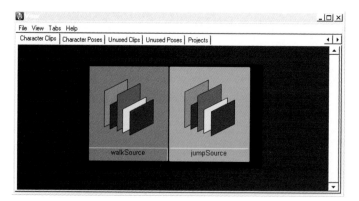

Pickup source clip in Visor

• Select the *jumpSource* clip.

• **RMB** on the clip and select **Export.**

• **Save** the clip as *jumpExport* in the project *clips* folder.

Note: *Since you are in a new project, you can either copy the other walkExport.ma file from the second project or export it again from here.*

- **Close** the Visor**.**

4   **Save your work**

- **Save** this scene to *22-moreAnimation_03.ma.*

Conclusion

You have now completed a type of animation that requires much more artistic input. As you can see, a lot of practice is required to achieve good animation in an efficient manner, and you might have to correct rigging problems as you work.

In the next lesson you will use nonlinear animation techniques to experiment with various ways of creating an animated sequence.

Lesson 23
Nonlinear
Animation

So far in this book, you have animated Romeo and created two Trax clips from the animated sequences. In this lesson, you will create a more complex motion by joining the walk clip with the jump clip in the Trax Editor.

The advantage of working with Trax' nonlinear animation lies in the ability to move, edit, connect, and reuse multiple clips freely, without having to edit multiple time curves. You can also add sound files to the scene using Trax.

You will also have a look at animation layers, which allow you to layer refinements on top of your existing animation. This technique can be very useful when modifying dense animation curves or motion capture data, or just to compare two animations easily.

In this lesson, you will learn the following:

- How to work with relative and absolute clips

- How to clip, split, blend, and merge clips

- How to use time warp

- How to redirect animation

- How to use sound in Trax

- How to use animation layers

- How to animate a two-node camera

Initial setup

1   **Scene file**

- **Open** the file you saved at the end of the last lesson.

  OR

- **Open** the scene file *22-moreAnimation_03.ma.*

2   **Set up the work area**

- Set the **Playback Frame Range** to go from **1** to **200**.

- From any panel menu, select **Panels** → **Saved Layouts** → **Persp/Trax/Outliner**.

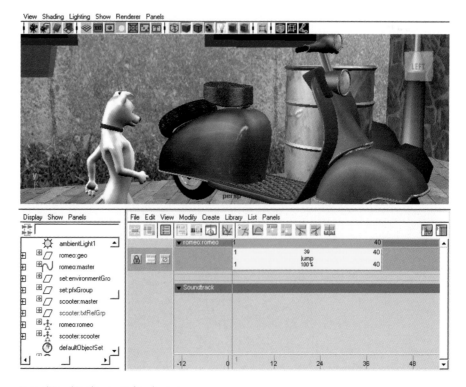

Persp/Trax/Outliner window layout

Generate the animation

The following exercise uses several Trax commands that will establish the new character animation. The animation you want to achieve in the scene goes like this:

Romeo walks up to the scooter and is looking around. He then jumps on the scooter and sits comfortably waiting for some friends to pass by.

1   Load the first two clips

- Select the romeo character from the **Current Character** menu at the bottom right of the interface.

  The Trax Editor will update, showing the jump motion from the previous lesson.

- From the Trax Editor, select **Library** → **Insert Clip** → **walkSource**.

  Both the walk and jump clips are now in the Trax Editor.

- Press **a** to frame all.

- **Click+drag** each clip in the Trax Editor so that the *walk* clip starts at frame **1** and the *jump* clip starts at frame **121**.

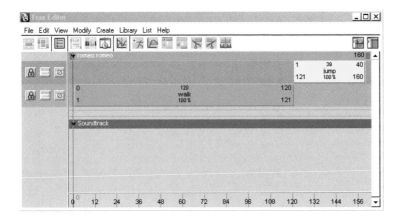

Walk and jump clips

Tip: *If a clip is not in your scene, you can import via the **File** → **Import Animation Clip** menu item in the Trax Editor.*

2   Trim the walk clip

- Scrub to frame **41** in the timeline.

    This is a good place to match the jump clip, since it is a pose similar to the start pose.

- Select the *walk* clip.

- Select the **Trim clip after current time** icon from the Trax menu to **trim** the clip after frame **41**.

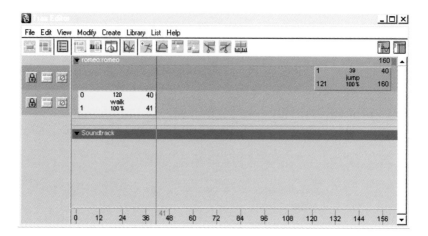

Trim the walk clip after frame 41

- **Move** the *jump* clip to its new starting position at frame **41**.

3   View the clips with absolute offset

- **Play** the animation by dragging the vertical time indicator in the Trax window.

    As the walk clip switches to the jump clip during playback, you will see the Romeo character snap back at its original keyframed position—or absolute offset.

Note: *You should also notice that the scooter animation needs to be offset, which will be seen later in this exercise.*

4   **Change the relative/absolute offset**

- Select the *jump* clip, then press **Ctrl+a** to open its Attribute Editor.

- Scroll to the **Channel Offsets** section and click the **All Relative** button.

- **Play** the animation.

    Now, as the walk clip switches to the jump clip during playback, you will see that Romeo does the jump animation from his new position at the end of the walk clip. This is because the clip's animation is relative to the end position of the clip preceding it.

Note: *It is normal at this stage that Romeo walks away from the scooter. You will offset the whole animation later in the exercise.*

5   **Ease out the walk clip**

At this point, you might notice a speed change between the end of the walk clip and the start of the jump. The following steps will help smooth this.

- Select the *walk* clip.

- **RMB** on the clip and select **Create Time Warp**.

    A time warp is a curve that controls the speed of the clip animation. Using this, you will slow down the walk to have Romeo slow down before jumping up.

- Click the **Open Graph Editor** button located at the top right corner of the Trax Editor.

- Scroll down in the Graph Editor Outliner and highlight the **Time Warp** attribute.

- Select the **first keyframe** and set its **Tangent** to **Linear**.

- Select the last keyframe, and then select its left tangent manipulator.

- Press **w** to select the Move Tool, and then **MMB+drag** the tangent down a little so it is not perfectly flat.

    If the tangent is perfectly flat, then the animation will gradually slow down in order to be a complete halt on its last frame. Moving the tangent down a little makes the animation slow down, but does not stop completely.

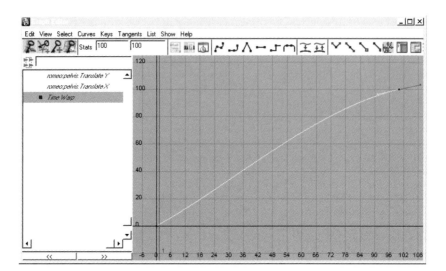

The time warp curve

- Click the **Open Trax Editor** button located at the top right corner of the Graph Editor.

- If you scrub in the animation, you will notice that Romeo is now slowing down before jumping up.

6   **Blend between the two clips**

- Select the *walk* clip, then **Shift-select** the *jump* clip.

- Select **Create → Blend → ❏**.

- In the option window, set **Initial Weight Curve** to **Ease in out**.

- Click the **Create Blend** button.

- Select the *jump* clip on its own and **drag** it so that it starts at frame **36**.

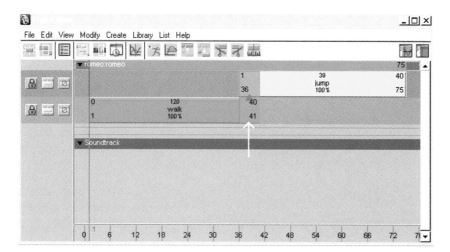

The newly created blend area

- **Playback** the animation. You will notice that the animation is now much more fluid.

Tip: *To frame the animation from the Trax Editor in the main Time Slider,* **RMB** *in the Time Slider and select* **Set Range To** → **Enabled Clips**.

7   Merge all the clips

- Select all the clips by **click+dragging** a selection box over the clips in the Trax Editor.

- Select **Edit** → **Merge** → ❑.

- In the Merge option window, set the following:

    Name to *RomeoAnim*

    Merged Clip to **Add to Trax**

- Click the **Merge Clip** button.

    The newly merged clip is now in the Trax Editor, and has replaced all the previous clips.

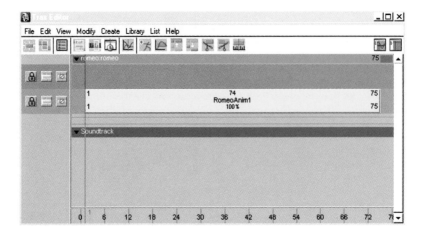

The new merged clip

Redirect the animation

Next, you will change Romeo's position so that he walks up to the scooter properly.

1   Animation timing

Since you moved the timing of the jumping-up motion, the scooter animation is happening too early.

- Select scooter's *master,* then select **Edit → Select Hierarchy.**

  You should now have selected everything that was animated outside the actual character.

- In the Graph Editor, select all the nodes on the left and then select all visible animation curves.

- **Offset** the animation curve by **35** frames, which is the exact time when the jump clip starts in the Trax Editor.

  Doing so fixes the timing of the scooter animation.

Tip: *Make sure the Time Snap button is enabled in the Graph Editor. Doing so will make sure that you drag the keyframes on exact frame numbers.*

2   **Change the animation orientation**

- Select Romeo's *master* node.

- From the Animate menu set, select **Character** → **Redirect** → ❏.

- Select the **Translation only** option, then click the **Redirect** button.

  Doing so creates an override that allows you to move the animation to the proper place.

The Redirect node

- Go to frame **75**.

  This is where Romeo is seated on the scooter.

- With the *OffsetTranslateControl1* still selected, set the following:

  Translate X to **-13.5**;

  Translate Y to **0.0**;

  Translate Z to **-21.25**;

  Doing so will change the placement of the entire animation.

The correctly placed animation

3   **Save your work**

- **Save** the scene as *23-nonlinearAnimation_01.ma*.

Animation layers

You have already experienced the flexibility of working with nonlinear animation clips. To further refine the motion, you will add animation layers to the animation. Animation layers allow you to set keyframes on top of the existing animation.

1   **Remove the Trax clip**

For the rest of this lesson, it is unnecessary to leave the clip in the Trax Editor, so you will remove it and keep the existing animation.

- In the Trax Editor, **RMB** on the *RomeoAnim1* clip and select **Activate Keys**.

  Doing so puts the keyframe found in the clip into the Time Slider.

- With the *RomeoAnim1* clip highlighted, press the **Delete** key on your keyboard to delete the clip.

  The clip is now gone, but the animation is still in the scene.

2   Remove the offset control

- Change the active character set to **None**.

- Select the Romeo *master*.

- Highlight the **Translate** attributes in the Channel Box.

- Select **Edit** → **Keys** → **Bake Simulation** → ❑.

- In the option window, select **Edit** → **Reset Settings**, then set the **Time range to Start/ End**, with a **Start** time of **1** and an **End** time of **75**.

- **Click the Bake** button.

  The translation animation will be baked at every frame on the master node.

- **Delete** *OffsetTranslateControl1* node.

- Set the **Playback Frame Range** to go from **1** to **75**.

3   Add an animation layer

- In the Layer Editor, select the **Anim** radio button.

  Doing so will display the Animation Layer Editor.

- In the Animation Layer Editor, select **Layers** → **Create Empty Layer.**

  There is now an empty animation layer and a base animation layer visible.

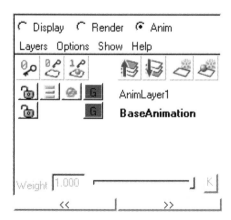

The Animation Layer Editor

4   **Add body parts to the animation layer**

- Click the *AnimLayer1* to highlight it.

- Select the *neck1*, *head* joints, and the *lookAt* locator.

- Select **Layers → Add Selected Objects.**
  Doing so will add all keyable attributes on the objects to the animation layer.

Note: *Notice that when you highlight the BaseAnimation layer, the baked keyframes are visible in the timeline, and when you highlight the AnimLayer1 layer, the timeline is free of all keyframes, allowing you to keyframe layered animation.*

5   **Add keys to modify the head position**

- Highlight the *AnimLayer1* layer.

- Select the *neck1* and *head* joint.

- Go to frame **10** and press the **s** hotkey to keyframe the joints position.
  You will notice a new key has been placed in the timeline.

- Go to frame **20** and rotate the joints so Romeo looks to his right.

- Press **s** to keyframe the joints.

Note: *If Auto Key is on, you do not have to manually key the rotation after you have set a key once.*

- Go to frame **35** and rotate the joints so Romeo keeps looking to his right.

- Press **s** to keyframe the joints.

- **Playback** the results.
  Now Romeo's head is deviating from his original animation, but notice how the animation is now changed for the rest of the animation. This is because the last offset put on the joints remains beyond frame 35.

6   Set zero keys

When setting layered keyframes, you need to set default keys before and after the region where you want to alter the animation. If you do not set those keys, the offset you keyframe will remain throughout the animation.

- Go to frame **45**.

- Select the *neck1* and *head* joints.

- Click the **Zero Key Layer** button in the Animation Layer Editor.

  Notice how the animation goes back to its original position.

- Select all the keyframes at frames 10, 20, 35, and 45 in the timeline, then **RMB** and select **Tangents → Flat** to set the tangents of the selected keyframe.

- **Playback** the results.

  Now the character goes back to his original animation past frame 45.

7   Modify the lookAt

- **Repeat** the last steps in order to correctly animate where Romeo is looking throughout the animation.

Romeo looking around

Note: *These keys are not altering the original animation in any way. In fact, these keys can be deleted or moved around and the base animation will remain intact.*

8   Changing the weight of a layer

If you would like to see what the animation would look like with only a fraction of the added animation, you can keyframe the weight of an animation layer.

- With the *AnimLayer1* layer highlighted, change the **Weight** slider at the bottom of the Animation Layer Editor.

- Press the **K** button to the right to keyframe the value.

9   Merging the animation layers

If you would like to merge the layered animation together with the base animation, simply do the following:

- Highlight all the animation layers using the **Ctrl** key.

- Select **Layers** → **Merge Layers.**

10   Save your work

- **Save** the scene as *23-nonlinearAnimation_02.ma.*

Adding sound to Trax

The Trax Editor offers you the ability to import and easily sync sound files to your animation.

You can import *.wav* or *.aiff* sound files into Trax to synchronize motion and audio. More than one audio clip can be imported into the soundtrack, but you will be able to hear only one file at a time upon playback. The audio file at the top of the soundtrack display will take precedence over those below.

You will now import an existing sound file into your scene.

1   Set playback preferences

- Select **Window** → **Settings/ Preferences** → **Preferences.**

- In the **Time Slider** category under the **Playback** section, make sure **Playback speed** is set to **Real-time [24 fps].**
  If this option is not set to Real-time, the sound might not be played.

2 **Add a sound file**

- From the Trax Editor, select **File** → **Import Audio...**

- From the *sound* directory, select *hop.wav.*

3 **See and hear the sound file**

- **RMB** in the Time Slider.

- From the pop-up menu, select **Sound** → **Use Trax Sounds.**

  A green indicator bar will appear on the global timeline and the clips will display an audio waveform.

4 **Sync the sound to the animation**

- **Play** the animation with the sound.

- **Click+drag** the sound clip so that it syncs up to when Romeo jumps on the scooter.

  The sound clip should be somewhere around frame **29**.

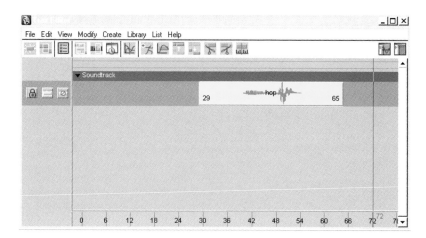

Sound clip in Trax

Note: *When you playblast your animation, the sound will be added to your movie as long as the soundtrack is selected in the Time Slider.*

Animating a camera

You will now add a new camera to the scene and animate it so that you can follow Romeo as he walks.

A camera can be created on its own or with additional nodes that provide control over the *aim point* and *up direction*. Most cameras only need one node that lets you key the camera's position and rotation. You will create a camera to control both the *camera point* and the *view point*. Both of these nodes can be keyed individually.

1   **Set up your panel display**

- Select a **Two Panes Stacked** view layout.

- In the *Perspective* view, make sure Show → Cameras and Show → Pivots are **On**.
  You will need to see these in order to work with the camera.

2   **Create a two-node camera**

- Select **Create** → **Cameras** → **Camera and Aim**.

- In the bottom pane, select Panels → Perspective → camera1.

- Press **6** to view the textures in the *camera1* view.

- In the *camera1* view, select **View** → **Camera Settings** → **Resolution Gate**.

- Still in the *camera1* view, select View → Camera Attribute Editor...

- Change **Fit Resolution Gate** to **Vertical**.

3   **Frame the character**

- Go to frame **1**.

- In the *camera1* view, select **View** → **Select Camera**

- Select the **Show Manipulator Tool** by pressing the **t** hotkey.

- In the *Perspective* view, position the *camera* and *camera1_aim* handles as follows:

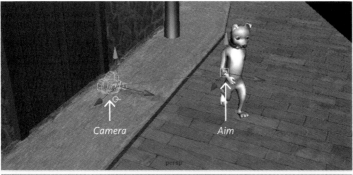

Camera manipulator handles

> **Note:** *You can position the camera using the usual viewport hotkey if wanted.*

4   Follow the action

You will now set keys on the camera point to follow the character from frames 1 to 60.

- Go to frame 1.

- Select the *camera1* and *camera1_aim* nodes.

- Press Shift+w to keyframe the current position.
  Doing so sets a keyframe for the current camera position.

- Go to frame 45.

- Move the *camera1_aim* node so that it is again looking at the character, framing both the character and the scooter.

- Select the *camera1* and *camera1_aim* nodes.

- Press Shift+w to keyframe the new view position.

View at frame 45

5   **Dolly around the scooter**

The camera animation now frames the first portion of the animation correctly, but the second part of the animation could be better. You can set keys on the viewpoint node to fix this.

- Go to frame 75.

- Move the *camera1* node from the *Perspective* view to the left of the scene.

- Adjust the framing to your liking.

- Select the *camera1* and *camera1_aim* nodes.

- Press Shift+w to keyframe the new view position.

- If you do not like the framing in the in-between frames, you can reposition the camera and set new keys. **Repeat** this until you get the camera movement you want.

6   **Playblast the animation**

You can now playblast the scene to test the motion. This will give you the chance to confirm the camera animation.

7   **Save your work**

- **Save** the scene as *23-nonlinearAnimation_03.ma.*

View at frame 75

Tip: *Make sure you maximize the camera view by tapping the spacebar and displaying only NURBS surfaces and polygons. You can also set Romeo's **smooth** attribute found on the master to be high resolution, and set any NURBS smoothness to its finest setting.*

Conclusion

In this lesson, you completed your first nonlinear animation using both Trax and the animation layers. You have also inserted sounds through the Trax Editor.

In the next lesson, you will animate Romeo riding the scooter in the alley using a motion path.

Lesson 24
Motion Path

In this lesson, you will animate Romeo riding the scooter in the alley. To do so, you will use a motion path to determine the trajectory of the scooter, then keyframe some secondary animation to refine the motion.

In this lesson, you will learn the following:

- How to constrain the character to the scooter

- How to make a surface live

- How to define a motion path

- How to shape the path to edit the animation

- How to update the path markers

- How to constrain about the normals of a surface

- How to keyframe secondary animation

Path animation

Path animations are created by assigning an object or series of objects to a path. This creates a special *motionPath* node that allows you to key its motion along the path.

1   Scene file

- **Open** the scene file *20-lightEffects_04.ma* from the last project.

- Set the frame range to go from **1** to **300**.

- **Save** your scene as *24-motionPath_01.ma*.

2   Make live

- Select the *ground* surface.

- Select **Modify → Make Live**.

  When making a surface live, it is displayed in green wireframe. You can then draw a curve directly on the surface, which will create a curve that follows the shape of the alley.

3   Draw a path animation curve

- Go to frame **1**.

- Select **Create → EP Curve Tool → ❑**.

- **Make sure to reset the options of the tool.**

- **Draw** a curve starting at the front of the alley, which goes all the way to the back, as on the following page:

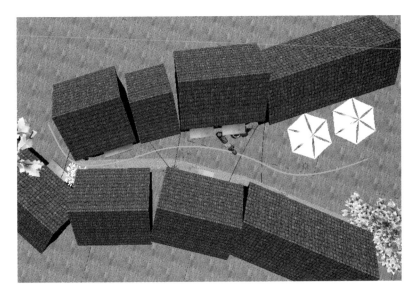

Path curve

- When you have finished, press **Enter** to complete the curve.

- Select **Modify** → **Make Not Live** again to remove the live state of the ground surface.

Note: *When using the Make Live feature on a NURBS surface, the resulting curve is projected on the surface. Thus, you could change the shape of the curve by perfectly following the surface's shape. When using the Make Live feature on a polygon surface, the curve is only approximating the surface and maintains no construction history.*

4   **Constrain Romeo**

Before you go on with animating the scooter, you must set up Romeo to be perfectly synchronized with the scooter. The easiest way of doing this is to constrain Romeo's master node to the scooter node.

- Set the *Romeo* character to be the active character set.

- Open the Trax Editor and **delete** the *walk* clip.

- **Pose** Romeo on the scooter and **keyframe** the *Romeo* character set.

Romeo moved into position

- Select the scooter *frameGrp*, then **Shift-select** Romeo's *master* node.
  You are constraining to the frame group because you need Romeo to perfectly follow the engine cover, regardless of how you animate the master or its overrides.

- Select **Constrain** → **Parent** → ❑.

- In the options, make sure that **Maintain Offset** is set to **On**.

- Click the **Add** button.

- Test the constraint by moving the scooter's *master.*
  Romeo should follow the scooter perfectly.

5   **Constrain the hands**

In order to be able to animate the steering and have Romeo's hands follow properly, you need to constrain the hand manipulators on the scooter handles.

- Select the left scooter *handle*, then **Shift-select** Romeo's *lHandManip* node.

- Select **Constrain** → **Parent.**

- Repeat for the other hand manipulator.

- Test the constraints by rotating the *frontWheelGrp.*

6   **Remove attributes from character set**

In order to attach an object to a motion path, you need the translation and rotation attributes to be freed. At this time, the scooter master's attributes are part of the scooter character set. Here you will remove these attributes from the character set.

- Make sure the *scooter* character set is active.

- Select the scooter *master* and highlight the **Translate** and **Rotate** attributes in the Channel Box.

- Select **Character** → **Remove from Character Set.**

  The attributes should now be free for the Motion Path node.

Note: *The Channel Box attributes are color coded to let you know the various states of an attribute.*
   Locked : Grey
   Nonkeyable : Light gray
   Muted : Brown
   Blended : Green
   Keyed : Light orange
   Expression : Purple
   Constrained : Blue
   Connected : Yellow

- If the attributes are colored in orange, it means you have a keyframe on the *master* node. To remove the keyframes, select **Edit** → **Delete by Type** → **Channels.**

7   Scooter pivot

When an object is attached to a motion path, the pivot of the object will move and follow the curve perfectly. If in your scene file the pivot of the scooter is not located at the base of the scooter, place it in line with the base of the rear wheel.

Note: *You are placing the pivot at the base of the rear wheel because the front wheel will be rotated to steer the scooter.*

8   Attach the scooter to the path

- Make sure the **Time Slider** range goes from **1** to **300** frames.

- Select the scooter's *master* node using the Outliner, then **Shift-select** the path curve.

- Go to the **Animation** menu set.

- Select **Animate** → **Motion Paths** → **Attach to Motion Path.**

- **Playback** the results.

Note: *For simplicity reasons, this lesson will not cover wheel animation.*

9   Edit the Motion Path Input node

The scooter is moving down the path, but it is not aimed in the correct direction. You can change this using the *motionPath* Input node.

- With the scooter *master* selected, open the Attribute Editor.

- Click the tab for *motionPath1* and set the following:
    Follow to **On**;
    Front Axis to **Z**;
    Up Axis to **Y**.

- **Playback** the results and notice how the scooter now points in the direction it is traveling.

Scooter attached to path

10   Banking

You can also use the Bank attribute to have the object automatically roll when following the path.

- With the scooter *master* selected and the *motionPath1* tab selected in the Attribute Editor, set the following:

    Bank to **On**;

    Bank Scale to **10.0**;

    Bank Limit to **60.0**.

- **Playback** the results and notice how the scooter banks when turning.

11 Edit the path's shape

Edit the shape of the path using the curve's control vertices and the object will follow the path.

- Select the path curve.

- **RMB** on the path curve and select **Control Vertices** from the context menu.

- **Move** the CVs in order to tweak how the scooter follows the street.

- **Playback** the results.

12 Path timing

Notice the start and end markers on the path. They tell you the start and end frame of the animation along the path. You can insert new time keyframes and decide where the character should be on a certain frame.

- Go to frame **100**.

- Ensure that the **Auto Key** button is turned **On**.

- Select the path curve.

- In the Channel Box, click the *motionPath1* Input node.

- Still in the Channel Box, click the **U Value** channel name to highlight it.

  Notice the two keyframes in the Time Slider at the first and last frame. Those keyframes are defining the animation of the motion path from start to end.

- Hold down **Ctrl** and **click+drag** the **MMB** to change the path value at the current frame.

  This specifies a new location where the scooter should be on the path at that frame.

- Use the virtual slider to move the scooter forwards on the path.

  *You have just set a key on the motionPath's **U** value. Moving the value higher basically speed up the animation before that frame.*

100

300

New keyframe marker

Updated path position

13   **Manipulator**

Instead of using the virtual slider, you can use the motion path manipulator.

- Go to frame **200**.

- With the *motionPath* still highlighted in the Channel Box, select the **Show Manipulator Tool** by pressing **t**.

  A manipulator appears with handles for positioning the object along the path. You will use the handle on the path to move the scooter forward, so that it speeds up as it goes down the street.

- **Click+drag** the center marker of the path manipulator handle to move the scooter down the street, just before the scooter turns the corner.

  Another path marker is placed on the curve and a new key is set.

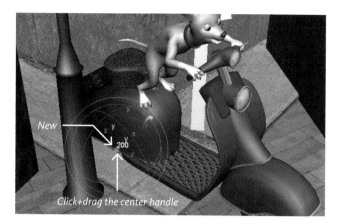

New path marker

Tip: *It is always good to remember that Input nodes may have manipulators that you can access using the Show Manipulator Tool.*

14 **Edit the path marker's position**

The position of the markers can be moved to edit the animation of the scooter.

- Click the **Auto Key** button to turn it **Off**.

- Select the **Move Tool**.

- To select the path marker that is labeled as **200**, click the number without touching other objects or the curve.

  This will select the marker on its own.

- **Click+drag** the marker to change the position of the scooter.

  The marker is constrained to the curve as you move it.

15 **Edit the timing**

Since the marker points are simply keys set on the U Value of the *motionPath* node, you can edit the timing of the keys in the Graph Editor.

- Select the scooter *master* using its selection handle, and then click the *motionPath* Input node in the Channel Box.

- Highlight the **U Value** in the Channel Box, then select **Edit** → **Graph Editor** in the Channel Box menu.

- Press **a** to frame all in the Graph Editor window.

  The position of the attached object in the U direction of the curve is mapped against time. You can see that a key has been set for each of the path markers.

- Select the key at frame **200**.

- In the Graph Editor's **Stats** area, change the time from **200** to **190**.

- In the Graph Editor, select **Tangents** → **Spline**.

  You can edit the effect of the path keys' in-between frames using the same techniques as for normal keyframes.

- Tweak the curve's tangents to your liking.

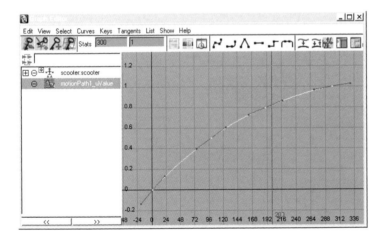

Edited path curve

  *You can see that the path marker is now labeled as **190** in the view panel.*

16   **Save your work**

- **Save** your scene as *24-motionPath_01.ma*.

Secondary animation

Now that you have a basic animation for your scooter, you can add secondary animation on top of what you already have. Secondary animation usually adds life to an animation, making the scene more natural. For the scooter, you will create a tangent constraint so it follows the path curve, and then keyframe some bumps along the road.

1   **Steering locator**

You will first connect the steering rotation to a locator.

- Select **Create → Locator**.

- **Rename** the new locator *steeringLocator*.

- **Parent** the *steeringLocator* to the scooter's *master* node.

- Set the **translation** and **rotation** attributes of the *steeringLocator* to **0**.

- **Offset** the *steeringLocator*'s **Translate Z** so it is in line with the front wheel.

- Select **Window → General Editors → Connection Editor**.

- **Load the** *steeringLocator* on the left side and the *frontWheelGrp* on the right side of the editor.

- **Connect** the *steeringLocator*'s **Rotate Y** to the *frontWheelGrp*'s **Rotate Y**.

2   **Tangent constraint**

You will now use a tangent constraint with the path curve to retrieve the rotation to apply to the steering locator.

- Select the path curve, then **Shift-select** the *steeringLocator*.

- Select **Constrain → Tangent → ❑**.

- **Set the Aim Vector option** to **0, 0, 1**.

- Click the **Add** button.

- **Playback** the animation.
  Notice how the steering now rotates according to the curve path.

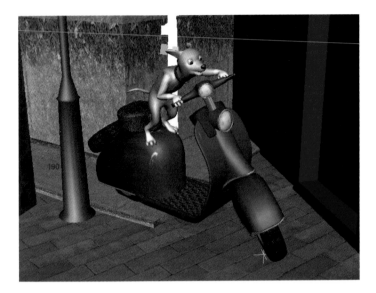

The normal constraint effect

3   **Scooter animation**

- Make sure **Auto Key** is turned **On**.

- Go to frame **40**.

- With the scooter *transOverride* node selected, press **Shift+w** to set a keyframe in translation.

- With the scooter *rotOverride* node selected, press **Shift+e** to set a keyframe in rotation.

- From the *top* view, move the *rotOverride* pivot so it is located under the rear wheel.

- **Rotate** the scooter so the front wheel is in the air.

- Go to frame **50**.

- **Rotate** the scooter so the front wheel is on the ground.

- **Translate** the scooter using the *transOverride* to put some weight on the scooter as it lands.

Riding on one wheel

- Scrub in the timeline to a place where the scooter should be back in control.

- Set the translation and rotation of the scooter back to **o** in all directions.

4   Other animation

- Spend some time animating Romeo's reaction to the scooter animation.
  Doing so will add lots of realism, rather than having just a stiff character following the scooter.

5   Save your work

- **Save** your scene as *24-motionPath_02.ma*.

6   Playblast or render the animation

Index

Rendered scene

Conclusion

You are now more familiar with animating using motion paths, constraining, and keyframing secondary animation. As a result of your work, Romeo is now riding a scooter down the street.

In the next lesson, you will learn about rigid bodies, which will allow you to create realistic animation using dynamics.

TurboSquid 3D Marketplace

Save time and save money with 3D models from TurboSquid

With over 200,000 stock models from some of the world's greatest 3D artists, TurboSquid's goal is to revolutionize the way that 3D products are bought, sold and delivered through digital marketplaces. We offer the largest library of royalty-free products, quality guarantees on all purchases and 24/7 technical support, so give us a try today on your latest project and see how much money we can help you save.

The Tentacles plug-in

Access TurboSquid from inside your Autodesk 3ds Max or Maya applications

Powerful search capabilities

Side-by-side product comparisons

Dynamic shopping cart

Unpack and import models directly into your 3D application

SIX WAYS TO OPTIMIZE YOUR
AUTODESK SOFTWARE INVESTMENT

Autodesk® Subscription is a maintenance and support program that helps you minimize costs, increase productivity, and make the most of your investment in Autodesk® software.

With Autodesk Subscription, you can:

1. Save on periodic upgrade costs: The annual fee includes any upgrades or product enhancements released during the Subscription term.

2. Extend your usage rights: Flexible licensing terms mean you can use your software on both home and office computers.*

3. Run previous versions: Use the current release and certain previous versions of your Autodesk licensed software (up to 3 versions back for most products).

4. Leverage exclusive educational materials: Get interactive training tools, self-paced e-Learning lessons, AU course material, video podcasts, and more.

5. Tap into the Autodesk® Knowledge Base: Access this unified search capability to more than 2 million content sources.

6. Receive web support direct from Autodesk: Get help with installation, configuration, and troubleshooting 24/7. Track your support queries so your entire team can benefit from the answers you receive.

Visit www.autodesk.com/subscription for a complete overview and online tour or contact your local Autodesk Authorized Reseller at www.autodesk.com/resellers.

Autodesk Subscription

A FREE SUBSCRIPTION LETS YOU
DISCOVER MANY WAYS TO DEVELOP
YOUR SKILLS—AND IT PUTS YOU
IN TOUCH WITH THE EXCITING AUTODESK[(R)]
3D ANIMATION COMMUNITY.

TUTORIALS & TIPS

DOWNLOADS

ARTISTS' SHOWCASE

COMMUNITY NETWORK

AREA

WWW.THE-AREA.COM   < GO

Autodesk®

PUBLISHED BY: AUTODESK, INC.
111 MCINNIS PARKWAY
SAN RAFAEL, CA 94903, USA

Foundation

Autodesk Official Training Gu

Autodesk
Maya

2010

Learning **Autodesk® Maya®** 2010

A hands-on introduction to key tools and techniques in Autodesk® Maya® 2010
software, based on the Yash Raj Films and Walt Disney Pictures feature film
Roadside Romeo.

Autodesk®